THE LONDON SURVEYS
OF RALPH TRESWELL

THE LONDON SURVEYS

of

RALPH TRESWELL

Edited by

JOHN SCHOFIELD

London Topographical Society

Publication No. 135

1987

Publication no. 135 of the
London Topographical Society
3 Meadway Gate, London NW11

ISBN 0 902 087 25 8

PRINTED IN GREAT BRITAIN BY
W. S. MANEY & SON LTD, HUDSON ROAD, LEEDS

CONTENTS

ABBREVIATIONS

Assize of Nuisance	H. M. Chew & W. Kellaway (eds) *London Assize of Nuisance 1301–1431*, London Record Society 10 (1973)
b.	breadth
CAD	*Descriptive Catalogue of Ancient Deeds in the Public Record Office* (6 vols, 1890–1915)
Cal LB A, etc.	R. R. Sharpe (ed.) *Calendar of Letter-Books preserved among the archives of the Corporation of the City of London: Letter-Book A to L* (11 vols, 1899–1912)
Cal P R	*Calendar of Patent Rolls* (14 vols, 1894–1916)
Cal P & M	A. H. Thomas (ed.) *Calendar of Plea and Memoranda Rolls preserved among the archives of the Corporation of the City of London, 1323–1437* (4 vols, 1926–43) and P. E. Jones (ed.) *1437–82* (2 vols, 1953–61)
Cal Wills	R. R. Sharpe (ed.) *Calendar of Wills enrolled in the Husting* (2 vols, 1889–90)
CCO	Clothworkers' Company Court Orders
CD	Clothworkers' Company Deeds
CDW	Clothworkers' Company Book of Deeds and Wills
CHMB	Christ's Hospital Court Minute Books, GL MS 12806: 1, 1556–1563; 2, 1562–1592; 3, 1592–1632; 4, 1632–1649
CH Treas Accts	Christ's Hospital Treasurer's Accounts, GL MS 12819: 1, 1552–58; 2, 1561–1608; 3, 1608–1616
CH View Book	Christ's Hospital View Books, GL MS 12834/1–2
Charity Comm	*Report of the [Charity] Commissioners*, vol 32 Part VI (1840)
CLRO	City of London Record Office
Comm Court 1374–1488	M. Fitch (ed.) *Index to the Testamentary Records in the Commissary Court of London, I, 1374–1488* (1969)
d.	died
E	East
Evidence Book	Christ's Hospital Evidence Book, GL MS 12805
GL	Guildhall Library
HG	*Historical Gazeteer of London before the Great Fire*: D. Keene & V. Harding, *1, Cheapside* (1987); D. Keene & M. Carlin, *2, St Botolph without Aldgate* (forthcoming); D. Crouch *et al, 3, Walbrook* (forthcoming)
HR	Husting Roll(s) (CLRO)
HTP	G. A. J. Hodgett (ed.) *The Cartulary of Holy Trinity Aldgate*, London Record Society 7 (1971)

Inq PM	G. S. Fry (ed.) *Abstracts of Inquisitiones Post Mortem relating to the City of London returned into the Court of Chancery, Part I, 1485–1561* (LAMAS, 1896); S. J. Madge (ed.) *Part II, 1561–1577* (LAMAS, 1901); G. S. Fry (ed.) *Part III, 1577–1603* (LAMAS, 1906)
Journal	Journal of the Court of Common Council (CLRO)
l.	length
LAMAS	London and Middlesex Archaeological Society
Memorials	H. T. Riley, *Memorials of London and London life in the XIIIth, XIVth and XVth centuries* (1868)
N	North
PCC 1558–1583	S. A. Smith & L. L. Duncan (eds) *Index of wills proved in the Prerogative Court of Canterbury, III, 1558–1583 (1898, repr. 1968)*
PCC 1584–1603	S. A. Smith & E. A. Fry (eds) *Index of wills proved in the Prerogative Court of Canterbury, IV, 1584–1604* (1910)
Plan Book	Clothworkers' Company, Plan Book ('Book of Treswell Surveys')
PRO	Public Record Office
QW	(Clothworkers' Company) Quarter Warden
Repertory	Repertory of the Court of Aldermen (CLRO)
RW	(Clothworkers' Company) Renter Warden
S	South
Stow	J. Stow *Survey of London* (1598) ed. C. L. Kingsford, 3rd edn (2 vols, 1971)
Sudbury Register II	R. C. Fowler (ed.) *Registrum Simonis de Sudbira, 1362–1375* (Cant & York Soc., 2 vols, 1927–38)
W	West

ILLUSTRATIONS

PLATES

FIGURES

ACKNOWLEDGEMENTS

I am grateful to many people and institutions for assistance in the production of this study. First I must thank the custodians of the surveys for permission to publish them: the Worshipful Company of Clothworkers, Christ's Hospital and Guildhall Library, the Leathersellers' Company, the Trustees of the British Museum and the Governing Body of Christ Church, Oxford. Photography of the plans has been by Godfrey New (with the exception of Figures 15 (British Museum) and 36 (Bodleian Library)). I am especially grateful to Ralph Hyde who has provided the Table of all Treswell's known works, urban and rural, from his own researches.

For discussion of points raised by the plans and criticism of the text I am extremely grateful to Peter Barber, Caroline Barron, Frank Brown, Alan Carter, Tony Dyson, Richard Harris, Negley Harte, Derek Keene, Eric Mercer, Tim Tatton-Brown, Janet Taylor, Sarah Tyacke, and David Wickham. Figures 1–3 and 16 have been prepared for publication by Tracy Wellman.

The Worshipful Company of Clothworkers have made it possible to illustrate this volume with twelve pages of colour plates instead of the four originally intended. For this generosity, the author and the London Topographical Society are most truly grateful.

JOHN SCHOFIELD

INTRODUCTION

1. The life of Ralph Treswell

Ralph Treswell was the son of Robert Treswell alias Baker of St Albans and Margaret Langley.[1] His date of birth is not known, but he died in 1616. The first known reference to him at work is 1567–8, and it might therefore be suggested that he was born about 1540, reaching an age of nearly eighty.

He was by trade a Painter-Stainer. The Stainers were an established craft in London by the mid-thirteenth century;[2] they stained cloth to resemble tapestries. The Painters are known as a fraternity from 1283; their main occupation was the painting of saddle-bows, though by Treswell's time they also painted signs and portraits. The two companies were amalgamated, at their joint petition, in 1502.[3] At the incorporation of the Painter-Stainers' Company in 1581, freemen were classified as Face Painters, History Painters, Arms (heraldic) Painters and House Painters;[4] unfortunately no specification can be attached to Treswell's name itself.

Treswell is mentioned a number of times in the records of the Painter-Stainers. In 1532 Sir John Browne, Serjeant Painter to Henry VIII, had conveyed his house to the company to become their hall.[5] As was usual, the hall site was passed from one group of trustees, often predominantly members of the craft, to another whenever circumstances required it. Thus the trustees were renewed in 1549, 1580 and 1605; and Ralph Treswell appears as one of the receiving trustees in 1580, and as one of those releasing the property in 1605.[6]

Treswell's conventional work as a painter of banners is mentioned twice in other company records. In 1567–8 the Carpenters' Company paid him £8. 10s. for painting three streamers and a banner;[7] and in 1603 the Clothworkers' Company paid him the same amount to make a new banner of the King's arms for this Company's use, to find silk and fringe and all things thereto pertaining. But if it happen that the banner be not done as the King shall bear it at his Coronation, then the said Mr Treswell to alter or make it new at his own charges.[8]

The painting of a 'story' in the Carpenters' Company parlour in 1571 by one Baker has also been attributed to Treswell, on the grounds that he may have used his father's alias;[9] this painting has not survived, but the character of such work may be seen in the contemporary painting in the hall, still largely surviving as three painted panels at the present Carpenters' Hall.[10]

From at least 1580 Treswell was also carrying out pictorial surveys. His earliest surviving surveys are a series of plans of estates of Christopher Hatton (Chancellor 1587–91) at Kirby Hall, Northants. During 1580–9 Treswell also surveyed Hatton's estate at Wimbledon. Throughout his career Treswell surveyed rural estates in southern England; a list of the known surveys is given below (pp. 5–7). He also surveyed fortifications, though these were not a frequent subject: Corfe Castle for Hatton, and in 1593–4 he probably accompanied Sir John Norris on his second expedition to Brittany, surveying the area in the process.

Treswell's earliest work in London dates from 1585, when he produced a drawing of St Michael le Querne, at the west end of Cheapside, and the adjoining Conduit (**12**) (Plate 1). In the following year he produced a survey of lands in the parishes of St Martin in the Fields and St Giles', and a lease-plan for Christ's Hospital property in Tothill Street, Westminster (**52**) (for full concordance, see below, p. 5). His main commissions in central London were in 1607–11 for Christ's Hospital (of which he had been appointed a governor in 1603) and for the Clothworkers'

Company in 1612. He also produced single surveyed plans for the Leathersellers' Company (1614 (**27**)), and Christ Church Oxford (1610 (**32**)). These London surveys (i.e. of properties in the City of London, Southwark and Westminster) are reproduced in the present volume.

Treswell apparently also made at least one sun dial, though it cannot now be traced. The Society of Antiquaries possesses a rubbing of a fragment of a Flemish brass, showing the lower legs of a shrouded figure; such latten scrap was imported into England during the later sixteenth century. The reverse of this plate, of which no representation is extant, had been reused to make a sun dial, signed by R. Treswell and dated 1582.[11] Nothing further is at present known about Treswell's work, if any, in this field.

Treswell married three times. His first wife was Cicely Cresley, by whom he had three sons: Robert, who became Somerset Herald in 1597, Ralph and Christopher. His second wife was Anne, widow of Robert Kentish; and his third wife Elizabeth, widow of Edward Bachelor.[12] From 1577 he is recorded as living in Aldersgate ward.[13] In 1603–4 Ralph Treswell senior (identified by the fact that the arrangement terminated with his death in 1616) took a lease of a house in Aldersgate, part of the estate granted to Christ's Hospital by Robert Mellish.[14] In the Hospital surveys of *c.* 1607–11 two of the tenants shown in the properties granted by Mellish are Robert Treswell (beneath Trinity Hall in Aldersgate Street) (**2**) and 'R Treswell' nearby, in one of the houses opposite St Botolph Aldersgate church (**1**), both sites being within the parish of St Botolph and the ward of Aldersgate. The latter survey is dated to 1610 or later since it includes a partial plan of the conduit set up immediately outside Aldersgate in that year. In November 1613 the shops in the block containing Trinity Hall (**2**) were leased by the City to Roger Jenkins, barber-surgeon, Roger Taylor, gentleman, Ralph Treswell, painter-stainer, Humphrey Westwood, goldsmith, John Haughton, saddler, and Tewthe Roberts, vintner.[15] Roger Taylor had been a tenant at the time of Treswell's survey a few years before (below,

p. 36). It seems likely that Treswell senior moved into the tenancy of his son Robert, who stopped paying rent in the same year.

Wherever he actually lived, Treswell had been playing his part in the local community for some years. In 1583 he appeared as one of the inquestors at the Wardmote of Aldersgate Ward, verifying indentures;[16] he also was one of fourteen men commissioned to produce a catalogue of all the copied indentures held by the ward.[17] In 1598 he was appointed Petty Collector for the ward,[18] and in 1600 he became a Common Councilman, one of six for the ward.[19] He was elected churchwarden of St Botolph Aldersgate for the years 1597–1600,[20] and continued being a vestryman from 1601; in this year he, fellow painter Richard Crewlett and two others were ordered to conduct a survey of parish lands and rents in Lamb Alley, Aldersgate.[21] In 1606 he was named deputy in the parish records, which indicated he had become the senior Common Councilman of the ward; this title continued with him until his death.[22]

He attended his last vestry meeting on 2 April 1616[23] and his last court meeting of the Hospital on 1 July 1616, when a minute records that Treswell was to assist with a court at Horley in Surrey.[24] Thereafter his name disappears from the parish and ward records; a new deputy was named. He attended no more Court meetings of Christ's Hospital. In March 1617 Scholastica [*sic*] Treswell renounced administration of his estate in the Archdeaconry Court of London, and administration was granted to Ralph Treswell junior;[25] Treswell had apparently died intestate.

2. Treswell's work in London

CHRIST'S HOSPITAL

Treswell's earliest known survey for Christ's Hospital, that of land at Rickling in Essex, dates from 1597 (see Concordance, below).[26] Treswell first appears as a governor of Christ's Hospital in 1603–4;[27] throughout the period 1604–16 he took part in views of hospital property and adjudicated disputes between hospital tenants in London;[28] he also went into surrounding counties on behalf of the hospital. In 1604 the Treasurer recorded payment of £1 to him 'for his charges for horse hire for himself and his man when he did ride to Horley [Surrey] to keep Court there'.[29] In 1606 the hospital paid £2. 13s. to him for riding to Gainscolne in Essex to mark what scathels and storers (trees and saplings to be left standing) should be left in Oxney Wood;[30] his survey of Colne Engaine had been undertaken in 1602. In 1611 Treswell was paid £62 'for surveying the lands in Berden and Clavering and Rickling [parishes in north-west Essex] and all the lands in and about London, and for making the plots and entering them into a book'.[31] Evidently this large fee covered some past services, for the Berden survey dates from 1600. The fact that making the plots is mentioned as well as surveying is significant, since many surveys continued to be written documents only at this date. A further unspecified sum was given to Treswell in 1612 'for his pains taken in riding into the country diverse and sundry times to keep courts there'.[32]

The Evidence Book of Christ's Hospital (GL MS 12805) is a manuscript volume of about 500 un-numbered pages measuring 16¼″ by 10¼″ in a mid-sixteenth-century tooled leather binding, with late-medieval paste-downs and a painted late seventeenth-century fore-edge. The binding, ciphered LR, has been attributed to a London workshop of *c.* 1536–*c.* 1622 known as the Blank Book Binder. The workshop produced blank books with stamped bindings on a large scale; its London clients included four city companies, government departments, a city church, and the Inner Temple.[33] The first twenty-five pages of the Evidence Book are taken up by a register of Hospital property and tenants in London and the surrounding counties, as the first page states,

collected and taken out of sundry evidences and books, being mingled with other matters diffusedly and without order. But now with regard and diligence, truly gathered, and made perfect in the time of Mr Robert Cogan.

Most of the volume thereafter consists of blank pages. At the back of the book is a section of folios (numbered 1–22 in pencil); on these are eighteen

water-colour plans of twenty-one blocks of property in the City, Southwark and Westminster, ranging from single houses grouped three to a page (**10**, **37** and **38**, but regrouped into alphabetical order of address in the present volume) to large blocks of property which stretch over two adjacent pages (**3**, **53**). This group of plans is preceded in the book by late seventeenth-century plans of three of the same properties, all rebuilt (**8**, **36** and **50**), evidently drawn in the book at a later date. One plan of the major group is signed by Treswell and dated 1610 (**3**). The close resemblance of style to Treswell's other major set of surveys for the Clothworkers' Company reinforces the conclusion that these are the surveys Treswell was paid for.

On 17 December 1612 the Court ordered that 'there shall be a fair book made of parchment wherein shall be entered a note of all the evidences concerning the lands and annuities belonging to this house'.[34] If this refers to the Evidence Book, then more thrifty counsels prevailed; it is a blank book of paper. The first page of the text records that it was written, or at least begun, in the time of the treasureship of Mr Cogan; the date of his appointment, 1594, is placed in the margin. The date of his replacement, 1614,[35] is not mentioned in the Evidence Book. The written survey is incomplete, for it stops half-way through the Hospital's extensive holdings around Horley in Surrey; it also does not cover several pre-1594 bequests of city property which are known from other hospital records.

The plans which each occupy two pages were clearly drawn before they were bound into the volume. Further, the paper on which the plans are drawn shares the same watermark as the rest of the blank book. It therefore seems likely that the book was made up by the binder when Treswell had drawn some, and probably all, of the existing surveys. The written survey at the front was however compiled in the made-up book; the prick-marks of the last written page show through to the following blank page.

Though Treswell had produced maps of the Hospital estates in Essex and Surrey, only surveys of London property (including houses in Southwark and Westminster) are included in the back of the Evidence Book. There is no apparent reason for this except for the obvious practical consideration: the rural surveys were drawn on very large sheets, whereas the urban properties were generally small and compact. The advantages of such handy individual surveys had already been apparent, since it is evident that some of the plans were originally drawn up to accompany leases, and only later transcribed by Treswell to form the 1611 series. The earliest of these is of property in Tothill Street, Westminster, probably of 1586 (**52**). A signed copy of the plan is attached to a lease of that year (Plate 2);[36] in comparison with the plan in the Evidence Book, the lease-plan shows houses running along the street in both directions in addition to the frontage of the Christ's Hospital property. This plan, like the one in the Evidence Book, is undated, but the tenants' names and those of the abutting owners are as in the lease. In two cases lease-plans, both probably of 1607, have survived. In the first case (**7**) the plan is mentioned in a lease of that year as 'the plot hereunto annexed' but is absent, having been removed to be now attached to a subsequent lease of 1661; in every detail except the colouring, which is a plain brown ink and wash, it resembles the plan in the Evidence Book. In the second case (**26**) the plan, signed by Treswell and dated 1607, is attached to a lease of 1712 (the lease of 1607 not surviving); the plan is in the same brown tones as the other lease-plan. In comparison with the copy transcribed into the Evidence Book, however, the lease-plan shows the door of one of the two houses in a different position. In two further cases, what may be either lease-plans or drafts have also survived (**32**, **53**).

Thus it seems likely that some at least of the original surveys were drawn in 1607 as lease-plans; one, in Treswell's 'rural' style (**52**) probably dates from 1586. One survey (**3**) was signed and dated in 1610; evidence of tenants' names would date two other Christ Hospital surveys to 1603–1609/10 (**53**) and before 1611 (**25**). One further plan (**33**) must date from 1610 or later.

General comparison of tenants' names with the Treasurer's Accounts indicates that Treswell carried out the majority of his surveys for the Hospital in 1610–11.

THE CLOTHWORKERS' COMPANY

Treswell's association with the Clothworkers' Company is first recorded in 1603, when he painted their banner for James I's coronation, as described above (p. 1). Like Christ's Hospital, the Company was growing increasingly concerned that it should have a written and if possible drawn survey of all its lands; like the Hospital, the major livery companies had by the end of the sixteenth century acquired substantial amounts of property by bequest or purchase, much of it chantry lands or ex-monastic in origin. Some lay in the City and its suburbs, some comprised far-flung rural manors. In 1607 the Clothworkers' Company resolved that the bounds and limits of all its lands should be taken down and set in writing.[37] This does not seem to have been immediately effected, since in 1609 a carpenter named Anncell was asked 'to draw a plot and the measure shall be exactly taken and set down in writing, of all the Company's lands and tenements, and the number of rooms in every particular house.'[38] This in turn seems to have been without result, since Treswell was asked to do it on 24 September 1611.[39] He presented his surveys on 3 September 1612; he asked for £50, but the Company gave him £35 and had him survey their lands in Sutton Valence, Kent, and Essex.[40] The title page of the Plan Book records that the surveys were carried out in July 1612; this must refer to the London plans only, and suggests that, as with the Evidence Book of Christ's Hospital, Treswell's surveys for the Clothworkers were drawn on loose sheets and later bound into a volume when he had completed the commission (one Essex plan follows the London series in the Book). The comparison of names of tenants shown on the surveys with those recorded in the Company's Renter Wardens' Accounts for 1611–12 makes it quite clear that Treswell conducted the London surveys in one operation, and without working from previous lease-plans, in 1612.

The Plan Book of the Clothworkers' Company, held at Clothworkers' Hall, comprises thirty water-colour ground-plans of company property in London and Essex, on paper in a modern binding 19½″ by 14½″ (the nineteenth-century binding was replaced in 1983). A number of the Treswell plans, and the eighteenth-century plans which follow them in the Book, were published by the London Topographical Society in 1938–42.[41]

OTHER INDIVIDUAL SURVEYS

Three other individual surveys of London properties by Treswell are included in the present volume. These are the drawing of the Conduit and pipes at the east end of St Michael le Querne, Cheapside (**12**) signed and dated 1585; property in Old Bailey belonging to Christ Church, Oxford in 1610 (**32**) and property of the Leathersellers' Company in London Wall, surveyed in 1614 (**27**).

Treswell's surveys of property outside London, including lands at Islington and Lewisham, are not described in the present volume, but have been catalogued in the list of all his known surveys.

3. Chronological survey of the drawings: concordance

Here, in tabular form, is summarised the known work of Ralph Treswell, including both his rural and urban surveys.

Table: Known surveys of Ralph Treswell

BY RALPH HYDE

SURVEY		DATE	DIMENSIONS	LOCATION
[*Planbook of the Hatton Estates in Northants. containing the following*][1]				Northants. R.O. Finch-Hatton MS 272
Fo. 1	The Survaye of Cottingham Woodes	1580	394 × 526 mm	
Fo. 5	The Survay of the Mannor of Kyrby [Kirby] with the grounds belonging to the same	1585	401 × 520 mm	
Fo. 6	The survay of the Mannor of Kyrby [Kirby] as it is now in ano.1587 . . . made since the exchange with Mr. Thomas Brundnell	1587	413 × 534 mm	
Fo. 7	The Survaye of the mannor of Gretton with the grounds belonging to the same	1587	420 × 534 mm	
Fo. 13	[The survey of Weldon]	n.d.	410 × 527 mm	
Fo. 59	The Survaye of the mannor of Holdenby in the Countie of Northampton[2]	1580	390 × 540 mm	
Fo. 62	The Survay of the manor of Holdenby[3]	1587	426 × 520 mm	
Fo. 63	[The survey of Brampton]	1584	426 × 530 mm	
Fo. 75	The Survay of the Mannor house of Ketteringe with the Demanes belonging to the same[4]	1587	420 × 515 mm	
Fo. 78	[The survey of Deanthorpe]	n.d.	400 × 493 mm	
[St Michael le Querne, at the west end of Cheapside with neighbouring houses][5]		1585	271 × 393 mm	British Museum, Dept. of Prints & Drawings 1800–11–13–3516

Table: Known surveys of Ralph Treswell — continued

BY RALPH HYDE

SURVEY	DATE	DIMENSIONS	LOCATION
[Lands in the parishes of St Martin in the Fields and St Giles in the Fields, including the area of Leicester Square, Soho, and Piccadilly][6]	1585	812 × 507 mm	PRO E.178–1391
[*Planbook of the Manors of Corfe Castle, Studland, Langton Wallis, Eastingham, etc., estates of Sir Christopher Hatton*]			Dorset R.O. (D/BKL)
Fo. 3 [Map of the Isle of Purbeck]	n.d.	522 × 392 mm	
Fo. 6 [Ground plan of Corfe Castle][7]	1586	529 × 415 mm	
Fo. 8 [Map of lands around Corfe Castle][8]	1585	535 × 406 mm	
Fo. 10 [Map of Newton Heath]	158[ ]	540 × 410 mm	
Fo. 24 The Survey of the Manor of Studlande in the Isle of Purbeck in the countie of Dorset	1586	538 × 418 mm	
Fo. 31 The Survey of the Mannor or Lordshippe of Langton Wallis in the Isle of Purbeck in the Countie of Dorset A Survey of the Mannor of Eastington . . .	1586	536 × 405 mm	
Fo. 34 [Map of Middlebury]	n.d.	544 × 418 mm	
[Friern Farm in the parishes of Downham, Ramsden, Bellhouse, Runwell, and Wickford, Essex][9]	1587	629 × 638 mm	St Bartholomew's Hospital
[Friern Manor Farm in the parish of Hatfield, Broad Oak, Essex][10]	1587	432 × 655 mm	St Bartholomew's Hospital
[Parsonage Farm, in the parish of Little Wakering, Essex and Hockerell at Bishop's Stortford].	[1587]	327 × 620 mm	St Bartholomew's Hospital
Soweware in Burneham [Burnham] Marshe [showing] Ringwood Channel alias Burneham Channell, the Lease of Oysters belonging to Burneham Marshe [Essex][11]	1587	359 × 508 mm	Royal Institution of Chartered Surveyors
[Part of Elkington, called Cockhills][12]	1587	193 × 145 mm	Northants. R.O. Finch-Hatton MS 272 f94
[*Inscribed*:] Old Map of Berry Green Farm and A Mappe of the lands of Mr. Tho: Palmer in little Hadham in the County of Hartford.[13]	1588	787 × 814 mm	Herts. R.O. 76558
[The Bridge House Farm, Ladywell][14]	1592	527 × 616 mm	CLRO Comptroller's Bridge House Plan, 204/3
Britanie [Brittany][15]	1594	369 × 482 mm	British Library, MSS Dept. Cotton Aug. 1 ii 58
[Wyllyotts Manor, South Mimms, and Potters Bar, Hertfordshire][16]	1594	807 × 1194 mm	GL Map Case 66

Table: Known surveys of Ralph Treswell — continued

BY RALPH HYDE

SURVEY	DATE	DIMENSIONS	LOCATION
[Land at Rickling, Essex][17]	1597	603 × 730 mm	GL MS 13766
Alice Robinson's 5th pte of the Manor of Cransley [Northants.]	1598	298 × 514 mm	Location of original not known. Colour photo in Northants. R.O. Mp. 1430
[Farm at Brockley Green, in Lewisham and Deptford][18]	[*c.* 1600]	387 × 585 mm	GL MS 22636/8
[Estate at Berden and Clavering, Essex][19]	[*c.* 1600]	676 × 1371 mm	GL Map Case 7
[Survey of Radstone, Northants.][20]	[*c.* 1600]	342 × 552 mm	Photo. in Northants. R.O.
[Colne Engaine, Essex][21]	1602	767 × 1130 mm	GL MS 12819/2
[*Inscribed on reverse:*] Survey of Horley in Surry[22]	[1602]	1054 × 2198 mm	GL Map Case 168
[Survey of an estate at Esher, Surrey][23]	1606	832 × 850 mm	Location of original not known. 19th-century tracing in private collection
[Survey of ground belonging to Christ's Hospital in Bishopsgate][24]	[*c.* 1607]	676 × 195 mm	GL MS 12949E
[Survey of ground belonging to Christ's Hospital in the Round Woolstaple, Westminster][25]	[*c.* 1609]	335 × 204 mm	GL MS 22635/21
[Survey of ground belonging to Christ's Hospital in Tothill Street][26]	[*c.* 1610]	350 × 175 mm	GL MS 13057
Chrystes church land in London in the olde baylye in the tenur of the lady lucy oxon	1610	560 × 410 mm	Christ Church MS Estates 45, 1
[Draft for the plan of 'Chrystes Church land in London in the olde baylye . . .,]	*c.* 1610	520 × 410 mm	Christ Church Deeds: London, St Sepulchre 4
Christ's Hospital Evidence Book (*The individual plans are described fully in the present volume.*)	1611	413 × 263 mm	GL MS 12805
[*Planbook entitled:*] A Survaye of all Lands and Tenementes belonging to the Worshipfull Company of Clothworkers of London . . .[27] (*The individual plans of properties in the City of London, Westminster, and Southwark are described fully in the present volume.*)	1612	495 × 368 mm	Clothworkers' Hall
Fo. 52 [Property in Islington]			
Fo. 54 A tenement . . . by the name of the Mill with desmaine land adjoining, lyeing in the parishes of Warley (?) and Upminster . . . Essex			
[Two plans of the Bridge House Close, George Lane, Lewisham][28]	1612	387 × 380 mm	CLRO Bridge House Plans, Nos. 43A and 43B
[Plan of property in London Wall]	1614	533 × 330 mm	Leathersellers' Hall

NOTE

The following Treswell items have yet to be located and may not have survived: a survey of the property belonging to St Bartholomew's Hospital at St Alban's, 1595; and a survey of the St Bartholomew's Hospital manor at Woolaston, Northants, 1592. The St Alban's survey is referred to in the St Bartholomew's Hospital manuscript Ha/1/3, 152v. It is possible that a survey of the property in the 'Llewellyn' planbook is a copy of it. It is also possible that the surveys of Clitterhouse Farm near Willesden, of a property near St Pancras, and of a property in Hethe in Oxfordshire are copies of Treswell plans.

NOTES TO TABLE

[1] The maps listed here represent those in the planbook that are either signed by Treswell or can be attributed with confidence to him.

[2] Reproduced and discussed in M. Beresford, *History on the ground* (1957).

[3] Réproduced and discussed in Beresford (*op. cit.*), and by M. Finch, 'Elizabethan and Jacobean Animals', *Northampton Past and Present*, 1 (1948–53), 37.

[4] Reproduced by F. W. Bull, *Supplement to the History of the Town of Kettering* (1908).

[5] E. Croft-Murray and P. Hulton, *Catalogue of British Drawings* vol. 1 (1960), 24–6, plate 17.

[6] See C. L. Kingsford, *Early History of Piccadilly . . .* (1925); LCC *Survey of London*, 31 (1963), 24–5, reproduced as plate 1 in vol. 32; 310 in *Maps and Plans in the Public Record Office*, vol. 1 (1967). For a redrawing of the map see LTS Publications 54–5.

[7] See G. T. Clark, 'Corfe Castle', *Archaeological Journal*, 22 (1865), 200–40, which includes a lithographic facsimile of the plan printed by F. G. Netherclift; T. Bond, *History and Description of Corfe Castle* (1883), which includes a facsimile photolithographed by James Ackerman.

[8] See T. Bond, *op. cit.*

[9] A copy of this map appears in the St Bartholomew's Hospital planbook. The plans in this volume have been attributed to Martin Llewellyn. Treswell's map, and the copy of it, are described in *Catalogue of Maps in the Essex Record Office*, 2nd suppl. (Essex R.O., 1964), 1–2.

[10] A copy attributed to Llewellyn appears in the St Bartholomew's Hospital planbook, *op. cit.* Treswell's map, and a copy of it, are described in *Catalogue of Maps in the Essex Record Office*, 1.

[11] A copy attributed to Llewellyn, described in *Catalogue of Maps in the Essex Record Office*, 2, appears in the St Bartholomew's Hospital planbook, *op. cit.* Treswell's original presumably strayed from the Hospital's records.

[12] Described in P. G. M. Dickinson, *Maps in the County Record Office, Huntingdon* (1968), 43.

[13] Described in *Catalogue of Manuscript Maps in the Hertfordshire Record Office* (1968), 43.

[14] Reproduced and discussed by P. E. Jones, 'Some Bridge House Properties', *Journal of the British Archaeological Association*, 3rd ser., 16 (1953), 59–73. The payment for surveying and plotting the Estates' Lewisham farm is recorded in the Bridge House Accounts (BH A/C 11, account for Mich. 1592–Mich. 1593).

[15] *Catalogue of the Manuscript Maps, Charts, and Plans, and of the Topographical Drawings in the British Museum*, vol. 2 (1844).

[16] Estate of the Worshipful Company of Brewers. A redrawn, reduced copy of the map by Helen M. Baker was published by Potters Bar & District Historical Society, 1978 (Pub. no. 4).

[17] Christ's Hospital estate, Ramsey Bequest.

[18] Christ's Hospital estate, Knott Bequest.

[19] Christ's Hospital estate, Ramsey Bequest. Described in *Catalogue of Maps in the Essex Record Office*, 2.

[20] Estate of Magdalen College.

[21] Christ's Hospital estate, Ramsey Bequest. There also exists a terrier — 'A Book of Survaye of the Manor of Colne Engaine . . . Made by Ralph Treswell, Surveyor' (GL MS 13568).

[22] Christ's Hospital estate, Ramsey Bequest. Payment for the survey is recorded in the Hospital's annual accounts, 1602 (GL MS 12819/2).

[23] No. 35 in *The Story of Surrey in Maps* (Surrey Branch of RICS, 1956).

[24] Richard Casteler's gift. the same property features in the plan on fo.19 in the Christ's Hospital Evidence Book. Unsigned.

[25] Sir Martin Bowes' gift. Now attached to a lease of 1661 but originally attached to lease of 1607. A smaller version of the plan appears in the Christ's Hospital Evidence Book, 22.

[26] Richard Casteler's gift. Attached to lease. A less detailed version of this plan appears in the Christ's Hospital Evidence Book, 20.

[27] See R. Weinstein, 'Clothworkers in St Stephen Coleman Parish, 1612' *London Topographical Record*, 24 (1980), 61–80.

[28] These plans were made in the course of a dispute between the Corporation of London and Sir Nicholas Stodard, lessee of the manor of Lewisham, regarding a right of way. One of the plans is reproduced in P. E. Jones, *op. cit.*

4. Treswell as a surveyor

SURVEYING AT THE BEGINNING OF THE SEVENTEENTH CENTURY

There are three personae to be considered here: Treswell the painter-stainer, the map-maker and the surveyor. Each skill had its own particular setting in the opening years of the seventeenth century.

A connection between the painting of banners, heraldry and map-making was nothing new. Local maps drawn in Netherlands in the late fifteenth and early sixteenth centuries were the work of painters or artists: Willem Croock, whose maps from the 1520s survive, also painted the standards for the warships of Emperor Charles V.[42] The combination of painter and estate cartographer in the same person was often found on the continent throughout the sixteenth century.[43] William Smith (*c.* 1550–1618), herald and topographer, drew a panorama of London in 1588[44] and produced six county maps in the years around 1600; and Treswell's own son Robert became Somerset Herald in 1597. In 1610 Robert was appointed Surveyor-General of Woods south of the Trent, and was to monitor the condition of all castles, forts, parks and lodges. His assistants were John Thorpe and John Norden.[45]

As Treswell was among the first modern land surveyors — i.e. men who were capable of preparing scale plans of estates as opposed to earlier surveyors, mainly lawyers, who prepared written surveys, or masons and artists who prepared sketch plans and perspective views — a principal point of interest must be where he acquired the necessary skills. Here three interrelated factors can be suggested: the spreading use of maps in the sixteenth century, Treswell's links with the merchant community in London, and his connection through Sir Christopher Hatton with the Court.[46]

During Treswell's youth the idea that maps (albeit not to scale) could be useful in a variety of practical ways (as opposed to being largely didactic tools, as medieval *mappemondes* seem to have been) was spreading. This found expression in the works of Machiavelli (*Arte della Guerra*), Castiglione (*Cortegiano*) and Elyot's *Boke named the Governour* (1531). Lawyers also began using sketch maps to clarify issues and for production in court from at least the fifteenth century.[47] The Ledger Book of the draper and alderman George Monoux, for instance, contains an elevation of a proposed almshouse (*c*. 1527) and a plan of fields bought by him, both in Walthamstow.[48]

From about 1550, London merchants and London companies came to act as patrons of cartography, particularly chart-making. Their special contribution was to encourage the collaboration of academic mathematical theorists, often from Cambridge (e.g. John Cheke, John Dee and their followers, but also country gentlemen like Leonard Digges) with mariners like William Borough and, after about 1560, with the earliest English instrument makers and platemakers in London.[49] Treswell would have been on the spot in London when the important works by Leonard and Thomas Digges on surveying were published in the later sixteenth century.

Apart from the drawing of St Michael le Querne and the lease-plan of Tothill Street, Westminster (1585–6), Treswell's work until about 1607 was predominantly the surveying of rural estates. The rise of the estate surveyor is a feature of the late sixteenth century, one of the consequences of the great transfers of land which followed the Dissolution and the Reformation.[50] At the beginning of the reign of Elizabeth in 1558, estate maps were a rarity; by the end of her reign they were commonplace. Maps of estates in the Home Counties survive in numbers from the late 1570s. Surveyors such as Thomas Clerke (died 1592) worked for institutional clients such as the Oxford colleges. Clerke was probably engaged in surveying for the Gresham family after the death of Thomas Gresham in 1587.[51] From 1587 Christopher Saxton was working in the counties, where his surveys included work for St Thomas Hospital, though from 1598 he seems to have worked exclusively around his own estate in Yorkshire.[52]

Here Treswell's early connection with the Court through Sir Christopher Hatton, his first known patron, is probably significant. Hatton was active as an investor in overseas voyages by such men as Drake, Frobisher and Hawkins. As such he would have been in regular contact with London merchants and this may even have been the manner by which he came into contact with Treswell. He was patron of a translation of Wagheneer's marine atlas into English in 1588,[53] and it is therefore not surprising that he should have commissioned scale mapping of his Northampton estates as early as 1580. Through Hatton — both as courtier and later as Lord Chancellor — Treswell would also have had access to the royal working collection of maps dating back to the pictorial maps of the late 1520s by Vincent Volpe and Hans Holbein.[54]

Though none of Treswell's work was engraved, it is also worth mentioning that engraved maps were published in London from the middle of the sixteenth century. It is not known where the copperplate map of *c*. 1560 was produced, but a copperplate map of England ascribed to George Lily was published in London (having been previously published in Rome) in 1555.[55] Saxton's maps were engraved and presumably printed in London from the mid 1570s.[56] In 1591 Jodocus Hondius migrated to London and set up as a type founder and engraver, joining an existing business run by his eventual father-in-law, Pieter van den Keere. Hondius later engraved some of the maps for Speed's county atlas; he returned to Amsterdam before 1600 and took over the business of the great Mercator.[57] Printed town plans of British and Irish towns were also in circulation: William Cunningham's plan of Norwich, 1559; Richard Lyne's plan of Cambridge, 1572; and in 1573 Braun and Hogenberg began publishing their *Civitates Orbis Terrarum* which included plans of London, Cambridge, Oxford, Norwich, Bristol, Chester, Edinburgh, Canterbury, Exeter, York and Dublin.[58]

A further kind of survey was that drawn by the other kind of surveyor, the architect. Several surveyors/architects of the 1590s produced surveyed plans which have survived: John Thorpe,[59] John Symonds[60] and Simon Basil,[61] for instance. Their drawings have a greater air of accuracy because they used rulers to draw lines, which Treswell did not; they noted more details, especially of window openings and sometimes vaulting arrangements. Being more interested in the whole plan of buildings, their drawings often include upper floors, which are totally absent from the Treswell surveys, concerned as he was chiefly with the extent of the property. The carefully drawn architectural surveys were not however made only for building work; the Symonds plan of Holy Trinity Priory, Aldgate, probably drawn in 1592, seems to have been made for Burghley at the time of an application to alienate the former precinct;[62] and the only other dated ground-plan of a City of London property of this period outside the Treswell series known to the writer is an anonymous 'grounde plat' of 1596 of the Erber, Dowgate, then belonging to the Drapers' Company, which is of the Symonds-Thorpe architectural kind.[63]

There are two possible coincidental or circumstantial connections between Treswell and John Thorpe, who was to become his son's assistant as Surveyor-General of Woods. In 1580 Treswell surveyed the grounds of Holdenby House, Northamptonshire, for Sir Christopher Hatton. Hatton completed a rebuilding of the house in 1583,

and the grounds were re-surveyed by Treswell in 1587;[64] the house was surveyed in detail by Thorpe at an unknown date, but possibly 1607.[65]

The evidence for a second case of the two men's work coinciding is not so clear. In 1594 Treswell surveyed the manor of Wyllyotts, South Mimms; the map has survived.[66] The patron was probably Robert Taylor, who acquired the manor in that year.[67] In Thorpe's book of drawings is the plan of a house for 'Mr Tayler at potters bar'.[68] Sir John Summerson took this to be a plan, never executed, for a house at Wyllyotts;[69] the Victoria County History, however, holds that this was a plan for the nearby Cattall House, which Taylor also acquired.[70]

FEATURES OF STYLE IN TRESWELL'S PLANS

Treswell's rural surveys, encompassing as they did large tracts of land, used the contemporary technique of a bird's-eye view, showing houses as tiny sketches, sometimes in elevation, more often in crude three dimensional form. The tradition of bird's-eye views of towns apparently spread from Italy to other countries of Europe towards the end of the fifteenth century;[71] one of the earliest bird's-eye views of an English town is of Bristol about 1480.[72] Treswell used this convention in the 1586 Tothill Street plan, which was of a sizeable property, but not in the surveys, concerned with central London.

All the Treswell surveys are drawn to a scale; a ruler-scale is not present on the Christ's Hospital surveys, but present on those of the Clothworkers' Company. Various scales are used, from 6′ to the inch to 22′ to the inch; the most common are 10′, 11′ or 12′ to the inch. The earliest surviving post-Roman map with a scale drawn on it is a plan of Vienna of about 1422.[73] Scaled maps were produced in Germany in the second half of the fifteenth century;[74] they may have profited from the spreading use of the magnetic compass to measure directions on land. Scaled maps were drawn up in England by military engineers in the reign of Henry VIII, and it is clear that concern with fortifications hastened the development of surveying skills.[75] The map of Portsmouth in 1545, for instance, includes outline ground-plans of blockhouse and bastions, with details of embrasures. These plans are the immediate predecessors of the detailed ground-plans of individual stone or brick buildings by Symonds, Thorpe and others in the 1580s and 1590s. The inclusion of a pair of compasses above the scale, as practised by Treswell in some of his surveys, both rural and urban, appears in early sixteenth-century German maps.[76] It is also found on maps of Britain (e.g. the 'Cotton' map of 1534–46; Mercator's map of the British Isles, 1564),[77] on English military plans and estate plans of the sixteenth century.

Other conventions, such as the colours used for walls of brick, timber and stone (Plates 3–10), were also derived from the general stock of the Elizabethan and Jacobean map-maker or surveyor. Borders formed of a simple double line, as employed by Treswell, are found on Saxton's work;[78] Treswell did not employ the cabled border used by Martin Llewellyn, who possibly drew up the plans of St Bartholomew's Hospital properties in the City in *c.*1617; plans which resemble the drawing of St Michael-le-Querne by Treswell.[79]

The cardinal points (North, South, East and West) are given usually in Latin, though occasionally in English, within the borders. Cardinal points were sometimes marked on the appropriate edge of medieval picture-maps. On both continental and English maps this was normally in Latin, but in at least one case an English picture-map of the fifteenth century had English terms.[80] The use of Latin terms persisted in France even when the explanatory text was in French.[81] In England, Christopher Saxton's county maps from the 1570s had the cardinal points named in Latin, within a thin decorated border.

Thus although there are a number of resemblances to the work of Saxton (whom Treswell must have known, since the City managed both Christ's Hospital and St Thomas's Hospital, for which Saxton did some work), Treswell could have acquired the features of his style from several sources.

5. The surveys as studies of London houses

The sites of the buildings surveyed by Treswell for the two institutions in the years 1607–12 are shown in Figure 1. The property of the Clothworkers' Company and Christ's Hospital spread throughout the city, on major and minor streets.

Many of the sites fall within the area almost totally devoid of later records of above-ground medieval domestic buildings, the area devastated by the Great Fire of 1666 (shown by a dashed line in Fig. 1).

CONVENTIONS

Apart from the single plan-view of property in Tothill Street, Westminster (**52**) and the unusual early drawing of St Michael-le-Querne (**12**), all the plans are groundplans of buildings with details of doorways, chimneys and stairs, together with their yards and gardens. Window-openings are shown in only three plans (**32, 33, 53**) in contexts which suggest they were exceptionally large and fine examples. Nearly all the walls are coloured grey, and most are represented as less than a foot thick, presumably indicating timber framing. Some thicker walls were evidently of stone and are occasionally so labelled (**43**); unfortunately the same colour is used as for the thinner walls (Plate 9). A bright red is used for chimneys, wells and some further walls, occasionally exterior walls of buildings but more often garden walls, which were presumably of brick. All chimneys (i.e. fireplaces) are red in colour, but perhaps this did not preclude the occurrence of stone mantels and surrounds in the more prestigious houses.

TYPES OF HOUSE

Four types of post-medieval London house can be seen in the surveys; these are presented here in order of increasing size of ground-floor plan. Houses only one room in plan (Type 1; Fig. 2) are

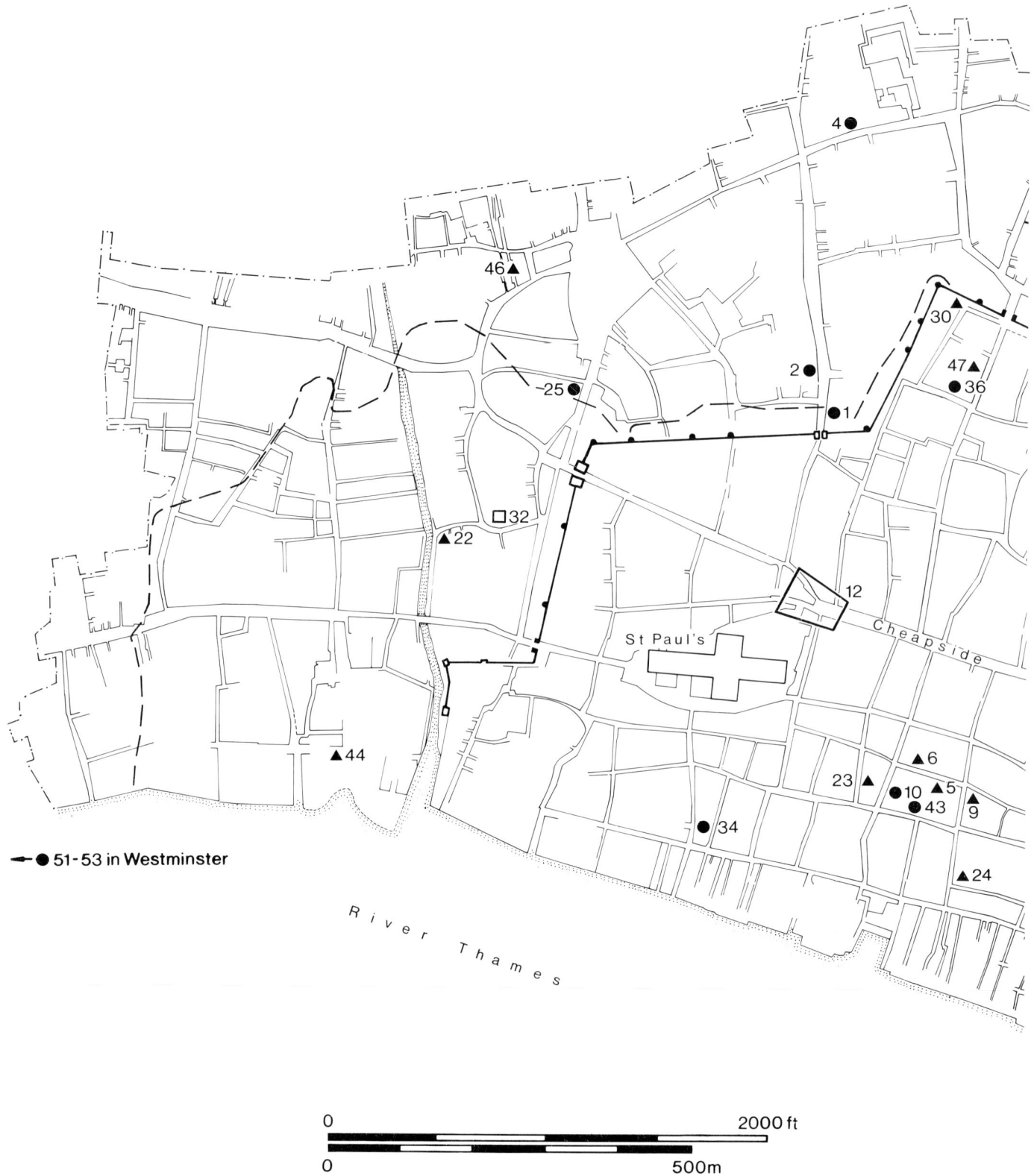

Figure 1. Map of the pre-Fire City of London, showing sites of the houses surveyed by Treswell.
The limit of the Great Fire of 1666 is shown by a dashed line.

N

● 7   8 ●

27 □

▲ 13-15

11 ▲

42 ▲

● 26 3
Aldgate

▲ 17
Cornhill

45   16 ▲
● ▲
33

37 ●

21 ▲
▲ 20
▲ 29
31 ▲
19 ▲   18 ▲

▲ 41

▲ 28

▲ 40   ● 35
▲ 39 ● 38

Tower

● 49-50 in Southwark

Bishopsgate

▲ 48 →

TYPE 1

TYPE 2

TYPE 3

Figure 2. Types of house in the Treswell surveys: Types 1–3

KEY TO FIGURES 2 AND 3

C	Cellar	Sh	Shop
Ch	Chamber	St	Study
H	Hall	W	Warehouse
K	Kitchen	Wa	Waterhouse
P	Parlour	Y	yard
Sd	Shed		

found both on principal streets, where they formed a screen for the larger houses behind (**21**), or in courtyards where they could assume awkward, angular shapes to take up every inch of space (**30**). On principal streets a one-room-plan house could reach five and a half storeys (**38**). While apparently similar in plan, houses of this type forming a single row could be of different ages. The row of predominantly small dwellings along Billiter Lane (now Street) (**21**) (Plate 6) was composed in 1612 of units partly rebuilt in stages since company records began in 1528; building accounts survive for rebuildings of 1538 and 1557.

The second and much more numerous type is the two-room house on three or more floors (Type 2), such as those in Abchurch Lane (Fig. 2; shown in context, Fig. 3). This type is known from documentary and archaeological evidence in London from the early fourteenth century.[82] The five houses of this type at Abchurch Lane (**31**) may be those built on the site by John Basse, draper, in or shortly before 1390. In Type 2 houses the ground floor is a shop and warehouse, sometimes with the two rooms thrown together to form one, or a tavern (**50**). The hall of the tenant is on the first floor at the front, overlooking the street. In the Abchurch Lane examples, probably because they were of the older medieval form, the kitchen is a separate building, but in the majority of the type as surveyed by Treswell the kitchen occupies a back room on the first floor.

More variety was possible in the planning or development of larger houses, and they fit less well into types. Two types can be suggested: that in which the house is of three to six rooms in ground-floor plan (Type 3; Fig. 2 and Plate 4) and a miscellaneous group of larger properties (Type 4) which includes courtyard houses (Fig. 3 and Plate 4) (**21**, **31**) and inns (**3**). The large house, probably still medieval in layout and substantially so in form, though adapted and rebuilt with more chambers and sometimes divided into tenancies, is shown four times in the Clothworkers' Company survey (**21**, **22**, **31**, **43**) (Plates 4, 6) and once in the Christ's Hospital plans (**34**) (Plate 3). Foxe's Court, (St) Nicholas Lane (**31**, Fig. 3) was entered through a three-storey street range. The house comprised a hall, entered by steps, on a cellar; the original hall appears to have been subdivided to provide a parlour. On the other side of the original screens passage lay a kitchen with a stack which occupied nearly the whole gable end.

The range fronting Nicholas Lane had first- and second-floor galleries on its inner, court side, with access to the court. Each floor of this range had several rooms running the width of the range, each room entered separately as in galleried inns.

Although there are several examples of lobby-entrance houses on the outskirts of the city (e.g. **13**, **15**, **46**) (Plate 5) they need not be regarded as a separate Type. The occurrence of a side entrance against a chimney-stack was evidently more appropriate in buildings where gable-ends did not front upon the street. Such houses may be classified instead by the number of their ground-floor rooms, usually as Type 2.

Apart from showing a range of domestic buildings of various sizes, the plans are valuable for providing examples of specialised buildings. There are taverns (**43**, **50**, **51**), two inns with extensive stables (**3**, **4**) and the row of what was certainly in one case and probably in all cases cookshops at Giltspur Street, near Smithfield, known as Pie Corner (**25**) (Plate 7). A nearby block of Clothworkers' Company property, fronting on to the open space of Smithfield itself, included several houses with large kitchens strongly suggestive of cookshops servicing the market area to the east (**46**) (Plate 5). Each collection has at least one company hall: the Clothworkers' Company had their own hall surveyed (**29**), and the large house nearby in Fenchurch Street had functioned briefly as Fullers' Hall in 1520–8 (**21**) (Plate 6). The Christ's Hospital portfolio included a second-floor room used as Woodmongers' Hall (**34**) (Plate 8). Each institution had one set of almshouses surveyed: those at Whitefriars bequeathed to the Clothworkers' Company by the Countess of Kent in 1540 (**44**) and a courtyard of six almshouses built at St Peter's Hill by David Smith, embroiderer to

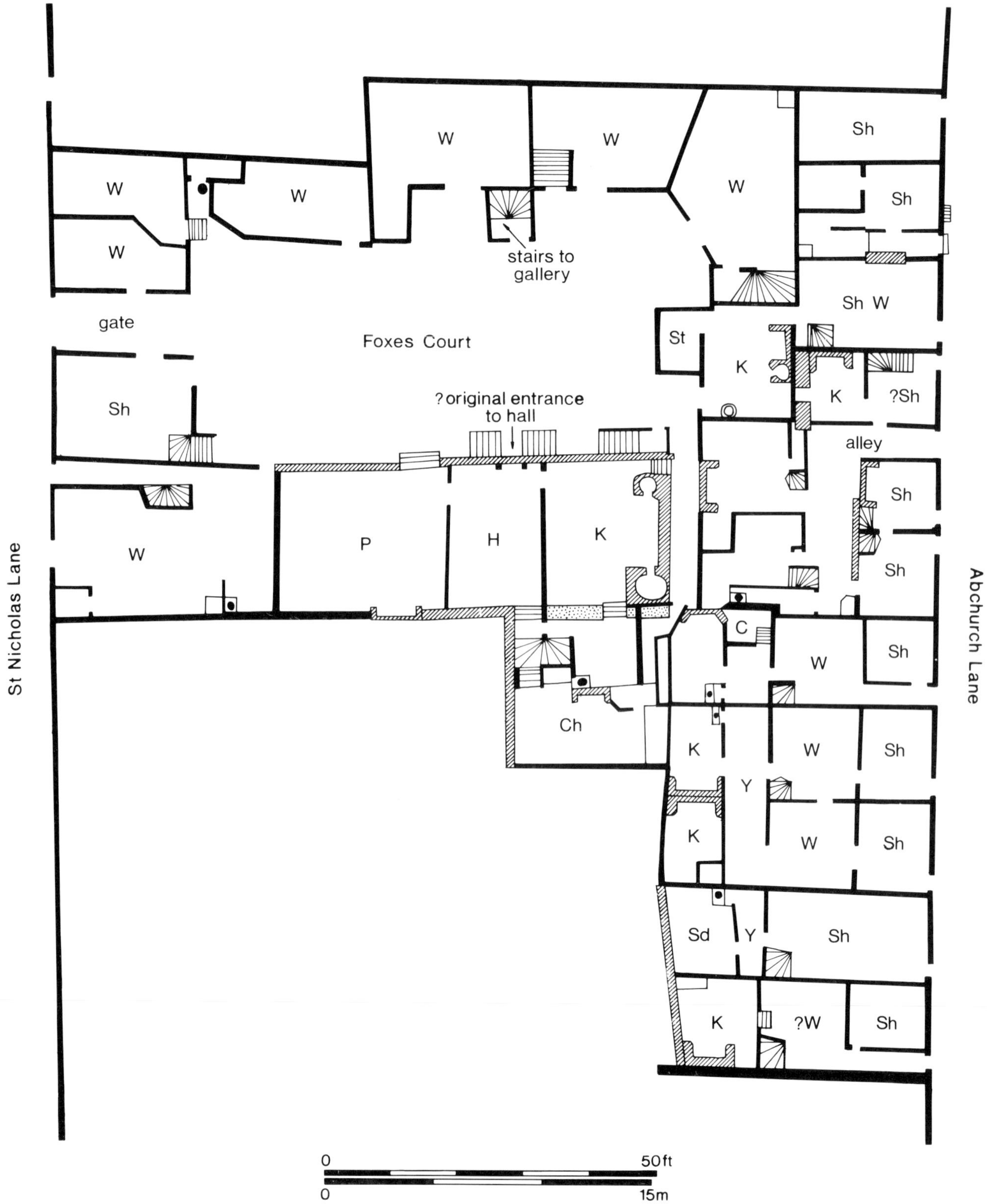

W

W

W

W

W

stairs to
gallery

W

W

Sh

Sh

Sh W

St

gate

Foxes Court

K

?Sh

alley

Sh

?original entrance
to hall

Sh

P

H

K

Sh

St Nicholas Lane

W

C

Sh

W

Sh

Ch

K

W

Sh

Y

Abchurch Lane

K

W

Sh

Sd

Y

Sh

K

?W

Sh

0   50ft

0   15m

Figure 3. Foxe's Court, Nicholas Lane and 23–5 Abchurch Lane (**31**)

Elizabeth I, in 1576 and bequeathed to Christ's Hospital (**34**) (Plate 8). Clearly the property portfolio of each institution comprised a wide range of properties.

It should be noted that Treswell is describing individual tenancies rather than houses, though the two are often the same. Some of the plans and texts show the advanced nature of property subdivision in central London.

CHIMNEYS AND HEATING

Although examples of central hearths are found on archaeological excavations in medieval London, it is clear that the wall-fireplace and chimney developed early in the medieval period, aided by a pressure on land use which encouraged the division of open halls into several chambers and the development of the first-floor hall and kitchen during the fourteenth century. Contemporary ordinances against chimneys of wood indicate the adoption of more durable materials for this purpose — at first stone, tiles and plaster, and later brick.[83] Chimneys in gable-ends of stone are specified in a contract for building the Peter and Paul tavern, Paternoster Row, in 1342.[84] Double chimneys are specified in a St Paul's contract for a block of shops in 1370,[85] and is likely that the axial stack shown in some of the Treswell plans (**7, 49**) became common in London in the fifteenth century, as it was in Norwich by the end of that century.[86] A building lease for a house belonging to Eton College in King Street, Westminster specifies the building of a double chimney between parlour and kitchen in 1459.[87]

The Treswell plans show that even the smallest houses in early seventeenth-century London possessed a chimney and several heated rooms. The kitchen invariably had the largest fireplace, often with an attached oven which might project into the yard or into an adjoining tenancy (**39**). A Type 1 house could have up to five hearths (called chimneys by Treswell) from its single stack, but generally two or three; Type 2 houses had a mean of between three and four hearths and Type 3 houses a mean of between four and five, with one

case of thirteen hearths. The smallest houses were however better heated, room by room, than the two larger types, since it would be relatively inexpensive to heat a large proportion (often all) of the rooms, because they could be serviced by a single chimney-stack. A cursory survey suggests that Type 1 houses had nearly two-thirds of their rooms heated, Type 2 had a little over a third of their rooms heated and Type 3 about half. Thus the small and medium-sized houses of London in 1612 seem to have had fireplaces in about half their rooms, a luxury not found in other English cities.[88]

HALLS

Evidence for the layout of medieval tenements in London is not substantial, and it is at present an assumption that the general classifications applied to other medieval towns by previous scholars[89] will apply here. By 1400, in general, the hall of the most prestigious tenements would lie at the back of or to one side of a courtyard, that of a long tenement, such as those excavated on the waterfront, along the side behind a street range.[90] The majority of central London properties, however, were neither large nor long. In the smallest medieval houses the hall is found on the first floor from the early fourteenth century;[91] in houses of two-room plan (i.e. Type 2 in the Treswell surveys) the hall was usually the front room overlooking the street. This would enable the shop beneath to expand or be serviced by a warehouse occupying the rear ground-floor room (as at Abchurch Lane (**31**)). Halls on the first floor are known in Exeter houses from the fifteenth century.[92]

In Treswell's surveys the hall took one of two forms:

(a) in larger properties, the ground-floor hall could be found at the side or at the inner end of a courtyard (**31, 21** respectively) in the medieval tradition. On long but wide properties, the hall could still be found along the side of the property behind the street range (**20**, de Bees; **3**). The company hall still preserved the medieval form of hall with screens passage, dais and twin oriel windows at high table end, as at Clothworkers' Hall (**29**); by Stow's time (1598) there were about fifty such halls, nearly all courtyard houses, scattered throughout the city.[93] One larger private house had an oriel in the hall, but set in the middle of the side, perhaps placed there to give a view down into, and to be seen from, the narrow approach courtyard (**21**, Darcy).

(b) The majority of the houses surveyed by Treswell were however those of two-room plan (Type 2) or its variants; and in these the hall lay on the first floor, always in the front room over the street when the position is specified. Usually this chamber would have a chimney, but there are some cases, in houses which may have been old (**20**, Jennynges, Robertson and Yeoman) where the hall was not heated.

There are some indications that the hall was coming to be regarded as a vestibule in larger houses (**31**, Foxe's Court); and that the room which functioned as the centre of the household was now being called the parlour (e.g. **30**).

PARLOURS

Documentary references to 'a locutorium called parlour' or an 'interloquitorium' in better houses (i.e. those which figure in wills) begin in the second quarter of the fourteenth century in London.[94] In the 1370s William Langland complained that 'now hath each rich man a rule to eaten by himself in a privy parlour . . . or in a chamber with a chimney, and leave the chief hall, that was made for meals, and men to eaten in',[95] showing that parlours were widespread in grand houses by the third quarter of the century. During the fifteenth century many livery company halls were provided, either by addition or refurbishment, with a parlour as a standard element. In the surveys of 1612 the parlour was still a room found mostly in the larger or well-appointed houses. It could be found in two main positions, and in a number of further, exceptional locations:

(a) in the largest houses, the parlour could be found at the upper end of the hall, in its medieval position (**21**, Darcy). This was the normal position in livery company halls, though the parlour of 1594 at Clothworkers' Hall (**29**) lay at the other end of the hall and could be reached through the screens passage. This was because the hall was open to the roof and the storeyed elements were placed together at the screens end, so that both kitchen and parlour supported two further storeys, forming a range at right angles to the hall.

(b) In both medium-sized and large houses, the parlour overlooked, and occasionally had access into, the garden of the house. Where no hall is mentioned, proximity to the garden (or at least away from the street) seems to have been influential in the placing of a parlour (**22**, Lady Wood; **43**, Fishburne; **34**; **36**, Cowndley). This proximity is often emphasised by a prominent window overlooking the garden; in one house, a quasi-octagonal window took up much of the gable end of the room (**13**, Butler). The parlour at Clothworkers' Hall had a canted window near one end which was carried up through the storey above.

(c) In small to medium-sized properties the parlour was rare but not completely absent (**1**, Elliott). It could be found on the first floor, next to a hall (**40**, **45**); and in one probably exceptional case, was the front room in a small tenancy and entered directly from the street (**20**, Sutton). Normally the parlour, in all situations, was buried deep within the property, whether on the ground floor or on an upper storey. Even within a tavern it was a secluded withdrawing room; Treswell's plan of the Sun at Westminster (**51**) shows that a parlour lay behind the normal drinking rooms.

There are some indications within the Treswell surveys that the parlour was beginning to take over some of the functions of the hall. At Foxe's Court, Nicholas Lane (**31**), the partitions and positions of doorways (both in use and apparently blocked) strongly suggest that the main range formerly comprised a large medieval hall which had been subdivided, with two-thirds becoming a parlour and only one-third called the hall. The hall now functioned as a vestibule, leading to the main staircase. A smaller house in Bell Alley, Coleman Street (**14**, Colley) had on its ground floor a parlour and kitchen, and no hall. This arrangement is repeated in the medium-sized house attached to, or perhaps formerly part of, the Hermitage of St James at Monkwell Street (**30**). Here the tenant, Beastney, had a principal ground-floor chamber called a parlour, with kitchen and buttery adjoining. This parlour had three entrances, indicating that it was not in the medieval style of an inner chamber with only one entrance. In these examples we may be seeing the gradual diminution and change in function of the medieval hall noticed elsewhere.[96] A view of 1631 of the houses at Trinity Hall, Aldersgate, mentions, in one of them, a 'dining chamber next the street with a chimney in it' on the first floor. Although this term is not used by Treswell, it was being used of his 'hall' rooms within twenty years. In 1634 the term 'dining chamber' is used in an inventory of a house in Covent Garden;[97] it is also used in nine Exeter inventories from 1590 to 1675, with a main concentration in the years 1620–30. In most of the Exeter cases it is synonymous with hall or parlour, on ground or first floors, in inns or houses of prominent merchants.[98] In certain London houses of the late sixteenth century, it may be suggested, the ground-floor hall was a relic of the past, and in certain houses had already become a vestibule; the social life of the family, especially entertaining, took place on the first floor.

KITCHENS AND BAKEHOUSES

Among large courtyard houses the medieval sequence of hall–screens–service rooms–kitchen was still found in 1612, no doubt partly influenced by the conservatism imposed by a large kitchen chimney-stack (**31**). In some cases the kitchen would be in line with the hall (**21**, **31**); in others, where space was restricted, the kitchen lay at right angles to the hall, sometimes along one side of the entrance court (**22**, Lady Wood; **29**). In one Type 3 property (**20**, de Bees) a medieval arrangement for medium-sized properties can be seen: the former hall along the side of the property behind the street range, with its kitchen beyond the hall. In the surveys kitchens assumed a variety of

positions in small and medium-sized properties, however, and it is likely that most of these positions were also developments of the medieval period. These were:

(a) On the ground floor, behind the shop; especially in Type 2 (two-room plan) houses, forming the back room of the ground floor. For examples see **20**, Jennynges, Yeoman; **26**; **50**.

(b) A related position was that in which a kitchen formed half of a two-room unit, but the other room was a hall or parlour. This was found in the outskirts of the built-up area, where the houses were different in several ways (**13**).

(c) On the ground floor, in a separate building, usually across a small yard. This type, which is seen at Abchurch Lane (**31**), Trinity Lane (**43**, Fryth) and Pudding Lane (**35**), may be a relic of the medieval practice of separate kitchens for fear of fire (and at a time when chimneys in the rest of the house were not widespread); the Abchurch Lane examples may have been constructed as part of a documented rebuilding shortly before 1390. Although such kitchens may have been of a single storey when built, they were not so by 1612; all the separate kitchens had chambers above, some reached by a gallery crossing from the main house at first-floor level (see below, galleries). The separate kitchen had been incorporated into the house complex, a process which could well be also of medieval date.

(d) On the first floor, behind the front room. Where the shop took up all the ground-floor space in smaller houses, particularly those of Type 2, the kitchen had joined the hall on the first floor from at least the beginning of the fourteenth century.[99] By 1612 this was a common arrangement in London, not only in central, congested properties but also in peripheral areas where space was no problem (**10**; **11**; **38**; **42**, Johnson; **47**; **15**, Ramsey, Myles). In several cases the room to the front of the house is called the hall, and it is clear the hall and kitchen functioned together as related rooms (**10**, **38**, **48**).

(e) On the first floor, but in a separate building. There are no examples of this arrangement in the houses surveyed by Treswell, but it should be noted that this arrangement, in which the separate kitchen lay on the first floor and was approached by a gallery, is known from a plan and survey of Eton College property in Bread Street in 1617,[100] and still survives at the mid-seventeenth-century Hoop and Grapes, Aldgate.

(f) In a variety of other positions, though these are rare. At West Smithfield a kitchen could be found in a cellar (**46**, Seger); this was a corner tenement, so perhaps special structural influences prevailed, but it nevertheless lay two floors below the first-floor hall. In Thames Street (**38**) a tiny house one room in plan and 5½ storeys high had its hall on the first floor and the kitchen on the third floor.

Several kitchens shown in the ground-floor plans of 1612 had substantial ovens. In the case of Clothworkers' Hall (**29**), where there may have been two large fireplaces in line and a pastry room within the stack (i.e. intentionally hot), such grander facilities were clearly for communal feasting. In other cases the ovens were probably used for brewing, dyeing and the commercial production of food. Two types of oven are shown in the plans: a normal domestic oven at the side of a hearth, which could be quite large and therefore used for non-domestic purposes (West Smithfield (**46**), Campion's brewery in Haywharf Lane (**40**)); and the larger commercial oven, in which an oven or vat has its mouth in the back of the hearth (**4, 25**). This larger type of oven was usually sited so that the body of the structure, of brick, tile and clay, lay outside the building. The occurrence of four such ovens in adjacent premises (two worked by one tenant) at Pie Corner, Smithfield (**25**) suggests a row of cookshops, but the derivation of the name is said to be from an inn sign, that of the Magpie, rather than from the shops' function.[101] These houses were on the corner of Giltspur Street and Cock Lane, and a corner site for a cookshop may well have been prized; a single corner shop at the junction of Fenchurch Street and Philpot Lane (**19**, Richardson) included two hearths and a substantial side-oven, perhaps for commercial production of food on a similar scale.

The fittings of the kitchen, whether solely domestic or with commercial overtones, are largely absent from the Treswell surveys, but there is one notable inventory of 1588 which describes a kitchen in detail (**53**). In a second case it is known, from an inventory of 1587, that the kitchen of the large house in Needlers (later Pancras) Lane (**33**) had a cistern and pump in it; but otherwise wells, when shown, were to be found outside the kitchen.

In several cases the ground-floor privy could be found within or adjacent to the kitchen block. In some cases the privy was part of the structure, but entered by a separate door from the yard (**31**); in other cases, the privy was approached through or off the kitchen (**21**; **36**, Cowndley; see also **31**, Foxe's Court). This proximity aided, and was perhaps intended for, the disposal of food waste from the kitchen. Larger pieces of food waste and kitchen utensils are often found in medieval cesspits on archaeological sites in the city.

BUTTERY, PANTRY AND LARDER

Although the pantry and larder are mentioned very occasionally in the surveys, the principal service room was clearly the buttery, which was present in many houses of all sizes. Its usual medieval position in larger houses is shown at Clothworkers' Hall and at Darcy's tenancy, Fenchurch Street (**29, 21**); in the latter two butteries are found between the hall and main kitchen. One is a simple small room with one entrance; but the other, depending upon interpretation of the plan, may be a kind of through-passage with two doors. The buttery was a small chamber, as the measurements show; but it could be attached to kitchen or hall. Whether on ground floor or at first floor, the kitchen often had an adjacent buttery (**50**, Aldriche; **1**, Percival; **17**; **42**, Colyer). Alternatively the buttery was attached to the hall (**42**; **24**; **46**, Drewery); or was a small presumably partitioned area within a hall (**20**, Sutton). In one further case a first-floor buttery was entered from a room called merely a chamber (**15**, Fizardett).

CLOSET

In fashionable European houses of the late six-teenth and seventeenth centuries any small room might be called a closet (*un cabinet*), but the main purpose of the closet was to be a small chamber off the bedroom, where the occupant could retire for privacy or rest.[102] A closet is mentioned twenty-one times in the two Treswell surveys, in a variety of contexts; it could be found on any floor except the ground floor, even in a garret (**50**, Red Bull). It could be found in all types of house, from 'a chamber with a chimney and a little closet over into Fleet Lane' at a Type 1 tenancy of 3½ storeys in Fleet Lane (**22**, Bulman), to the courtyard house at Foxe's Court, Nicholas Lane (**31**) which had two closets among its many rooms. As with the privy, Treswell often lumped the closet together with other rooms on the same floor, so that it is difficult to determine whether the closet was in every case a separate chamber or merely part of a larger room. In some cases it certainly was part of a larger chamber or considered to be an appendage of one (**35**, Dorrell). The closet is not associated with the hall; presumably a small room off the hall was called either a study or a buttery.

The dimensions of the closet, when they are specified, indicate a small chamber along the lines recommended by Sir Roger Pratt in 1660: 'nine feet upon three and a half feet is the least you can allow to the closet'.[103] A 'little closet' at Pudding Lane (**35**) was 7½′ × 3½′, and another in a modest suburban house at Bishopsgate 13′ × 4′ (**7**, Walker).

STUDY

A study, or a larger room called a library, was often present in larger seventeenth-century houses in England and France; surviving pictures of Samuel Pepys' library in London, about 1693, show a medium-sized rectangular room with several pairs of free-standing bookcases, a reading desk, portraits in oil hung above the bookcases and canted forward, and a large map of Paris on the wall.[104] At the beginning of the century,

however, books were often kept in chests, some-times in the bedroom; or houses might have a small room called a study which, at least in noble households, served as a depository for rarities of all kinds, curiosities and collections.[105] Studies are mentioned sixteen times in the Treswell surveys; and although there are no clues as to what they were used for, several suggestions can be made about their general position within the house, their size and character.

The study could be found on all floors, from the ground (**1**, **30**) to a garret on the third floor (**19**, Chauncey). If on the first floor, it was sometimes entered from the hall (**6**; **20**, Sutton) or even stood within it (**17**). A study could also be found within a larger chamber on other floors (on the third at the Talbot, Wood Street (**47**), a second-floor garret at Swan Alley (**15**, Ramsey) and a third-floor garret at Fenchurch Street (**19**, Chauncey)). It was usually on the outside of the building, presumably to give the maximum of natural light; if on the ground floor, the study was often placed either jutting into a court (**31**) or next to the street (**1**, **3**), where presumably the increase in light was thought more important than the increase in noise, a position sometimes repeated in the upper floors ('the study hanging over the street' on the first floor at 20, Basing Lane (**6**); a second-floor chamber with a study situated over the gate to the tenement (**43**)). A position overlooking the rela-tive quiet of the garden does not seem to have been favoured, and was only present in one house which was in any case surrounded by open spaces (**13**, Burdges). In this semi-rural house there were two studies, one on top of the other.

In dimensions and shape the study assumed a limited number of forms. The smallest, and quite common, form was a very small squarish room about 3 or 4 ft square (**3**, **34**). Larger sizes were presumably a result of having a room spare for this purpose. The two studies in one house at Swan Alley (**13**) were 10½′ × 10′; what might have been Treswell's own study in Aldersgate Street (**1**) was 8½′ square. The largest was a ground-floor room at the St James Hermitage (**30**), where Beastney had a spare room across the entry from his house, 19' × 10'. This large study was not however heated; and in general studies were not provided with a chimney. All the studies shown in the ground-floor plans understandably shared one characteristic; they had only one entrance.

SHOP, WAREHOUSE AND COUNTING HOUSE

The great majority of small and medium-sized properties which had street frontages had a shop as the ground-floor front room. In some Type 1 houses this was the function of the single ground-floor room. Most of the variation in layout of shops, and their relationship with warehouses behind, is shown in Treswell's plan of Abchurch Lane (**31**; Fig. 3). There were three different types of one-room shop: a squarish room between 8 and 10 ft square entered directly from the street; the same, but entered from a passage; and a double-sized shop in which the partition between two ground-floor rooms had been removed. Where the partition had not been removed, the rear room might be a warehouse. In slightly larger houses, separate warehouses were to be found across small yards (**9**; **28**, Ivatt) or, in the largest houses, around a courtyard (**31**, **33**). Warehouses were always on the ground floor, and where space allowed could be independent structures of one or two storeys (**31**); but they were usually built into the congested building complex as one of many rooms. They were naturally a feature of houses on the principal streets (**31**, **33**), though also in new houses on the periphery of the market centres (**28** Ivatt, built 1562). On the northern periphery of the built-up area, and in certain larger houses, they were absent; presumably in the latter cases there was sufficient cellarage (e.g. Darcy, Fenchurch Street (**21**)). The frequency and disposition of cellars is considered below.

An associated room was the counting or compting house (both spellings are used by Treswell). This could be found at the back of a warehouse (**33**, Jackson) or at the back of a shop (**11**), both on the ground floor ; in these cases it was a small chamber about 6' wide and 7' or 9' long. At 16 Cornhill (**16**) it was probably smaller, apparently part of a gallery leading at first floor from the house to a chamber over the separate kitchen. At Clothworkers' Hall in Mincing Lane (**29**) were two counting houses; on the first floor was a large chamber, 41' × 16½' called the Dry Larder, within which at one end was a Plate Chamber and at the other end a Little Countinghouse. On the second floor a second counting house lay in or alongside a gallery, next to two gunpowder houses. Here presumably the counting house had special functions related to the storage of plate or arms common in Elizabethan and Jacobean livery company halls.

PRIVIES AND HOUSES OF OFFICE

Stone and timber-lined privies are documented and found on archaeological sites in the City from early medieval times. During the fourteenth century the surviving rolls of the Assize of Nuisance indicate a gradual adoption of the better-built stone cesspits, which might last, with periodic cleaning, for two or three centuries. In 1422 such amenities must have been considered basic, for certain small lodgings or rents in Bassishaw Ward were considered defective because none of them had privies.[106]

Although cesspits could be filled in when the privy's position within the house was to be changed, there must have been a natural conservatism imposed by the often substantial nature of the stone-lined pit, up to 12 ft deep and 10 ft square,[107] and it is therefore reasonable to suppose that the ground-floor privies shown in the Treswell surveys, both interior and exterior, may well have been in the same places for generations.

The first problem is one of definition. Treswell uses the term house of office almost to the exclusion of privy; was there a difference between a privy and a house of office? The Treswell surveys apparently suggest that there was not. It seems likely that the small chambers with privy seats shown on many of the ground-floor plans would be over cesspits, and were what we would call

1.   St Michael le Querne, Cheapside, 1585 (BM Crace Collection 1880-11-13-3516)

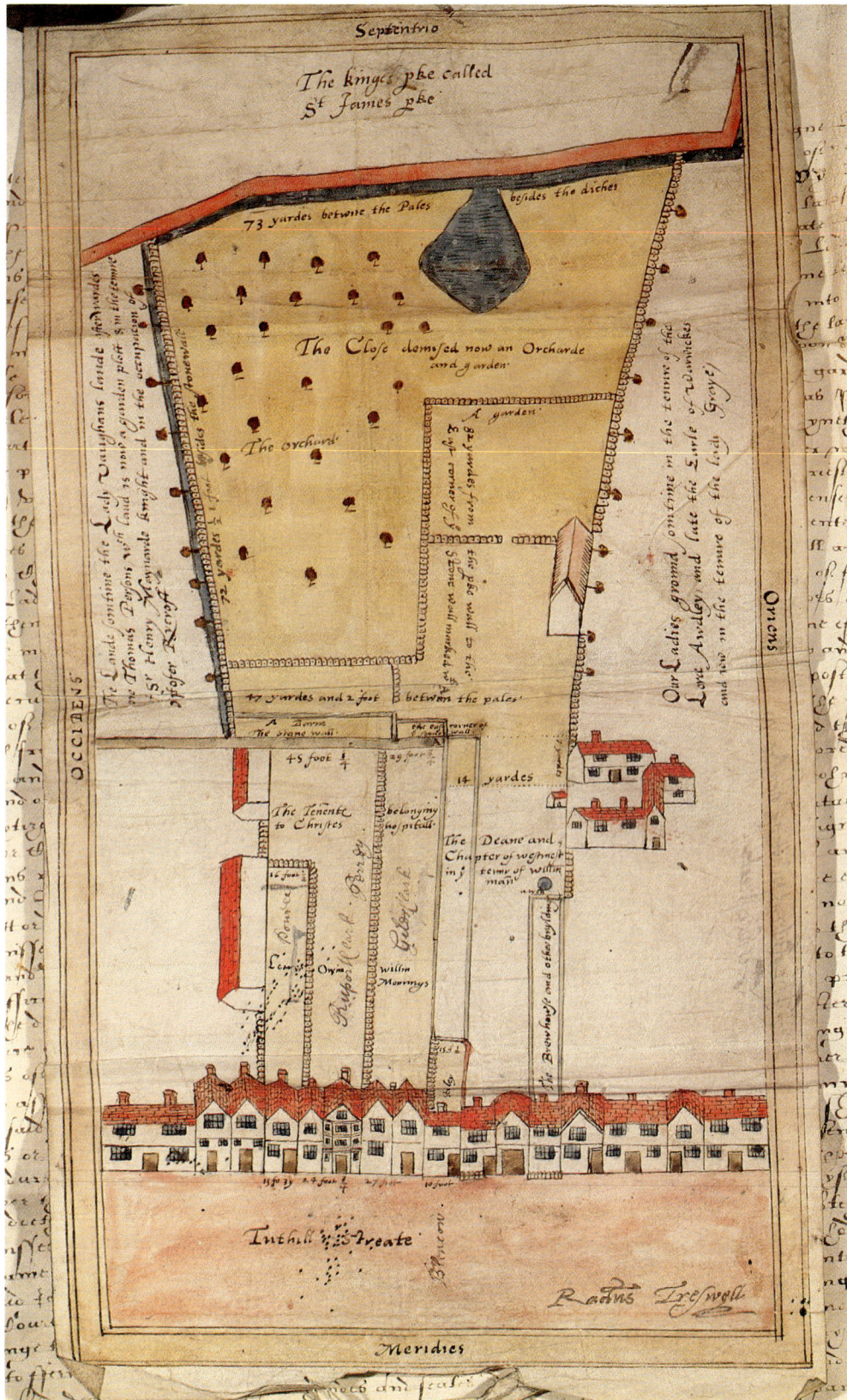

The map contains the following inscriptions:

Septentrio

The kinges pke called St James pke

73 yardes betwine the Pales   besides the diches

The Close demosed now an Orcharde and garden

A garden

The orchard

The Landes sometime the Lady Vaughans besides the Avords one Thomas Persons with land is now a garden plott 8 m thesemne of Sr Henry Maynarde knyght and in the occupacion of Phoster Kerof

Occidens

72 yardes 2 1 foo byds is 72 yardes 3 foot west topont 48

75 yardes 1 foo ovo wait mainted is 2 foot

Our Ladies ground sometime in the tenure of the Lord Awdley and late the Earle of Warwickes and now in the tenure of the Lady Graye

Oriens

47 yardes and 2 foot   betwin the pales

A Tearme the stone wall   the our coner of wall

48 foot 1/4   29 foot 1/2   14 yardes

The Tenente to Christes   belonging hospitall

Russell Wech   Brugy

Gelory Clark

The Deane and Chapter of wesmich in s teme of willm man

Lewis   Owin   Willm Mommys

the Brewhowse and other by the

16 foot

Tothill Streate

Brewen

Radus Treswell

Meridies

2.   Tothill Street, Westminster, probably 1585: the lease-plan version of the plan (GL MS 13507)

Nedelers lane in the p̃ishe of S̃ Pancrate   in lease to Petor
Ducane Esq̃r

24 foot

9 foot

M̃r
Baber

A warehowse
M̃r Halles

S̃t Thomas Hospitall
M̃r Crewe

A yarde

S̃t Stephen
Somes knyght

ouer heere is building
M̃r Halles
2 6 foot

11 foot 3 ĩnches   14 foot 4 ĩnches

M̃r Baber

M̃r Baber
A warehowse

M̃r Baber
A Warehowse

M̃r Baber

15 foot 4 ĩnches   M̃r Baber

M̃r Baber
A Buttrie   M̃r Baber A yarde

14 foot 4 ĩnch

Bakers
study   15 foot 6 ĩn

M̃r Baber
A kitchen

28 foot ½

A yarde M̃r Baber

18 foot 6 ĩn

M̃r Baber
A parlor or hall

M̃r Baber

27 foot ½

23 foot eache 3 ĩnches

A Butry
M̃r
Baber   M̃r
Baber

M̃r Baber A parlor

15 foot ½   A Chamb̃
M̃r Jackson

32 foote   17 foot

Common
howse

M̃r Baber
A garden   15 foot ½

29 foot

31 foot

M̃r Jacksons
warehowse

M̃r Jackson
a yarde

The grocers in the occupacion
of M̃r Dorington

M̃r Jackson

13 ½

M̃r Jackson

The Mercers   M̃r
Jackson

6 foot

8 foot

3.   3–4 Pancras Lane, 1611 (Christ's Hospital Evidence Book, 4)

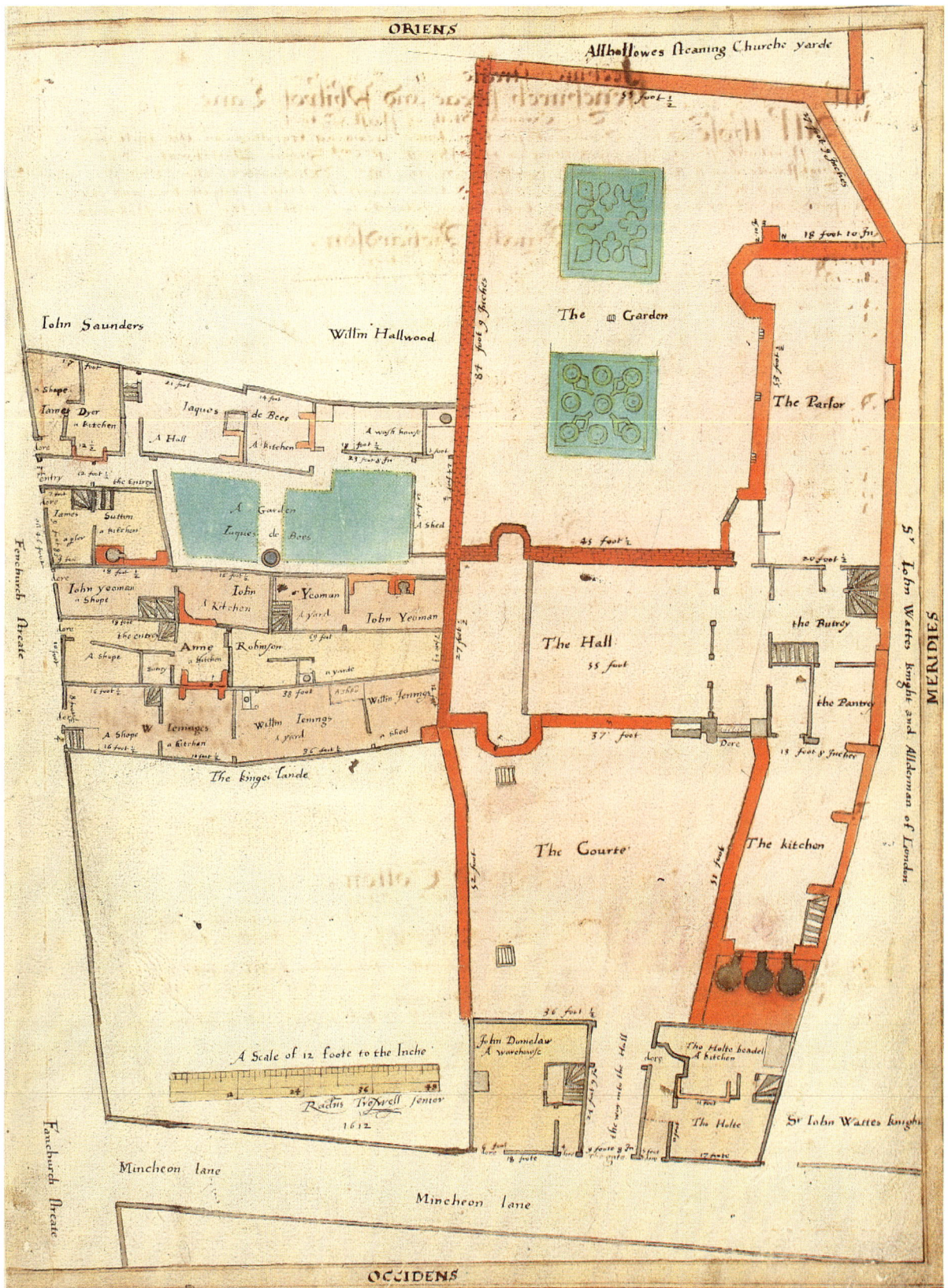

4. Clothworkers' Hall, Mincing Lane, and 47–8 Fenchurch Street, 1612 (Clothworkers' Company Plan Book, 3)

Blowbore Alley

Samson Pott

George Backhows

All is 9½ foote

Edward Drewry. A stable or shed.

E. Drewry

E. Drewry A kitchen

Edwarde Drewrey A shope

Charles Hill

Mr Webber

Phesante courte

E. Drewry A yard

E. Drewry

A yard

Christopher Askwith A kitchin

Christopher Askwith A Shope

Willm Ashpoole A chamber

A shed Shelston

G. Shelstone

George Shelstone

George Shelstone A shops

Phesant courte

Willm Procter A Chamber

Tho Welcott A yard

a shed

Tho Welcott kitchen

Thomas Welcote A shope

The Parrish land belonging to St Mary Ouery now in the tenure of Fremy Perkins All is 106 foote

A shed

Nic Ashley A chamber

Peter Clarke

Peter Clarke A yard

Peter Clarke A kitchen

Peter Clarke A shope

Smithfeelde penes

All is 85 foote

Richard Lighthurne

Richard Andrewe

Phesant courte

Willm Hallome

a shope

Tho Brettnor

Tho Brettnor

a kitchen

Tho Brettnor A shope

A shope

Tobias Haruille

The Brettnor entry

A shope

Robert Seger

Henry Perkins A Shope

Thomas Anderson A Shope

entry

John Showell

A shope

All is 86 foote

Cowe lane

Cowe lane

A Scale of 9 foot to the Inche

Radus Treswell senior 1612

ORIENS

5.   90–4 West Smithfield, 28–30 Cow Lane, 1612 (Clothworkers' Company Plan Book, 41)

6.   115 and 118 Fenchurch Street, 12–14 Billiter Street, 1612 (Clothworkers' Company Plan Book, 10–11)

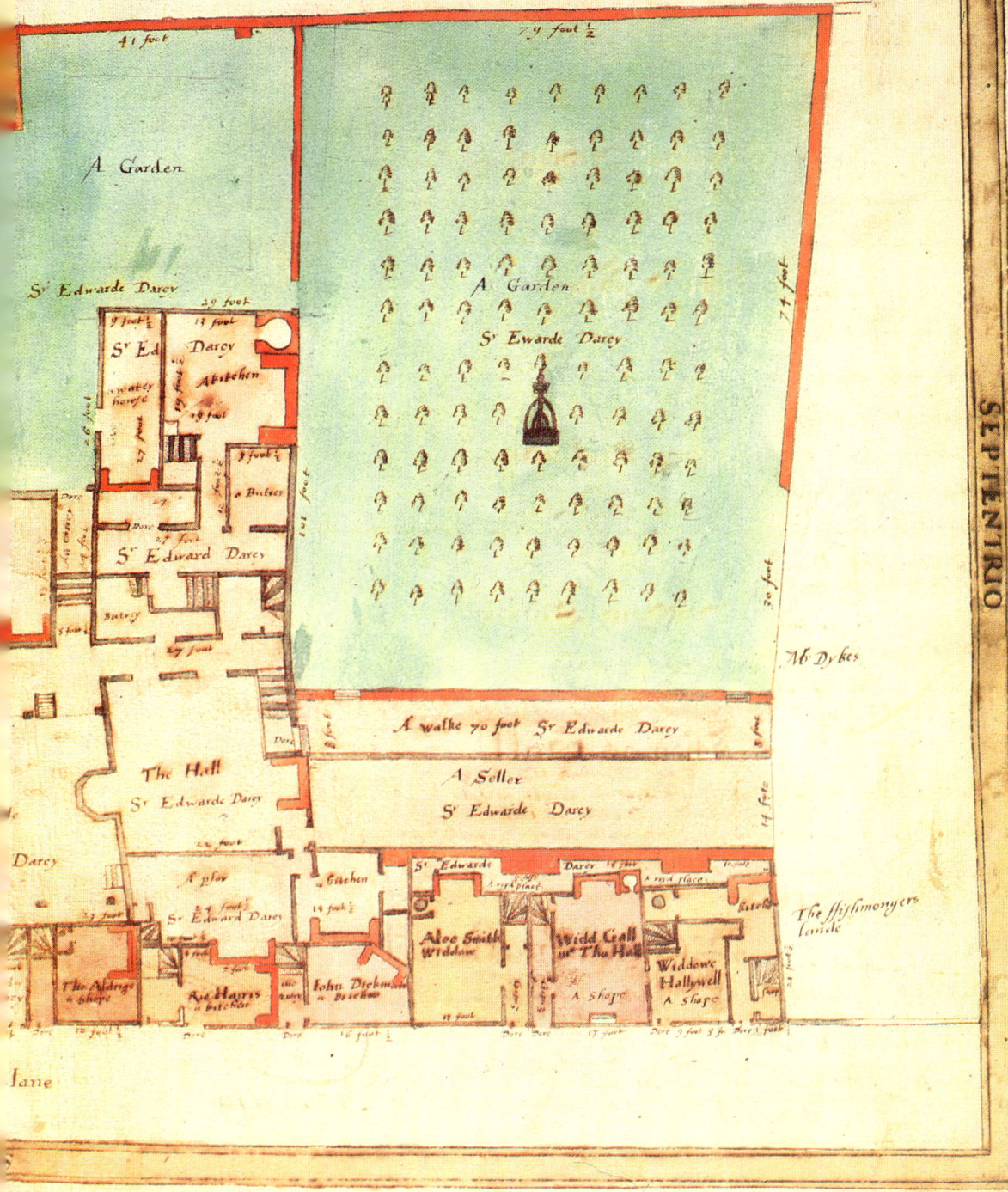

ngers Lande

The Fiſhmongers Land

41 foot

A Garden

Sᵗ Edwarde Darcy

29 foot

9 foot ½   13 foot

Sᵗ Ed   Darcy

water houſe   A kitchen

19 foot

Sᵗ Edward Darcy

Butrey

79 foot ½

74 foot

A Garden

Sᵗ Ewarde Darcy

30 foot

Mᵣ Dykes

A walke 70 foot   Sᵗ Edwarde Darcy

A Seller

Sᵗ Edwarde Darcy

The Hall

Sᵗ Edwarde Darcy

A plot

Kitchen

Sᵗ Edward Darcy

14 foot ½

Sᵗ Edward   Darcy 14 foot

The ffiſhmongers lande

The Aldrige a ſhope

Ric Harris a butcher

John Dichman a Brewer

Aloe Smith Widdow

Widd Gall m Tha Hall   A ſhape

Widdowe Hallywell A ſhape

Darcy

Iane

SEPTENTRIO

West

S.t Barthlmewes hospitall

Willm Norris

Tho Cobb 3 romes one ouer the other

11 foote 8 Inches

Margret Gryffin 3 romes one ouer the other

9 foote

7 foot

Andrew one Chamb ouer this pte

10 foote

Dauy Charles Bell a Chamb ouer this rome

13 foot 3 Inches

13 foot 3 Inches

Common privy 5 foote

8 foote 4 Inches

A Courte or yarde

7 foote ½

Charles Bell a Chamb ouer this

8 foote ½

5 foot

8 foot 4 Inches

Denis A Chamb ouer this and 2 foot ½ Charles Bell

10 foote

Willm Parret a yarde

27 foote 3 Inches

Jo welles

A yarde

Callaway

Callaway

13 foote ½

4 foote

North

Ouens

Ouens

7 foot ½

well

Robert Hollier a yarde

Robert Hollier A Chamb ouer this backe rome east and west 13 foot 3 Inch south and north 16 foote ½ Ouer the well a litle Chamb 8 foot ouer the Ouens a Chamb 11 foote ½

Robert Hollier

13 foote 4 Inches

Robert Hollier Ouer this rome is a Chamb with a Chimney, at the east ende 13 foote 3 Inches at the west end 14 foote ½ south and north 13 foot

S.t Barthlmewes hospitall

Cock Lane

a kitchen Willm Parret a Chamb ouer this

8 foote 3 Inches

8 foote 4 Inches

1 foote

7 foote

13 foot ½

a range

13 foot 2 Inches Edward Hurstes kitchen

W Parret a Chamber ouer this

John welles

R Hollier

Ouens

Ouens

9 foote

Willm Parret A Shopp A Chamb w.th a Chimney ouer the shopp and 2 yardes ouer the other Chamber and this, and a seller vnder this shopp

A Shopp John welles

R Hollier this pte to ye Ouens of excepted out of Holliers lease

Robert Hollier a shope Ouer this shopp is a chamb south 21 foot north 19 foot in west 15 foote East 13 foot and ouer Robt Holliers Chambers is 3 yardes in length 38 foot ½ In breadth 15 foote 8 Inches more a litle garret at the west end of this garret both in length 18 foot ½ breadth 13 foot 8 In

Edward Hurste a shope Ouer this shope and kitchen a hall at the east ende 13 foot ½ the north side 11 foot ½ to the Chimny on the south side 17 foot ½ also a garret one ouer ye hall the other ouer pte of Holliers Chamb 18 foot ½

10 foote ½

9 foote ½

6 foot 3 Inches

13 foote

14 foot

9 foot

8 foot

East

The howses at Pye corner

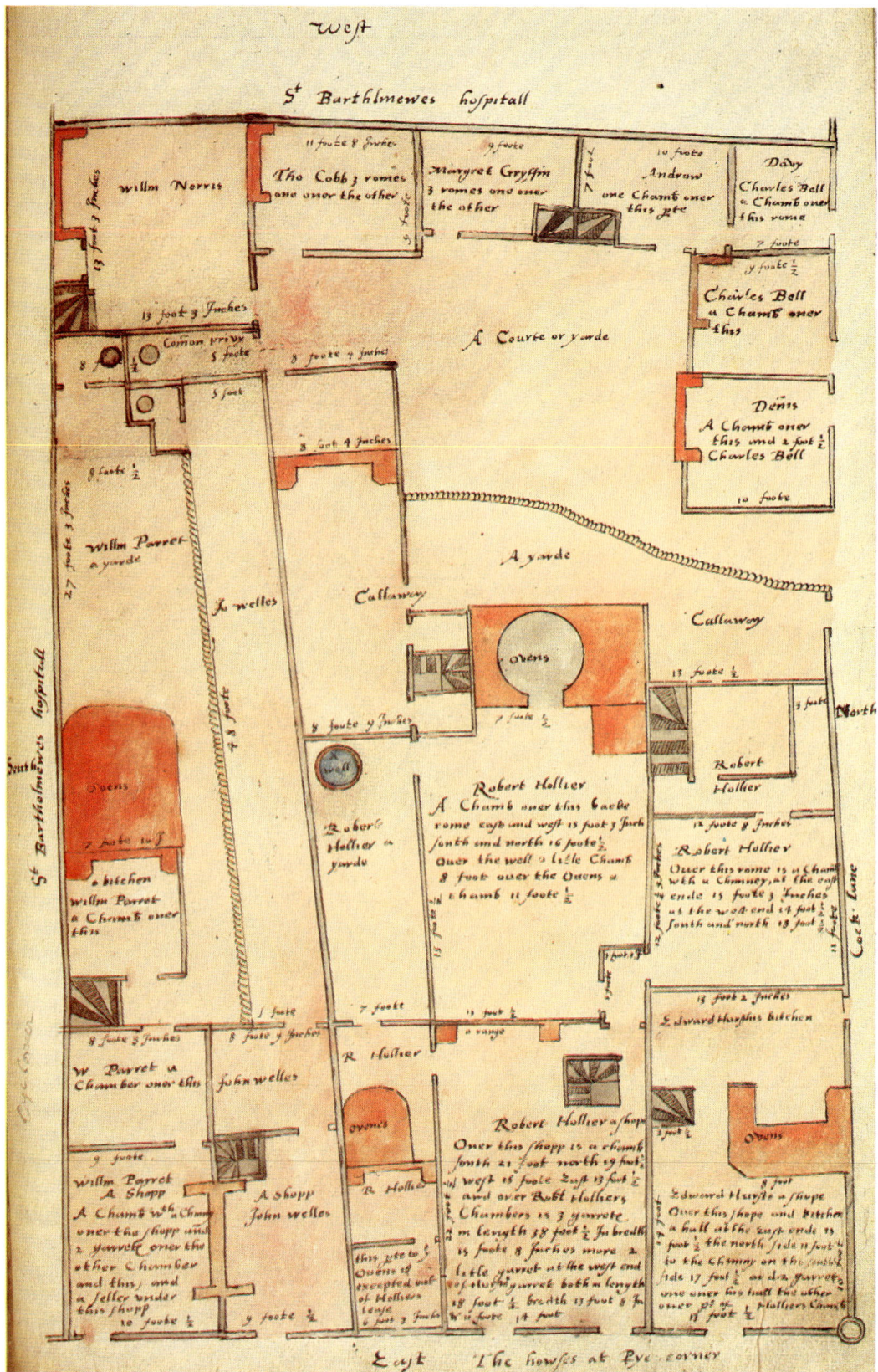

7.   Giltspur Street and Cock Lane, 1611 (Christ's Hospital Evidence Book, 17)

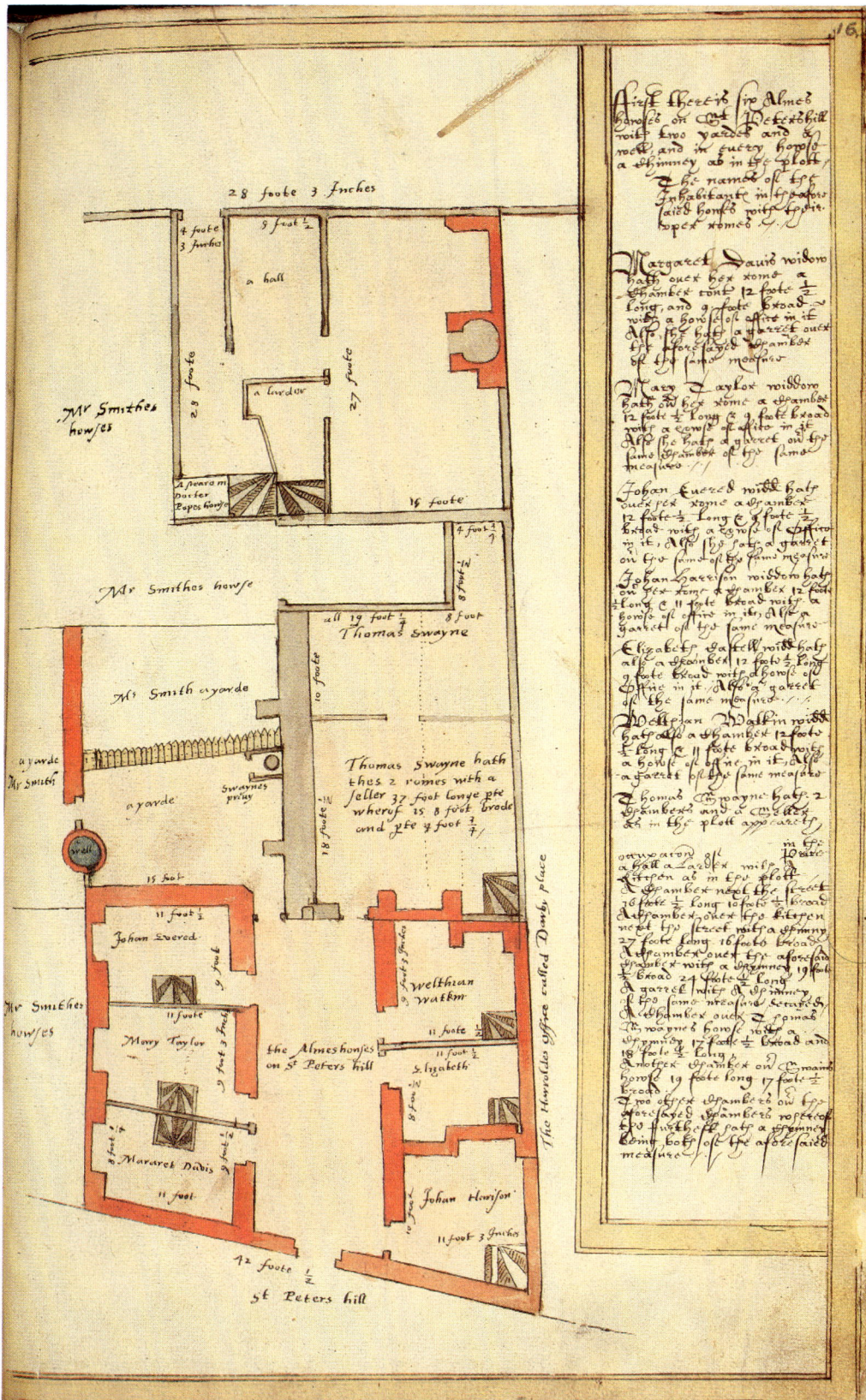

8. Smith's almshouses, St Peter's Hill, 1611 (Christ's Hospital Evidence Book, 16)

9. St James' Hermitage/Lambe's Chapel, Monkwell Street, 1612 (Clothworkers' Company Plan Book, 37)

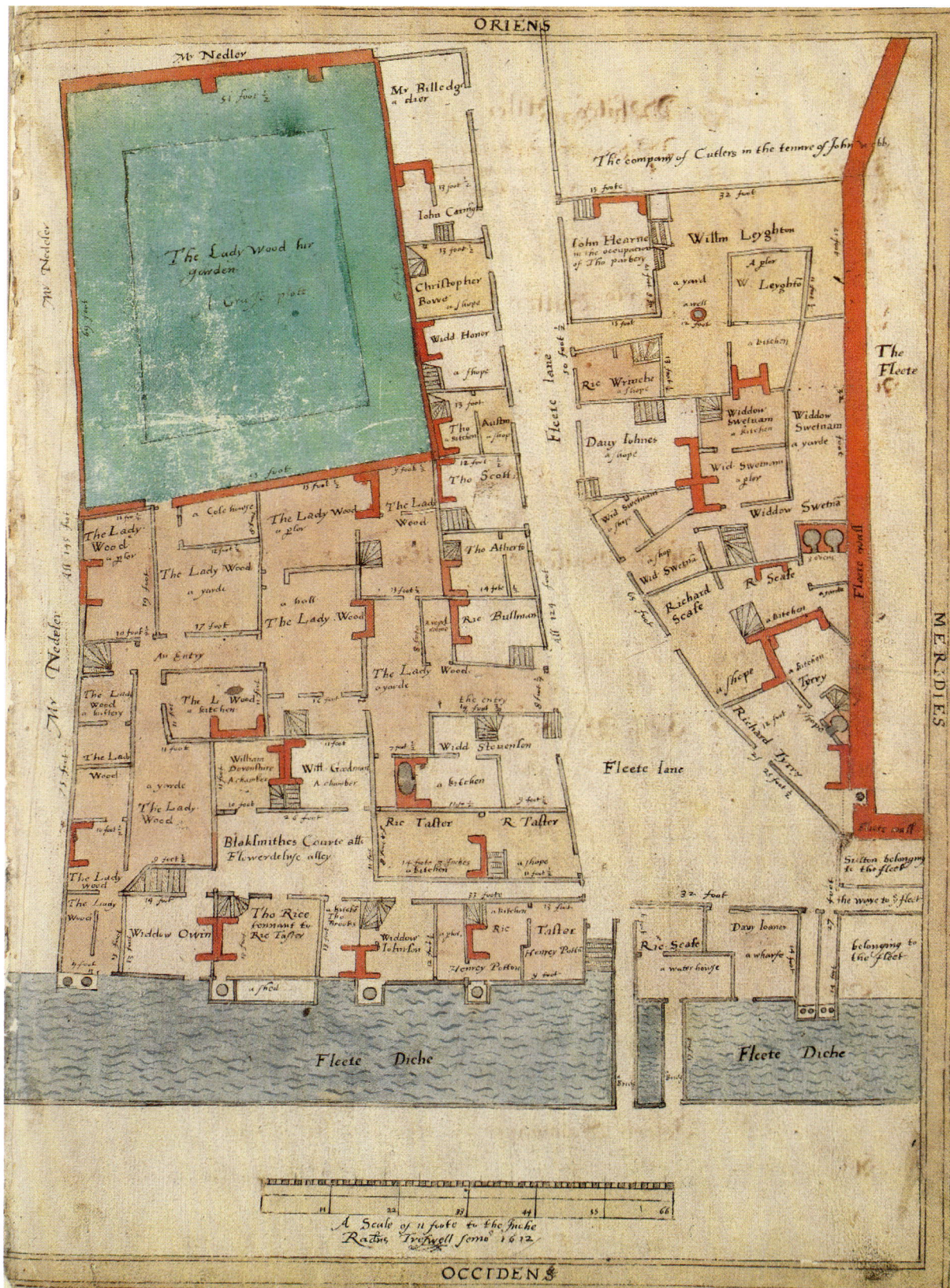

10.   1–6 Fleet Lane, 16–21 Farringdon Street, 1612 (Clothworkers' Company Plan Book, 47)

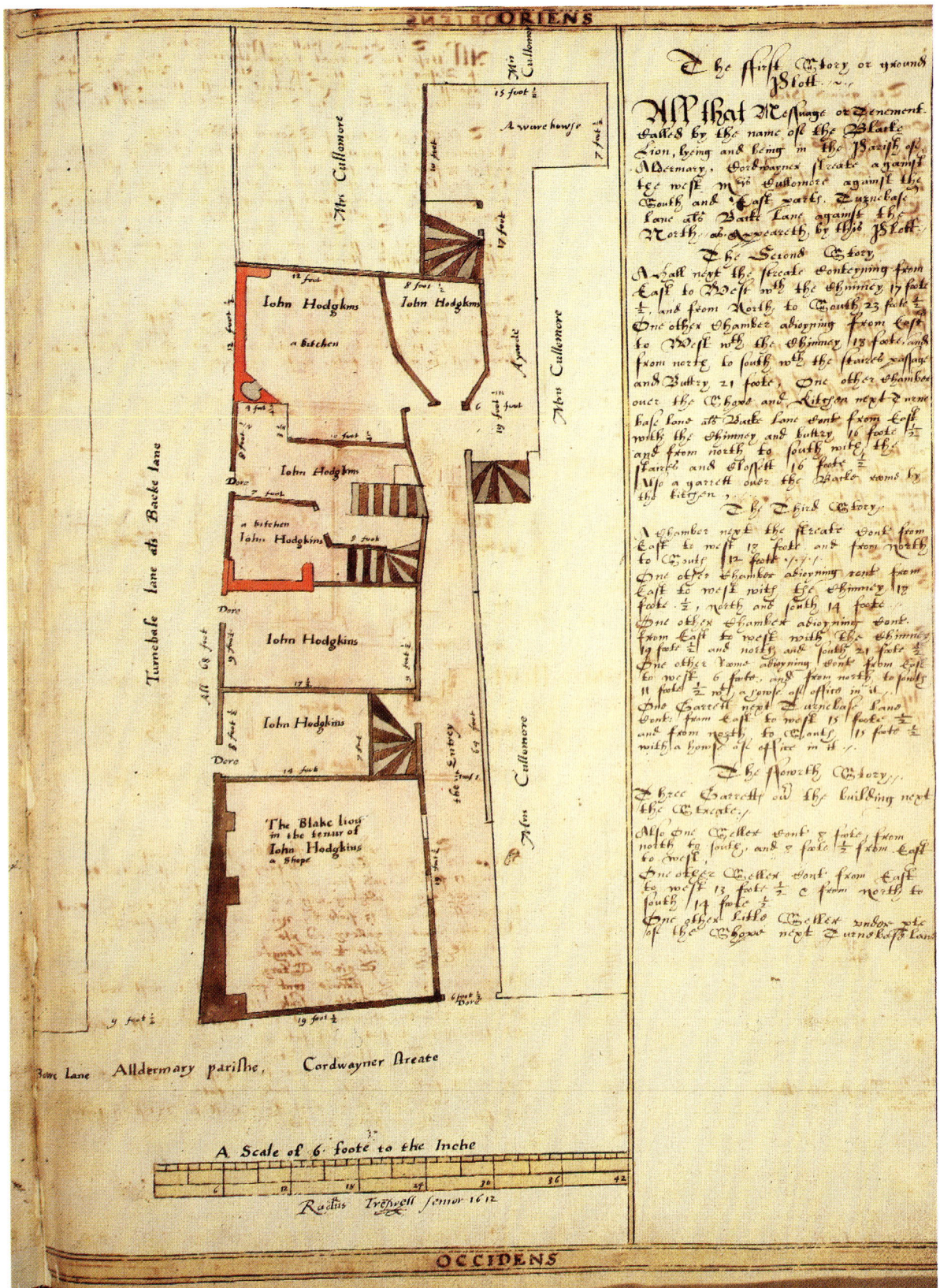

11. 34 Bow Lane, 1–3 St Thomas Apostle, 1612 (Clothworkers' Company Plan Book, 23)

privies. In one case, at Monkwell Street (**30**), a 'privy' of this kind is referred to (in the description of the storey above it) as the 'house of office'. It seems likely that both terms refer to a small chamber with structural connections to below-ground cesspits, rather than to temporary partitions, close-stools or other non-structural and more mobile arrangements. The term 'stool of ease' is used only twice: on the second floor of the tenancy of Thomas Holte, beadle to the Clothworkers' Company, who occupied the street range in front of the company hall in Mincing Lane (**29**), and in a second-floor garret of a house at Fenchurch Street (**19**, Chauncey). These stools may also have had structural connotations, since Treswell, acting as the company's surveyor, would not have officially been concerned with movable furniture. The term 'stool' could also refer to a seat of the privy-with-chute type. In 1543 the city Viewers examined a dispute between neighbours in St Dionys Backchurch parish in which they reported that the plaintiff had but one stool to a joint cesspit, whereas the defendant had three stools from separate chambers to the same pit.[108]

Treswell's ground-floor plans sometimes suggest that cesspits served more than one privy. Sometimes chutes to separate rooms within a tenancy are implied, but in other cases the privy construction suggests that the underlying cesspit served privies of adjoining tenancies. Joint cesspits are known in London from the twelfth century,[109] and were widespread from the fourteenth century.[110] A cesspit serving three tenements is mentioned in 1333.[111] Privies are grouped in some of the suburban houses in the Treswell surveys (**7**, **49**) or placed back-to-back on a boundary, indicating a common pit.

There is occasional evidence in the surveys that privies with chutes or funnels were present on the upper floors of these predominantly timber-framed houses. At 21–2 Trinity Lane (**43**) Rowse's tenancy included a first-floor room 'with a funnel of a privy out of the room above', and the plan of the adjacent tenancy of Alcocke shows two funnels going down the back of his ground-floor

privy, presumably to a communal pit. In properties of the Clothworkers' Company next to the Fleet (**22**) there were three cases of privies at first-floor level (shown by chutes) over a privy at ground floor.

Most houses had a privy, but usually not more than one. For houses with a privy on the ground-floor plan no further facilities were mentioned in the text of reference, which deals with the upper storeys; conversely, tenancies in which privies are mentioned in the text are almost invariably those for which there is no privy on the ground-floor plan. The only exceptions to this rule are a tenancy in Bell Alley, Coleman Street (**15**, Ramsey) where the several privies may have belonged to one tenant or, more likely, have been divided among the tenants in a way not recorded; and one medium-sized and two larger houses (**9**, **21** Darcy, **31**), where two privies are mentioned in the house. These four are the only certain occurrences of more than one privy in a single tenancy.

The privy could be found on any floor of the house including the garrets, but there are some indications that it was often placed at a distance from the main living rooms. Two cases of the house of office in a cellar are known in the Clothworkers' Company properties at West Smithfield (**46**, Brettnor, Showell). On the ground floor, the privy usually lay to the back of the building or at the far end of the yard; in suburban settings, this would be at the far end of a long garden (**7**, **49**). In one case only was the privy in the ground-floor front room (**35**, Dowsinge). In many cases, when on the ground floor, the privy was either next to or sometimes entered from the kitchen, as has been noted above (p. 20). In two cases the privy was on the staircase: in a staircase block on the first floor at Foxe's Court (**31**), and 'at the stairs head' in a smaller house in Aldersgate Street (**2**), described in a 1631 view of one of the buildings surveyed by Treswell. The observable preference for placing the privy in the garret in houses which otherwise had no yards or gardens is paralleled by the placing of privies in yards or gardens when they were available. Even in larger houses such as Darcy's 'great place' in

Fenchurch Street (**21**), the main double privy was next to the brick tower in the garden. This apparent trend to site the privy away from the main rooms of the house is in contrast to the medieval practice, in both rural and urban properties, of placing the privy off the solar or withdrawing room (known in London, for instance, in 1314).[112]

Since Treswell often included the privy in measurements of a group of chambers (e.g. 'a garret over all 15′ × 10′ with funnels of chimneys, stairs and a house of office'), it is not clear in many cases if the privy was entered from a communal space such as stair or passage, or was part of a larger chamber. In some cases it certainly was part of another chamber; but the number of doubtful cases is the majority. The inclusion of the privy without further specification in many cases also means that dimensions are often lacking, but those that are available show a wide variety of sizes. The privy need not be small: dimensions include 6′ × 3′ (**43**, Fryth) or 9′ × 4′ (**36**, Cowndley) and a rather elongated ground-floor room 32½′ long (**13**, Butler). The majority of the ground-floor privies, however, were about 3 ft square (**31**, **35**).

STAIRS, GALLERY AND PASSAGE

Access around the upper storeys of the houses surveyed by Treswell was by stairs, passages and galleries. In medieval and post-medieval London the following types of stair can be distinguished:

(a) exterior stair to a hall. Although an exterior stair of several steps, probably covered and in some cases with an oriel at the stairhead, is known to have been present on certain larger medieval London houses,[113] it is not evident in the larger houses surveyed by Treswell. The subdivided hall at Foxe's Court (**31**) had an entrance with two steps into the parlour, but the adjacent stairs suggest a former small exterior stair to a doorway, now blocked, into the hall.

(b) circular or semicircular newel stair or vice, within substantial walls, is absent from the above-ground floors in the Treswell surveys. The almost

total absence of stone walls above the cellar in the houses surveyed may account for this. It is however likely that some of the tight turning stairs down to cellars shown at the back of shops and warehouses were at least partly hollowed out of the masonry of the cellar wall, as is known in medieval cellars in London and elsewhere.

(c) straight flight of stairs, either between two walls or along one side of a room. This sixteenth-century form is shown many times in the Treswell surveys. Sometimes the stair used the chimney-stack for support as it reached first-floor level (**49**). In certain cases a flight of stairs gave access from the street or lane direct to the first floor (e.g. **42**).

(d) framed, enclosed, timber newel stair. This is the most common form of stair within a room, and is shown many times (e.g. **21, 22**). Sometimes the approach steps are lengthened, giving the impression of a dog-leg stair (**46**).

(e) newel stair in an external projection. This form, known in Essex from the late sixteenth century[114] is seen in several houses in the surveys. In a large house such as Foxe's Court (**31**) the former screens passage led to a square stair tower four storeys high crowned by a turret. A similar but more modest octagonal projection at Beastney's house at St James Hermitage, Monkwell Street (**30**) carried the stair up to the third storey, with a round turret above it.

(f) the stair rising by stages and half-landings round a solid core or an open stairwell — the truly framed staircase — is not shown in the houses surveyed by Treswell, though the form was present from the mid sixteenth century in grand houses such as the mansion carved out of the Charterhouse.[115] A framed stair in a stairwell is shown in the 1617 survey of Eton property at Bread Street.[116]

The term *gallery* covers several different types of sixteenth-century construction; a passage or corridor, a lobby or vestibule, or a long room intended primarily for exercise and recreation.[117] A further specialised use of the term was for a covered walk around one or more sides of a garden, such as that built for the Marquis of

Exeter's garden at his city house in 1530 by James Nedeham, afterwards King's Carpenter.[118] The term gallery in the Treswell surveys is restricted to two types of room: a passage, either between buildings at first-floor level and above or, as in galleried inns, along a range of separate chambers; and a 'long gallery' or recreation room.

First-floor galleries between buildings, often between the main house and a rear block, are known in London from the early fifteenth century[119] and in post-medieval Exeter[120] and Chester (e.g. Leche House). In early fourteenth- and fifteenth-century houses in Southampton the gallery was used to communicate between two blocks of two-storeyed buildings by running through the open hall which lay between them.[121] In central London properties where space was at a premium such galleries could be used while keeping a small open space between the two buildings (**5, 17**). In larger houses a gallery was found around one or more sides of a court, sometimes supported on posts (**19**, Chauncey; **21**, Darcy). The most elaborate arrangement of this type was at Foxe's Court in Nicholas Lane (**31**), where the range incorporating the gate to the Lane had, on the inner court side, galleries at first- and second-floor level. The first-floor gallery went on round part of the south side of the court, with a house of office at the corner. The 'long gallery' 44′ × 3′ on the second floor served three chambers which occupied the width of the range. A third gallery was placed on the third floor in the hall block on the north side of the court, giving access to five chambers. Here the term 'long gallery' may refer either to an access gallery or to the 'long gallery' of the more stately variety.

The 'long gallery' of the principal tenant at the Clothworkers' Throgmorton Street estate (**42**), Mr Fishburne, was certainly of a larger kind, 11′ wide and 30′ long 'beside the window', a rare reference to a window in the survey which implies a window at one end. Presumably this was the garden end, since the plan suggests the gallery lay over the buttery and parlour on the east side of the back yard of the house and terminated overlooking the large garden. An even larger 'long gallery'

could be found at the great house in Fenchurch Street (**21**, Darcy), which had served as Fullers' Hall in 1520–8. Here on the second floor of the range along one side of the garden was a gallery 68′ × 15½′; it occupied the entire top floor of the range. At Clothworkers' Hall itself (**29**), a gallery on the second floor of the parlour block was 53′ × 16½′, and had in it a chimney and a counting-house. Presumably these true long galleries (having a width greater than 6′ and so probably being intended for something more than communication between chambers) had the recreational functions attributed to them in royal palaces and noble houses. All three examples were alongside, or terminated with a view of, the private garden.

The term *passage* is used several times in the surveys. A ground-floor passage, whether outside or inside a building, was called an entry. A *passage* referred to similar corridors on upper floors, though in one case they are called entries (**42**, Fishburne). Measurements are never given, since the form of reference is always to 'a passage into the kitchen' or some other room which is then described. In one case, at Darcy's large house in Fenchurch Street, reference is made to 'the passage up out of the hall' to the parlour; the layout of the first-floor rooms suggests that after climbing the stair from off the screens passage, one walked along a passage to reach the parlour which was over the high end of the hall.

ROOF LEADS

In the congestion of the city centre it is not surprising that there are sixteenth-century references to roof leads which indicate that some domestic roofs were covered in lead, and were flat, enabling them to be used as walks or airing spaces. Later engravings and reconstructions of seventeenth-century houses show that in addition small balconies could be formed on any floor, but often on the attic floor, by recessing the front of a storey several feet behind the front wall of the one below. Such a balcony would be entered from the recessed storey by a door and fronted with a balustrade.

A 'lead' or 'leads' are mentioned eight times in the Treswell surveys. In seven cases the term refers to a rooftop walk on the second or higher floors. At St James' Hermitage (**30**), for instance, Mr Beastney had a door out on to a lead at the top of his staircase turret; his neighbour Mr Gray (or his subtenant Mr Hunte) was allowed to walk on the roof of the chapel itself. The leads at 36 Friday Street (**23**) were on the fifth storey. In the remaining case, at the Wildman, Cornhill (**17**), a lead is included in the first floor description without further detail; it could well have been a first-floor balcony overlooking the street, a feature of principal streets known from engravings and other surveys.

CELLARS

Though cellars in medieval London were used as taverns, stables and probably shops as well as for storage, these more 'active' functions for the cellar or undercroft seem to be generally absent from the buildings surveyed by Treswell. Only at West Smithfield were cellars lived in (**46**, Lee's tenancy mentioned as being under Hill) or in one case used as a kitchen for the house above (**46**, Seger). The purpose of the cellars in the surveyed houses was clearly for storage, though they may have had other more active functions in previous generations.

The storage capacity of a cellar could however be considerable. The 'Longe Seller' at Darcy's house, which lay at or near ground level and supported a range of buildings at right angles to the hall, was 70' long and 14' wide. In the same block the tenant of the 4½-storey range fronting Fenchurch Street, Arthur Harrison, had a long vault or cellar 83½' × 12' under his own and several other tenancies, stretching along Billiter Lane as far as the secondary gate into the large house, besides a second vault 25' long under the entry from Fenchurch Street (**21**). Others had cellars which went partly under adjacent tenancies: John Domelaw, the Clothworkers' tenant in front of the hall (**29**), leased the great cellar beneath the hall itself.

Many of the cellars had trapdoors or short stairs to the street, which are shown in the ground-plans; only in one case was the outside entrance to a cellar into a semi-private yard behind the house (**22**, Leyghton).

About a third of Type 1 houses had a cellar, but three quarters of the plot would be taken up by it. Since the cellar, like the upper rooms, would be measured internally, it is likely that much of the remainder of the small plot below ground would be taken up by thick cellar walls, especially if the cellar were old. Between half and two thirds of the Type 2 houses had cellars, but the cellar usually took up only half the ground area; a cellar under the front half of the building was common. About half the Type 3 houses had cellars, and the proportion of ground cellared was just under two-thirds. These rough figures suggest that the occupiers of all three types or size of house fell into two groups: those who had, and presumably used cellars, and those who did not, and that this did not bear much relation to the size of house.

Cellars were in addition not the only storage rooms in the seventeenth-century house: in London this function was shared with the garret which, as in small continental towns today, could communicate with the street via a hoist and keep stores relatively dry.

STABLES AND SHEDS

Four occurrences of stables are shown in the surveys. Two inns were surveyed: the White Horse, Barbican Street, and the Crowne, Aldgate. At the former (**4**) the absence of documentation including the text of reference makes analysis difficult, but it is clear that the eastern of the two halves into which the block had been divided contained two large stables among its buildings. To reach them the horse had to be led through the pedestrian entry from the street and through another building (which is not given a function on the plan, and may be a third stable). Both the larger stables had haylofts over. The stables at the Crowne (**3**) were on a more substantial scale; behind the public front yard of the inn, through a second gatehouse, lay a long yard surrounded by stables, all with haylofts over. Most had an entrance in the middle of a long side. At the far end of the yard was a small gate to the open spaces of the former extramural garden of Holy Trinity Priory. Even at this inn the main gateway to Aldgate was only six feet wide, which would have barely sufficed for carts or coaches, then coming into fashion. The survey of Christ Church property at Old Bailey (**32**) shows a stable yard at the back of the house, entered separately from Fleet Lane, and a building labelled 'stable and Coche howse'. Though the coach-house entrance was 10′ wide, the entry from the Lane was only 7′ wide.

At West Smithfield one example of a small domestic stable was surveyed (**46**, Drewery). This was an open-sided shed behind the house, and the horse (or other animal) must have been brought through the house, which in this case did not even have a side entry.

Smaller storehouses and sheds are to be seen in several of the ground-plans. Coalhouses are mentioned three times: at Pudding Lane (**36**, Kirkby and Dorrell, where the coalhouse is probably the unnamed chamber measuring 9′2″ × 6′ behind the house), in Thames Street (**41**), and at the Woolstaple, Westminster (**53**). At Throgmorton Street (**42**) and Trinity Lane (**43**) a 'coleyard' was fenced off immediately behind the house.

WELLS

By the late sixteenth century London had a comprehensive system of street pumps and conduits which provided the greater part of the domestic water supply. A partial plan of one of the newest conduits, that at Aldersgate, is shown in the plan of the adjacent Christ's Hospital property by Treswell (**1**). In addition wells were frequently found in yards, especially common alleys. On the Treswell plans their above-ground parts are always shown to be made of brick, but these may have been based in some cases on older structures of stone.

A well could be located in the middle of a yard (**22**, Leyghton), in an alley (**42**, Copthall Alley) or

in the corner of a yard or court (**25**, Hollier, **30**). Occasionally it was tucked away between buildings, with only one side available for access (**36**, Cowndley; **7**, Clapham). In several cases a well lay astride a boundary between two properties, or perhaps the boundary subdividing the property had been intentionally aligned through the well (**1**, Treswell; **4**, **23**). Joint wells, like joint privies, are known in medieval London.[122]

GARDENS AND PRIVATE OPEN SPACE; FACILITIES FOR SPORTS

Gardens were to be found only in some of the larger houses and in the peripheral or suburban areas. Most of the smaller properties on central streets had tiny yards, but the houses of one-room plan did not even have a yard. Three of the largest private houses, Darcy's tenancy in Fenchurch Street (**21**), that of Lady Wood in Fleet Lane (**22**) and the nearby Christ Church property of Lady Lucy's house entered from Old Bailey (**32**) had gardens; Darcy had two. Darcy's larger garden, perhaps an orchard or at least with small trees, had a fountain in the middle, and Lady Wood's is distinguished only by the words 'a grasse plot' which presumably indicates a cultivated lawn. In addition the garden at Clothworkers' Hall (**29**) was arranged in ornamental 'knots'.

Gardens of smaller houses are not detailed and are presented in outline only. Mr Beastney at Monkwell Street (**30**) could step into an adjacent bastion (B12, excavated in 1965 and now preserved in the Barbican estate) as part of his garden, and the houses in Swan Alley must have been surrounded by large garden spaces. In the suburban settings of Bishopsgate or Southwark, gardens could reach considerable lengths and were no doubt a source of income from market gardening. At Bishopsgate, also, Treswell surveyed an example of a separate garden with what may be a summer-house (**8**). Within the city, the parlour, when on the ground floor (as in the majority of the examples in the surveys) was nearly always to be found overlooking the garden, and it is clear the two went together; only occasion-ally is a parlour found without an adjacent garden.

The Clothworkers' Company did not want for sports facilities within its urban estate. At Fen-church Street was a tennis court, within their possession by 1535 and possibly dating from before 1481 (**21**). Two bowling alleys could be found in close proximity off Coleman Street, at White's Alley (**13**) and Bell's Alley (**14**). In all three cases the facilities were evidently the responsibility of the tenant rather than the Company.

BUILDING MATERIALS AND TIMBER-FRAMING

Clearly stone walls were a rarity in the early seventeenth-century London houses surveyed here, though stone underpinning walls or plinths were no doubt common. There is one case in the surveys of a large house with a hall which probably had three walls of stone, the fourth being of timber (**33**); in another case stone walls formed a property boundary at ground-floor level (**43**). The stone walls of the twelfth-century chapel of St James' Hermitage (**30**) (Plate 9) and possibly the wall below Woodmongers' Hall (**34**) were also medieval survivals. The measurements in the texts of reference are not exact enough to detect stone walls on any floor above the ground floor, since we do not know the basis on which Treswell measured the rooms.

There were in contrast several buildings partly or wholly of brick. Brick was used generally for garden walls, wells, chimneys and ovens, and occasionally for parts of the sides of buildings (**31**, Foxe's Court). The tower in Darcy's garden at Fenchurch Street (**21**) was of brick, but its date of construction is not known. The building dates of several other brick buildings are known: the courtyard of almshouses at Peter's Hill (1576) (**34**), and the hall (1549) and parlour (1594) of the Clothworkers' Company (**29**). Brick buildings, though scattered through the city, were still however a comparative rarity.

The majority of the houses surveyed by Tres-well were timber-framed; even some of the larger mansions (**21**, Darcy; **22**, Lady Wood) (Plates 6, 10). Known rebuildings which produced the houses in the plans occurred at Fenchurch Street in 1537 and 1557 (**21**), at 20 Basing Lane in 1560–1 (**6**), Mark Lane in 1562–5 (**29**), Mincing Lane in 1571–2 (**29**) and at Blackman Street in 1585–8 (**49**); in all cases timber frames are indicated or implied. Storey heights were spe-cified for the Blackman Street houses, and jetties can be calculated in two other cases; in the Mark Lane case the building jettied 2′ into the principal street and 1½′ into the side street. The medium used for infilling the frame is generally not known, but bricks were absent from the building accounts for 20 Basing Lane in 1560–1, suggesting that at this comparatively late date lath and plaster was used.

Perhaps in keeping with the many royal and civic regulations against subdivision of properties, creation of tenements in alleys and building on new ground from at least 1545–6,[123] jetties appear to have been going out of fashion in the second half of the sixteenth century, helped by some coercive local legislation. Most of the existing sixteenth-century timber-framed buildings in the City and its immediate environs have jetties of negligible dimensions;[124] jetties were discouraged in the City at this period.[125] A major problem with the hypothetical reconstruction of the upper floors of Treswell's houses is that we cannot tell how much of each floor jettied to the front and how much to the back; or whether there were passages or other spaces between rooms which he omitted to men-tion. It is probably only safe to experiment with the smallest houses; and reconstruction can only proceed on the tenuous assumption that first-floor partitions generally coincided with ground-floor partitions which are shown on the plan. Experi-ence with standing buildings suggests that this can be assumed only for load-bearing or party walls, i.e. not those in the middle of Treswell's buildings (e.g. the partition between the two rooms of a Type 2 house) from which measure-ments are calculated to create a jetty on the first and upper floors. Perhaps more surely, houses one room deep with a back against a property boundary could probably only expand towards the front (e.g. the row along Billiter Lane (**21**)). If we follow these guidelines, many of the houses surveyed seem to be jettied on the first and higher floors. This reinforces the supposition that many of the houses were built before 1550. Some in the Clothworkers' collection, being part of the Company portfolio in 1528 and of the Shearmen's Company estate before that, may largely have dated from 1520 or earlier (e.g. **20, 39**).

THE WIDER SIGNIFICANCE OF THE TRESWELL SURVEYS

The smaller houses surveyed by Treswell can be divided into three Types, though these are loose categories with variants. The Type 1 one-room plan house, either a 5½ storey tower-like construction or a 2½ storey urban cottage, was clearly widespread throughout the pre-Fire City. The latter form is known in the seventeenth century in several other towns such as King's Lynn, Norwich and Yarmouth.[126] In Norwich such cottages were on the one hand created out of the subdivision of existing larger properties in the seventeenth century, but are now seen to have been a late medieval form also.[127]

The two-room plan Type 2 house is known in London from the early fourteenth century[128] and elsewhere, in a less compacted form with the rear ground-floor room forming a hall, throughout the fifteenth century.[129] The design was so basic as to form the base of the Mark Lane houses built in 1562–5 (**29**), and the house of two rooms in plan became a standard small terrace form in brick in the later seventeenth century, after the Great Fire.[130]

The houses of Type 3, on a medium-sized plot and with 3–6 rooms in plan, are an amorphous group but some have parallels elsewhere, for instance in Norwich.[131] De Bees' house at Fenchurch Street (**20**) is of a general type known elsewhere from 1360 to 1560;[132] and Beastney's house at St James' Hermitage (**30**) was similar in

layout of chimneys and stair to others dated elsewhere to the period 1600–1700.[133]

Lobby-entrance houses, a very common rural form in south-east England by 1600,[134] were present in peripheral situations where a side-entrance was possible (**13–15, 46**).

The large house, here grouped loosely as Type 4, took various forms. A mansion such as that tenanted by Darcy in Fenchurch Street (**21**) could pass easily in and out of use as a company hall. These houses lay back from the street, and had large halls at the rear of courtyards (though the courts themselves were often encroached upon or difficult of access (**21, 22, 32, 34**)). They had large kitchens, and often the comparatively recent fashion of a long gallery for exercise, overlooking their large gardens. As in inns known in London and elsewhere, ordinary narrow galleries were used in external situations alongside ranges as well as for communication between buildings (the purpose of galleries in smaller complexes). In this group, perhaps, the robustness of the structural workmanship and materials (though little stone is in evidence) ensured that the larger house retained medieval forms longer than the smaller types. This was probably also due to the luxury of the high number of rooms. On the other hand, the halls in these larger houses were usually ceiled over with further chambers above (except at Clothworkers' Hall); perhaps the larger houses presented a striking contrast of new fashions such as long galleries in predominantly elderly fabrics.

In general, the larger the ground-plan area of the house in these surveys, the more likely it was to have a greater number of rooms, more chimneys and more private open space. But the proportion of rooms which were heated does not seem to have increased in similar fashion. Extra rooms generally meant unheated chambers in the larger houses, and the ease of heating the majority of rooms in a small Type 1 house from a single stack meant that the smallest house was best heated, room by room.

The surveys will repay careful study of the size of chambers and their functions. It seems to be the case, for instance, that the standard Type 2 house usually had its hall on the first floor at the front, overlooking the street; and this chamber was as a rule slightly larger than the others. Perhaps here the size of the hall might be used as an index of status — a common assumption among students of vernacular building. But the great variety in sizes of kitchens, on the other hand, with the inclusion of possibly specialist cookhouses, means that similar arguments about the relative sizes of kitchens do not hold; the size of the kitchen is no indication of the size of the house it served.

The size and distribution of cellars is probably subject to several influences. The Type 1 houses which had cellars were generally to be found on street frontages; those in courtyards behind the frontages, in the main, did not have cellars. Similarly, when the position of cellars within Type 2 and Type 3 houses can be established, they were near the street. It is clear that the provision of a cellar did not relate to house type, but to position.

Finally at the level of day-to-day archaeological analysis, it is useful to be warned that the contents of cesspits could be from more than one property, and would therefore represent a mix of social ingredients; or, if from a single household, the cesspit would serve the whole area of the house and not one part of it.

At a higher level, the plans are important and useful for providing a corpus of building plans dating to the early seventeenth century, which are otherwise not available in quantity for London and are rarely found in such quantity elsewhere. These surveys form a small corpus of buildings standing in 1612, to be compared with corpora of buildings still standing or recorded in historic towns. In the present collection will be found the seventeenth-century layout of rooms, for example shops, and the positions of stairs and fireplaces, to compare with surviving fabrics which have so often been changed in the centuries since the opening of the seventeenth. It is therefore hoped that the present edition of Treswell's London surveys will furnish a reference collection of building forms for future work in London and other towns.

NOTE ON EDITORIAL METHOD

Each site (numbered **1–53**) in the present study is given its street-name, with number(s) if possible, from its address *c.*1840 (when accurate modern street maps describe the City, still largely in its medieval form, before nineteenth-century improvements). Street-names applying at the time of the Treswell surveys, and later street-names and numbers are given when available. The detailed provenance of the plan and any previous publication of it are noted beneath the site name.

A brief site history forms an introduction to the survey and plan. No exhaustive research has been undertaken, for instance in the Husting Rolls in CLRO; the possibilities for further research are numerous.

The text of reference (see Plate 10) has been transcribed and edited to form the most concise description of the upper storeys of the buildings. This has made possible the omission of the text from the figures, which would otherwise have to be reproduced in many cases at a scale too small for comprehension.

The text of reference is supplied usually from one of the two main survey documents, the Clothworkers' Company Planbook or the Evidence Book of Christ's Hospital. If the text of reference is lacking, similar information is provided when possible from contemporary deeds or views, with a latest limit of about 1630.

The text includes, in round brackets, the number of the storey above ground in which each room was to be found, as recorded by Treswell or the accepted near-contemporary source. When the storey-number is in square brackets, this indicates that Treswell omits mention of the storey, or that it is unclear, and that the present author has suggested the number.

In the transcription of the text of reference, a number in brackets, whether round or square, always refers to the storey of that number above ground, e.g. (2) is the second storey, following Treswell's usage. The modern usage 'first floor' and cognate terms are however used in the site history and in the introduction. The following table therefore applies:

TERM USED BY TRESWELL	ALTERNATIVE MODERN TERM
ground	ground floor
second storey	first floor
third storey	second floor
fourth storey	third floor
fifth storey	fourth floor
sixth storey	fifth floor

The text has been modernised as regards spelling, and punctuation added; the words 'length' and 'breadth' have frequently been omitted, to be replaced by the × symbol ('A cellar under the parlour 17½′ × 12″'). Treswell's practice of beginning his description of each floor with a capital letter has been retained to show how the text is structured in the original.

Partly to improve the legibility of the plans, and partly because several of the Clothworkers' Company plans are already published in facsimile at original size, the plans here are reduced so as to show the buildings at uniform scales; mostly at 1:150 or 1:200, with certain of the larger areas at 1:300. This allows detailed comparison of house-forms and sizes.

Certain larger sites (e.g. **13/15, 21**) have been split for analysis into several blocks. This does not necessarily imply that they were so considered in the medieval or post-medieval period.

NOTES

[1] Harleian Society, *The Visitation of London 1568* (1869), 92.
[2] W. A. D. Englefield, *The History of the Painter-Stainers' Company of London* (1923), 13.
[3] *Ibid*, 46–8.
[4] M. Edmond, 'Limners and Picturemakers: New Light on the lives of miniaturists and large-scale portrait-painters working in London in the 16th and 17th centuries', *The Walpole Soc* 47 (1980), 63.
[5] Englefield, *op. cit.*, 51.
[6] GL MS 5670.

[7] B. Marsh (ed) *Records of the Worshipful Company of Carpenters IV: Wardens' Accounts 1546–1571* (1916), 208.
[8] CCO 1581–1605, 225v. Presumably there was some doubt about whether the king would like the product, as the new royal arms had not yet been issued.
[9] Marsh *op. cit.* xix, 244.
[10] E. B. Jupp *An Historical Account of the Worshipful Company of Carpenters* (1848), 232–42 and engravings; Royal Commission on Historical Monuments *London IV: The City* (1929), 37, pl. 85.
[11] J. Page-Phillips *Palimpsests* (1980), i, 70. I am indebted to Stephen Freeth for this reference.
[12] Harleian Society, *op. cit.*
[13] PRO E 179.
[14] CHMB 3, 74v. In 1601 a Ralph Treswell is recorded as living in the parish of Christchurch Newgate Street (which is in the ward of Farringdon Within), in a house bequeathed in that year by Margaret Sharles, widow, to her kinswoman Alice Sharles. Perhaps this refers to Ralph Treswell junior. See E. A. Fry (ed) *Abstracts of Inquisitiones Post Mortem relating to the City of London returned into the Court of Chancery Part III, 1577–1603* (1908), 290–1. From 1594–5 Robert Treswell was also living in a Christ's Hospital property, almost certainly that in Aldersgate in which he is found in the survey of 1611 (**2**), opposite his father's tenancy (CH Treasurer's Accts, *s.a.*).
[15] CLRO CL Grant Book I, 125.
[16] GL MS 2050/1, 15.
[17] *Ibid*, 10.
[18] PRO E179 146/372.
[19] GL MS 2050/1, 20v.
[20] GL MS 1454/97–/99.
[21] GL MS 1453/1, 1, 1v.
[22] GL MS 2050/1, 23v.
[23] GL MS 1453/1, 8v.
[24] CHMB 3, 188.
[25] GL MS 9050/5, 71v.
[26] Treswell had been working for St Bartholomew's Hospital since 1587 (see Concordance).
[27] CHMB 3, 72v.
[28] E.g. CHMB 3, 73v, 80v; for a dispute on site 26, CHMB 3, 142.
[29] GL MS 12806/1, 14.
[30] *Ibid*, 15.
[31] *Ibid*.
[32] *Ibid*, *s.a.* 1611–12.
[33] The binding is illustrated in J. B. Oldham, *English Blank-stamped Bindings* (1952) pl. xxxi; and discussed in J. B. Oldham, *Shrewsbury School Library Bindings* (1934), 28–31. I am grateful to Mr J. Cuthbert of Guildhall Library for discussing the binding with me.
[34] CHMB 3, 146v.
[35] *Ibid*, 174.
[36] GL MS 13057.
[37] CCO 1605–23, 19v.
[38] *Ibid*, 52v.
[39] *Ibid*, 79v.
[40] *Ibid*, 102v.
[41] London Topographical Society Publications LXXII (1938), LXXIII (1939), LXXIV (1940); 'The Clothworkers' Company: Book of Plans of the Company's property made in 1612', *London Topographical Record* 18 (1942), 51–97. See also V. Harding 'The Two Coldharbours of the City of London' *London Topographical Record* 24 (1980), 11–30; R. Weinstein 'Clothworkers in St Stephen Coleman Parish, 1612' *ibid* 61–80.
[42] P. Harvey, *Topographical Maps* (1980), 164.
[43] *Ibid*, 168.
[44] S. Tyacke and J. Huddy, *Christopher Saxton and Tudor map-making* (1980), 57–8.
[45] J. Summerson (ed) *The Book of Architecture of John Thorpe in Sir John Soane's Museum*, Walpole Soc 40 (1966), 9. The assertion that

Ralph Treswell senior was Somerset Herald in 1586 (P. Eden, *Dictionary of Land Surveyors and Local Cartographers of Great Britain and Ireland 1550–1850* (1975), 252) seems to be an error; Somerset Herald at the time was Robert Glover, who died in 1588. In 1590 William Segar was Somerset Herald (Sir Anthony Wagner, *Heralds of England* (1967), 206, 209–10). H. Colvin's calling Robert Treswell Ralph (*History of the King's Works IV: 1485–1660 (Part II)* (1982), 75, 77, 275) is also a slip.

[46] These paragraphs are based upon discussions with Peter Barber, to whom I am most grateful.

[47] R. A. Skelton and P. D. A. Harvey, *Local Maps in Medieval England* (1986), 247.

[48] British Library Add. MS. 18783 5v, 81.

[49] E. G. R. Taylor, *Mathematical Practitioners of Tudor and Stuart England* (1954), contains appendices on both instrument makers and their published works. The plane table was coming into use after about 1560; the theodolite is described by Leonard and Thomas Digges in *A Geometrical Practise, named Pantometria* (1571).

[50] There was a parallel expansion of surveying in Paris: *Greffiers des bâtiments* were men who surveyed, drew and valued property for church or corporate owners within the city and within the region. They were officially constituted in 1577, but their archives do not survive before 1610. I am grateful to David Thompson for this observation.

[51] P. Eden, 'Three Elizabethan estate surveyors: Peter Kempe, Thomas Clerke and Thomas Langdon' in S. Tyacke (ed) *English Map-Making 1500–1650* (1983), 68–84, especially 68–72.

[52] Tyacke and Huddy, *op. cit.*, 46, 48.

[53] *Sphieghel der Zeevaert* translated by Anthony Ashley (1588).

[54] Peter Barber comments: These were housed mainly in White-hall, either in the New Library or adorning the Privy Gallery. Fragments of the collection survive in the Cotton 'Augustus' maps in the British Library, but it seems likely that the bulk of them were destroyed in the Whitehall fire of 1697. The importance of this collection has not previously been fully grasped and it has been assumed that the earlier scale maps, produced by self-trained men (masons, gunners, mariners etc) working as military engineers, served purely military ends. This is not the case; by 1550 official maps were serving political, diplomatic and administrative ends and represented an enormous variety of techniques.

Almost certainly Saxton had recourse to this collection when he was mapping England, and it is possible that Treswell would have known of it; he did serve with English forces in Brittany (note the map of 1594 in the Concordance Table).

[55] R. V. Tooley, *Maps and Map-Makers* (1949), 49.

[56] Tyacke and Huddy, *op. cit.*, 36.

[57] Tooley, *op. cit.*, 33.

[58] *Ibid*, 67.

[59] Summerson, *op. cit.*

[60] On Symonds, see J. Summerson, 'Three Elizabethan Architects' *Bulletin of the John Rylands Library Manchester* 40 (1957) 209–16.

[61] On Basil, see A. P. Baggs, 'Two designs by Simon Basil' in *Design and Practice in British Architecture: Studies in architectural history presented to Howard Colvin, Architectural History* 27 (1984), 104–10.

[62] W. R. Lethaby, 'The Priory of Holy Trinity, Aldgate' *Home Counties Magazine* II (1900), 45–53.

[63] W. Archer-Thompson, *Drapers' Company: Property and Trusts*, I (1940), 121.

[64] For a study of these plans see J. Steane, 'The development of Tudor and Stuart Garden Design in Northamptonshire', *Northants Past & Present* V (1976), 1–23.

[65] Summerson *op. cit.* in note 45, 93–4 and pl. 85.

[66] GL Map Case 66; see also GL MS 5884/1.

[67] VCH *Middlesex V* (1976), 284.

[68] Summerson *op. cit.* in note 45, 102–3, pl. 105.

[69] *Ibid*.

[70] VCH *Middlesex V* (1976), 286.

[71] Harvey, *op. cit.*, 81.

[72] *Ibid*.

[73] *Ibid*, 80, fig. 41.

[74] *Ibid*, 146.

[75] *Op. cit.*, 169; see also M. Merriman, 'Italian military engineers in Britain in the 1540s' in Tyacke, *op. cit.*, 57–67.

[76] R. A. Skelton, *Decorative Printed Maps of the 15th to 18th Centuries* (1952), 17; Harvey, *op. cit.*, fig. 86.

[77] Tyacke and Huddy, *op. cit.*, figs. 5–6.

[78] *Ibid*, 48.

[79] That Martin Llewellyn, steward of St Bartholomew's Hospital, was the author of the plans of *c.* 1617 in the Hospital archives was suggested by T. Campbell, 'Atlas Pioneer', *Geographical Magazine*, 1975, 162–7. It is possible that some of these were copies of earlier plans by Treswell; see notes to Concordance, above, p. 8.

[80] Harvey, *op. cit.* figs. 52–3, 55.

[81] *Ibid*, fig. 90.

[82] For a house of this type known from a building contract, see L. F. Salzman *Building in England down to 1540* (1952), 418; for archaeologically recorded examples of the 14th century, see J. Schofield, *The Building of London from the Conquest to the Great Fire* (1984), 101.

[83] E.g. *Cal LB L*, 85 (1469).

[84] Salzman, *op. cit.*, 432–4.

[85] *Ibid*, 443–4.

[86] Information M. Atkin; see also M. Atkin, 'Excavations at Alms Lane [Norwich]' *East Anglian Archaeology* 26 (1985), 253.

[87] N. Blakiston, 'The London and Middlesex estates of Eton College' *Trans LAMAS* 20 (1960), 51–5.

[88] Inventory evidence suggests that houses in Norwich, for instance, were generally smaller (information M. Atkin and A. Carter).

[89] W. Pantin 'Some medieval English town houses: a study in adaptation' in I. Foster and L. Alcock (eds) *Culture and Environment: Essays in honour of Sir Cyril Fox* (1963), 445–78.

[90] J. Schofield, 'Medieval waterfront buildings in the City of London' in G. Milne and B. Hobley (eds) *Waterfront archaeology in Britain and northern Europe* (1981), 24–31.

[91] Salzman, *op. cit.*, 418.

[92] D. Portman, *Exeter Houses 1400–1700* (1966), 4, 73–4, 91.

[93] Stow, *passim*.

[94] E.g. *Cal Wills* i, 332.

[95] William Langland, *Piers the Plowman*, (ed W. W. Skeat), 1886, i, 292.

[96] If they were to enjoy a bequest of 1591, the Master and Livery of the Fishmongers' Company were to eat in the parlour, separated from the rest of the company who were to eat in the hall (*Cal Wills* ii, 720).

[97] J. Bruce, 'Observations on a lease of two houses in the Piazza, Covent Garden, granted to Sir Edmund Verney, A.D. 1634', *Archaeologia* 35 (1853), 194–201.

[98] Portman, *op. cit.*, 35.

[99] Salzman, *op. cit.*, 418–9.

[100] N. Blakiston, 'Milton's Birthplace', *London Topographical Record* 19 (1947), 1–13.

[101] Stow ii, 22.

[102] P. Thornton, *Seventeenth Century Interior Decoration in England, France and Holland* (1978), 296.

[103] *Ibid*, 297.

[104] *Ibid*, figs. 295–6.

[105] *Ibid*, 306. A vicar in Sussex had a study in his vicarage in 1584, but this was rare among parsonages at the time: M. Barley, *The English Farmhouse and Cottage* (1961), 93–4.

[106] *Cal P&M 1413–1437*, 118.

[107] The dimensions of the double privies specified in the St Paul's building contract of 1370; Salzman *op. cit.*, 443–4.

[108] CLRO Viewers' Reports 1509–1546, 165.

[109] 'London Properties of the Cluniac Priory of St Pancras, Lewes, Surrey', *London Topographical Record* 18 (1942), 8.

[110] *Assize of Nuisance, passim.*

[111] *Ibid*, 325.

[112] *Ibid*, 214.

[113] E.g. Dean's House, Westminster (1385); Salzman, *op. cit.*, 478–82 (a contract of 1405).

[114] C. Hewett 'The development of the post-medieval house', *Post Medieval Archaeology* 7 (1963), 60–78.

[115] Royal Commission on Historical Monuments, *London II: West London* (1925), 25.

[116] Blakiston, *op. cit.* in note 106.

[117] H. Colvin (ed) *The History of the King's Works: IV, 1455–1660 (Part II)*, (1982), 17–21.

[118] Salzman, *op. cit.*, 576–7.

[119] *Ibid*, 480.

[120] Portman, *op. cit.*, Fig. xiii.

[121] C. Platt, *The English Medieval Town* (1976), 73.

[122] *Assize of Nuisance* 219 (1314), 534 (1367).

[123] E.g. Journal 15, 203 (1545–6); Journal 16, 126–7 (1551); Repertory 15, 333 (1564).

[124] For instance, the timber-fronted building of *c.* 1525 at Lincoln's Inn, and the frontage of Staple Inn to Holborn (*c.*1586) (Royal Commission on Historical Monuments, *op. cit.*, 46–8, 57).

[125] E.g. CCPR St Martin's Lane, 1591, where a house jettying a total of six feet by means of four successively jettied storeys was to be cut back; only the lowest, first floor jetty being allowed.

[126] V. Parker, *The Making of King's Lynn* (1971), 100–1; Yarmouth, B H St J. O'Neil, 'Some seventeenth-century houses in Great Yarmouth', *Archaeologia* 95 (1953), 141–80. For Norwich, see next note.

[127] Atkin, *op. cit.* in note 85, 252.

[128] J. Schofield, *op. cit.* in note 81, 101.

[129] E.g. in Norwich: A. Carter, 'The Buildings' in D. H. Evans & A. Carter, 'Excavations on 31–51 Pottergate [Norwich]', *East Anglian Archaeology* 26 (1985), 70–1; and generally in medieval rows in Coventry, Tewkesbury and elsewhere.

[130] A. Thompson, F. Grew and J. Schofield, 'Excavations at Aldgate, City of London', *Post Medieval Archaeology* 18 (1984), 1–149.

[131] E.g. Tenement D, Oak Street site, Norwich; M. Atkin and H. Sutermeister, 'Excavations in Norwich 1977/8: the Norwich Survey — Seventh Interim Report', *Norfolk Archaeology* 37 (1978), 35–44.

[132] For general similarities, see R. Brunskill, *Houses* (1982), 121.

[133] *Ibid*, 126–7 (type 8).

[134] E. Mercer, *English Vernacular Houses* (1975), 60–1.

THE SURVEYS

1. 7–10 Aldersgate

Evidence Book, 10

The Fraternity of Holy Trinity, which had been founded in 1367 in the church of St Botolph, Aldersgate (Basing 1982), owned four blocks of property at its dissolution in 1547:

 i. a fifteenth-century first-floor assembly hall, the land under it and five tenements to the S (**2**).

 ii. properties opposite St Botolph's church in Aldersgate Street (**1**).

 iii. properties in Barbican Street, later the White Horse Inn (**4**).

 iv. tenements in Little Britain, apparently sold off before 1612.

By Letters Patent in 1547 Edward VI granted the fraternity property to William Harvy, Somerset Herald at Arms (GL MS 10907). Property **1**, with **2** and **4**, was granted by Harvy to Robert Mellish in 1552 (GL MS 13472) and by Mellish to the City for the use of the poor in Christ's Hospital in 1553 (GL MS 13472). As with the other two ex-fraternity properties, there is no text of reference on the Treswell survey; there is no apparent reason why they should share this deficiency. This is especially noteworthy because one of the tenants in block was 'R' Treswell, presumably the surveyor himself (though he had a son of the same name); his other son Robert lived opposite, below Trinity Hall (see **2**).

The plan (Fig. 4) also shows part of the 'new conduit', built in 1610 from an endowment by Thomas Hayes; it was not replaced after the Great Fire (Strype 1720,i,25).

In a note on hospital property dated 1584, two tenements on the E side of Aldersgate were leased to Nowell Sotherton; in the plan the garden, formerly of Mr Baron Sotherton, is leased to a Mr Percivall, who shared the N property with Treswell. Treswell's tenancy is described in a view at the time of a lease of 1623 to Stephen Potts:

A cellar in 1. towards the street 21′ × 17′ in b. from the street backwards, within the walls of the house, the whole house on the street side 22′ × 24′ from the street backward to the farthest part of the house, which consists of these rooms following besides the cellar, viz. one shop towards the street 12½′ × 10′ from the street backward, a lesser shop adjoining 9½′ towards the street × 10′ from the street backward, a little entry going into the parlour and kitchen 8′ × 2′9″, the kitchen behind the one shop with a chimney and window glazed 7½′ × 13½′ backward, a parlour behind the other shop and window half wainscotted with a window glazed and a chimney 12′ × 10′, a little yard with party well 4′ at the N end × 2′ at the S end, a little room at the N end of the said yard 6′ × 5′; [2] A hall over the shops 21′ × 12½′ with a chimney, a bay window and two clerestoreys and a little buttery in the same room, which room is half wainscotted, a little room over the kitchen 7′ × 6′, a chamber over the parlour 16′ from the hall backward with a chimney and glass window × 12′, a staircase from the ground leading to the upper rooms with a little entry to land both ways 20′ × 9′; [3] a garret next the street made for lodging 22′ on the street side ×12′ from the street backward, another garret behind the former, used for lodging, with a little room 22′ × 16′ both which are with glass windows (CH View book I, 3–4).

It is clear that this description is only of the front part of the building, formerly Treswell's tenancy; no description is available for the tenancies of Percivall to the E or of Eliot to the S.

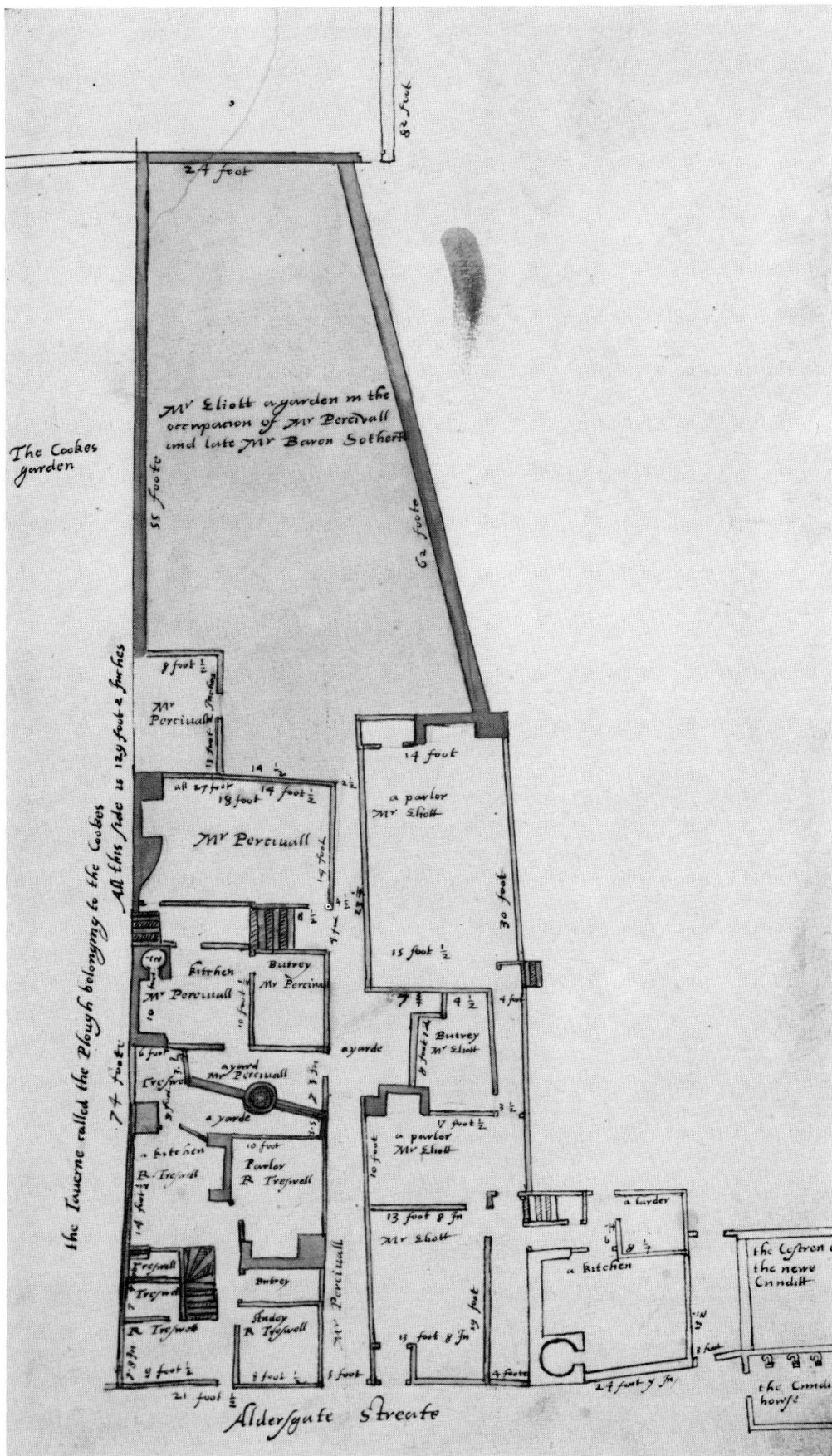

Figure 4. **1.** 7–10 Aldersgate (1:200). North is to the left of the plan.

2. 171–3, later 190–4 Aldersgate

Evidence Book, 11

This block of property, belonging to the Fraternity of the Holy Trinity, was granted to William Harvy in 1547 (see **1**). The northernmost building included the first-floor hall of the fraternity, which later plans and engravings (e.g. Schofield 1984, Fig. 94) suggest was rebuilt in the late fifteenth century. In 1548 Harvy leased the hall, two solars and a buttery to Roger Tailor and three other parishioners of St Botolph, Aldersgate for 'assemblies and Counsails'. The six tenements on the streetside and eight behind in Trinity Alley (not shown in the Treswell survey) were granted by Harvy to Mellish in 1552, and by him to the Hospital in 1553 (see **1**). The parish continued to lease the hall from the Hospital through trustees throughout the later sixteenth century (GL MS 10907). In 1612 it was leased to the Farriers' Company for 51 years (GL MS 10907A).

From N to S on Treswell's ground plan (Fig. 5), the houses were:

a. Robert Treswell: a ground-floor set of rooms beneath Trinity Hall itself, comprising hall, study, buttery and four chambers, yard and privy. The house is described in a view of 1630:

A parlour from E to W with the jetty whereupon the window stands that looketh into the street and the buttery and stairs leading into the cellar 26′ × 17′ 3″ from N to S from the ouside of the post next the street N to the breadth of the said parlour S, the hall and passage into the said parlour from E to W on the S side of the hall with the chimney and little buttery under the stairs 18′ × 10′6″ from N to S next the street, the kitchen from E to W with the stair room leading up into the chambers 18′ 8″ ×9½′ from N to S at the W end, a cellar arched with brick under the said parlour from E to W, beside the stairs going up into the street 22′ × 13′8″ from N to S; [2] A chamber over the kitchen with a chimney in it from E to W, with the staircase room, 19½′ × 11½′ with the chimney; [3] A chamber over the said chamber from E to W, with the staircase room, 22′7″ × 11′ from N to S within the walls, a chamber next the street over the chamber used with Farriers' Hall from E to W 16½′ × 11′6″ from N to S (CH View Book I, 95–6).

b. John Clarke: there is at present no further information about the rooms of Clarke or

c. Roger Taylor, presumably a relation of the parishioner who leased the property from Harvy in 1548.

d. Rowland Onions: when leased to Walters Rivers by the hospital in 1577, this house was described as containing a little cellar, a shop, one other shop on the S side of the first, both opening onto the high street [i.e. not as in the plan], one shed and a little yard backwards, wherein was a chimney and a privy, a hall over the shop with a chimney and a privy, a hall over the shop with a chimney, and a little buttery, two little chambers over the hall towards the street with two small chambers behind the hall, one of them over the passage into Trinity Hall (GL MS 13472). This arrangement is not shown in the plan; and as the tenancy was rebuilt by Onions in 1607–9 at a cost of £200 (CHMB I, 112), it seems likely that the plan shows the post-1609 arrangement. The tenement was rebuilt shortly before 1745 by one Nash, then its tenant; a plan of the new property was attached to his lease of that year (GL MS 13473).

e. John Edwards: when leased by the hospital to Richard Cadburie in 1580, this property comprised a cellar, a hall 'over the same' but on the second storey, (see below), a kitchen and chamber, one large chamber to the street over the hall and over the passage into Trinity Court [i.e. Edwards' tenancy sailed over the alley at the front, but Onions' tenancy did so behind], two backchambers, a chimney and privy on the same floor, with two garrets over the same chambers (GL MS 13472). The house is described in a view of 1631:

(2) A dining chamber next the street with a chimney in it and a little closet, a little chamber on the same floor at the W end of the said room with a house of office, another chamber on the same floor backward standing SW over Mr Waterhouses his house with a chimney in it; (3) Two bedchambers on a floor one with a closet in it, the other with a chimney in it, a garret with two partitions in it to lay in coals and other things (CH View Book I, 107–8).

f. Edward Waterhouse: in a lease of 1572, to John Jenkins, the southernmost property comprised a cellar, a hall over it to the street, a kitchen, chimneys in both, a chamber with a chimney over the hall and one other chamber on the same floor with a privy, with a garret

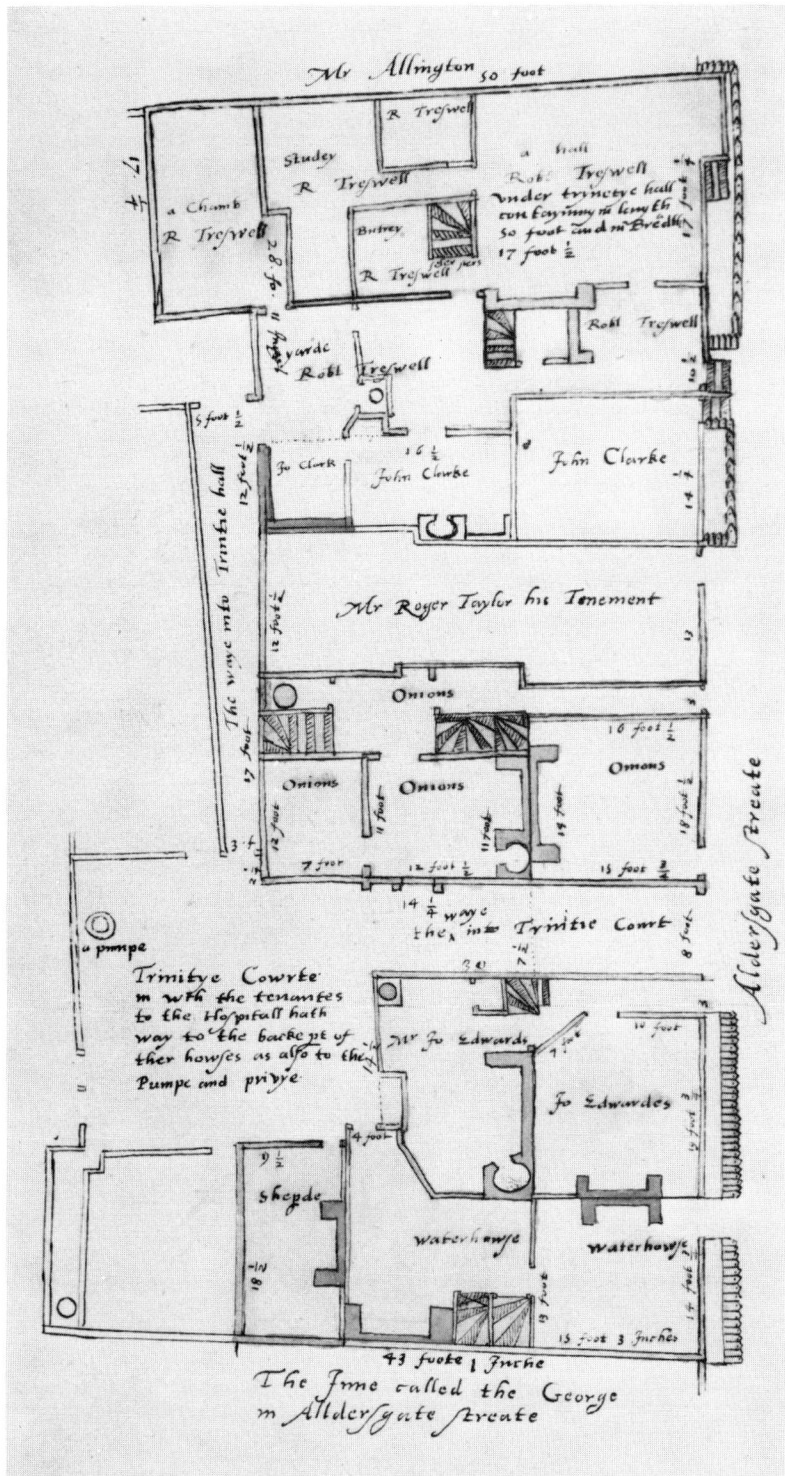

Figure 5. **2.** 171–3, later 190–4 Aldersgate (1:200). North is to the top of the plan.

towards the street and a backchamber (GL MS 13473). The house is described in a view of 1631:

(2) A hall next the street wainscotted round about with a closet, a bedchamber behind the hall with a chimney in it; (3) A bedchamber next the street wainscotted and matted with a chimney in it and a closet at the end, a bedchamber behind the said bedchamber with a chimney in it; (4) A bedchamber next the street with a chimney in it, another chamber behind that with a chimney in it, a house of office at the stairs' head (CH View Book I, 107–9).

It must have been natural to consider these S two houses together, for in 1689 it appears that a tenant, William Cleaver, had rebuilt them both and split them into four tenancies; the N (Edwards) house was split into two, and the back part of the S house on the S side of Trinity Court made into a fourth. All were of three storeys with garrets. There were still four separate tenancies in a lease of 1737, but by 1760 the two forming the N house (by now 172 Aldersgate Street) were reunited (GL MS 13473). A lease of 1786 includes a detailed schedule of fittings of both houses (*ibid.*).

3. Crowne, Aldgate

Evidence Book, 14

Between 1170 and 1197 Stephen, prior of Holy Trinity Priory, Aldgate, granted to Edric the Merchant land in the parish of St Botolph Aldgate, which Richard the chaplain had bought from Norman, son of Alfred Horeh, for 4*s*. p.a. (HTP, 887; *CAD* iv, A 7353). The priory cartulary records several owners paying the quit-rent until 1268, when Albreda, widow of Robert Lambard, granted the property to William son of Stephen de Sharnbrok; in this grant the property was described as extending from the king's highway (Aldgate) on the S to the priory garden on the N, and between the cemetery of St Botolph's church on the W and land of Mundekinus Trentmars to the E (HTP, 888–9). Subsequent payments of the quit-rent are noted in the cartulary until the early fifteenth century.

In 1316 John de Morce of Stebenheath quitclaimed his interest to Thomas le Bedell, and in 1317 William Derman, having been sold the property by le Bedell's executors, granted it to his father Richard Derman. In 1363, Thomas de Caxton, butcher, was in possession by right of his wife Alice, daughter of Nicholas Derman; he granted the property to William Cosyn, potter (*ollarius*). In 1398 Cosyn's heir Richard Knyght quitclaimed to Robert Burford, bellmaker. By 1458 the property had passed via Alex Sprot to the church of St Botolph to support a chantry. In 1546 Thomas Barlett and Richard Mody purchased it of the Court of Augmentations and sold it to John Margettson, brewer; two years later he sold it to David Gittins and John Lloyd, vintners. The tenement was then described as being 139′ long on the E, 179′ on the W, 73′ wide on the N and 47′ wide on the S (street) side. In 1563 Gittins and Lloyd sold the property to Johanne Turnbull, widow of Thomas Turnbull and formerly widow of Margettson. In 1569 she leased the Crowne to Richard Irme, woodmonger, and Johanne his wife for 30 years at £12 p.a. The attached schedule of fittings reads:

In the inner parlour: 7 panes of glass in the window there;
Great Parlour: 7 panes of glass, wainscotted round, settles and all the roof ceiled with wainscot;
Hall: 14 panes of glass;
Great Chamber: 16 panes of glass and a screen;
The chamber next the great chamber: 20 panes of glass;
Corner chamber: 3 panes of glass
Kitchen: a bar of iron in the chimney 'goinge throughout',
a long ladder of 18 rungs, a short ladder of 12, a bucket of 4 hoops of iron for the well, a wheel and rope;
12 doors with locks and keys and 2 bolts of iron, hanging windows and shutting windows to the parlour, hall and chambers
5 stables with racks and mangers

(All deeds in GL MS 13333; for a fuller documentary study see *HG*, 3, *St Botolph without Aldgate*, The Crowne, Aldgate (N side)).

The Crowne must have been inherited by Thomas Margettson, merchant-tailor, who sold it in 1581 to William Cooch, innholder (*ibid*). By Cooch's will of 1587 it passed to Christ's Hospital in 1594 (GL MS 13134). The plan by Treswell (Fig. 6) is the only dated example in the Christ's Hospital Evidence Book, signed in 1610.

Text of reference, Evidence Book (1610)

(2) One chamber with a chimney next the street 19½′ × 10½′, one other chamber next the street with a chimney N and S 19½′ × 13′, one other chamber next the street S and N 21½′ × 19½′ E and W, one other little chamber 13′, one other chamber next the churchyard 16½′ with a chimney × 12½′, one other chamber next the same 16½′ × 13′ with a chimney, one other chamber with chimney over the second gatehouse 18½′ × 17′, one other chamber next the churchyard with a chimney 19′ × 15½′, one other chamber next the yard with a chimney 19½′ × 17′, one other chamber with a chimney over the other chamber aforesaid 16½′ × [ ], one other chamber with a chimney next the churchyard 18½′ × 15′, one other chamber with a chimney 15½′ × 13½′, one other chamber over the second gatehouse 15′ × 11½′, one other chamber 18½′ × 9½′; (3) One other chamber

15½′ × 12½′ having a chimney, one other chamber with a chimney next the vestry house 24½′ × 18′, one other chamber next the street with a chimney 21½′ × 8½′, one other chamber next the street with a chimney 20½′ × 12½′, one other chamber over the first gatehouse with a chimney 20½′ × 13½′, the other chamber over the second gatehouse 13′ × 8½′; Three cellars, one 19½′ × 17½′, one other cellar next the churchyard 19½′ × 15½′ and the third cellar 15½′ × 14½′.

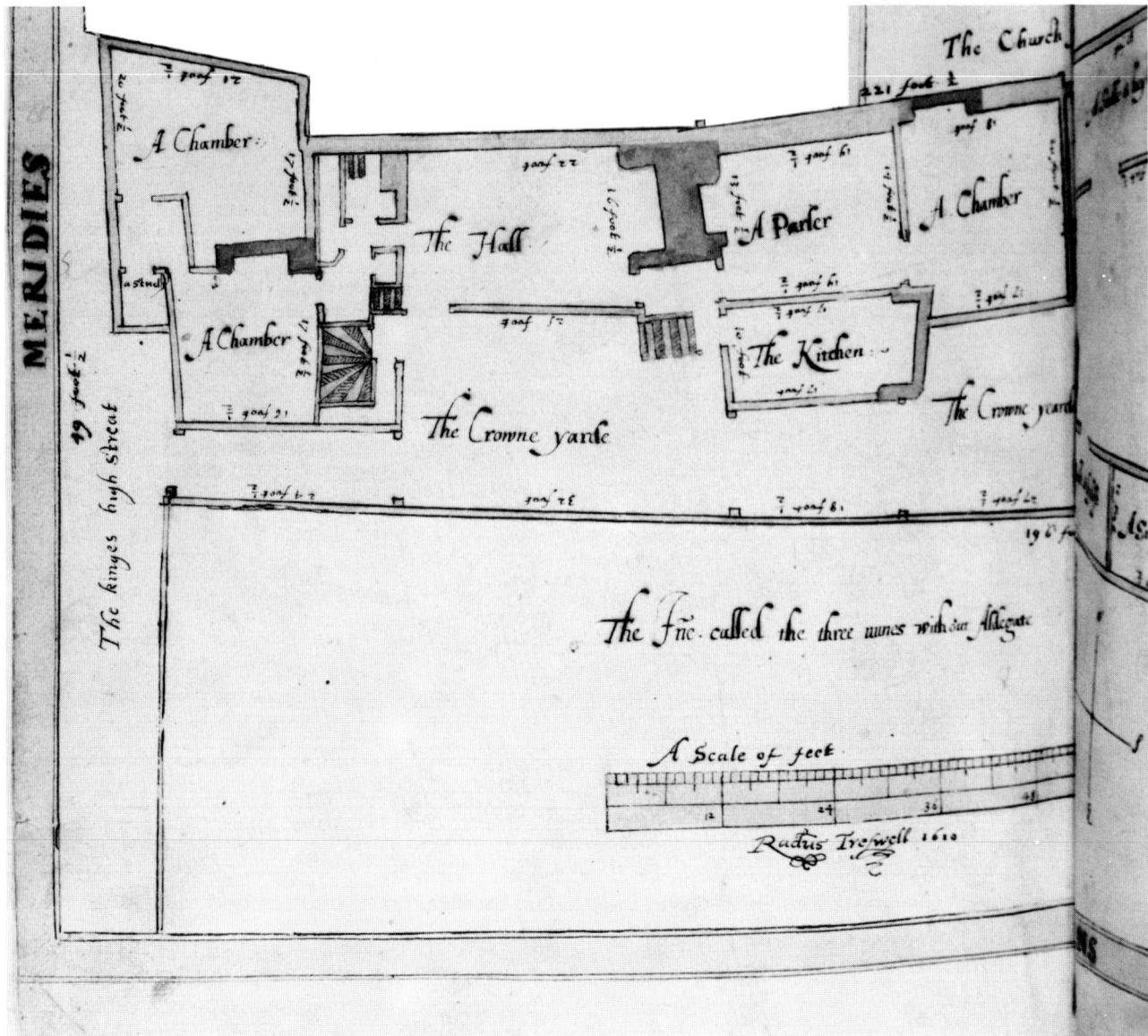

Figure 6. **3.** Crowne, Aldgate (1:200). North is to the right of the plan.

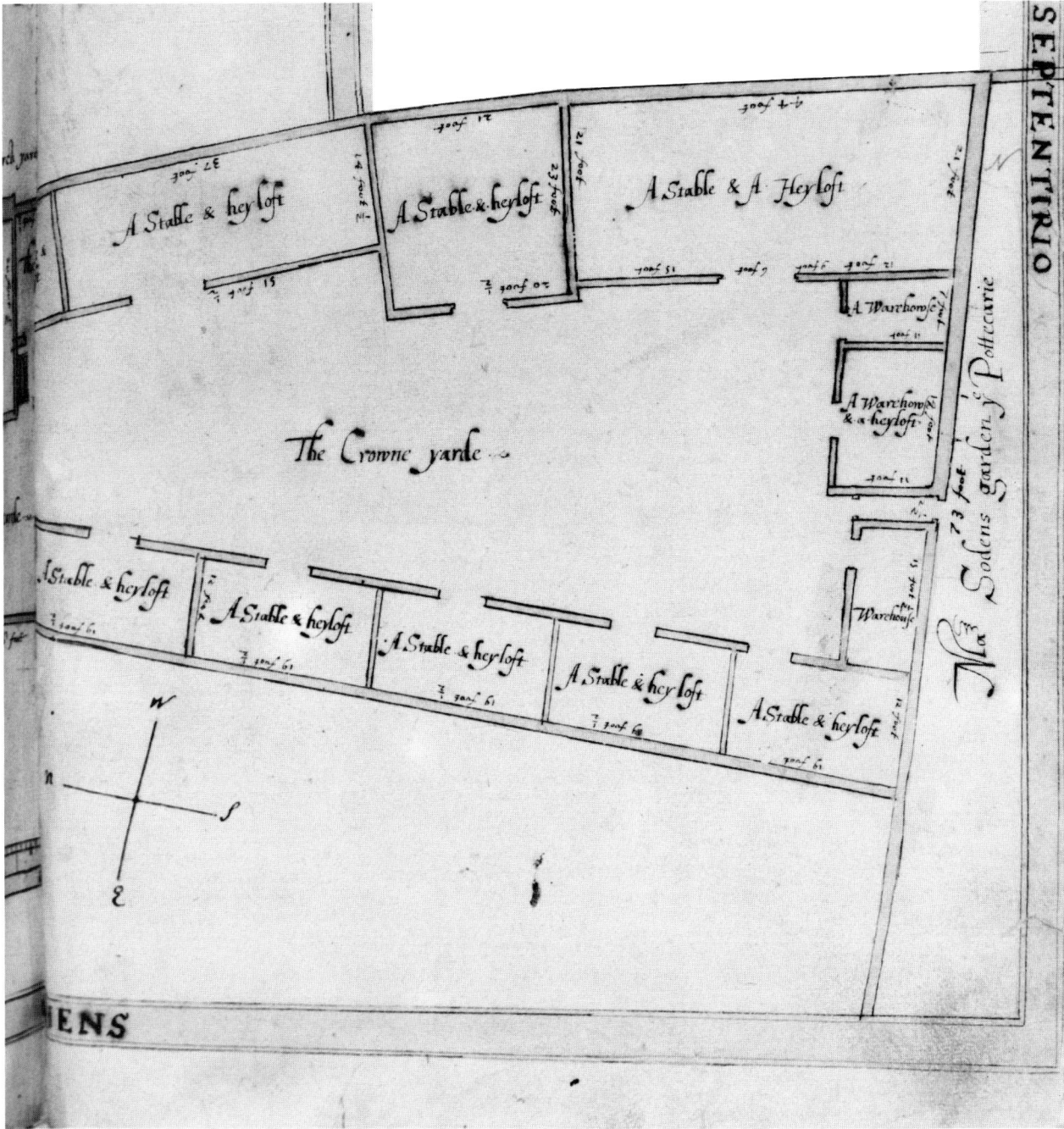

SEPTENTRIO

The Crowne yarde

A Stable & hey loft

A Stable & heyloft

A Stable & A. Heyloft

A Warehouse

A Warehowse & a heyloft

A Stable & heyloft

A Stable & heyloft

A Stable & hey loft

A Stable & hey loft

Warehouse

Mr Sodens garden & Pottecarie

ENS

4. White Horse Inn, Barbican Street

Evidence Book, 21

Two adjoining properties were transferred by Roger Elys to a group of trustees in 1394; by his will the trustees were made executors so that they could sell the property, and the surviving members conveyed the property to John Bradmore and his wife in 1397 (Basing 1982, 43–4). Bradmore remaindered the tenements, with others in Aldersgate, to the fraternity of Holy Trinity in St Botolph Aldersgate church, by his will of 1412 (*ibid.* xvii). Like the other fraternity property which eventually came into the possession of Christ's Hospital, the White Horse passed first to William Harvy in 1547 and to Christ's Hospital in 1553 (*ibid.*). Similarly, there is no text of reference with the plan (Fig. 7). The front of the property had been rebuilt by 1624, when it was viewed by Hospital officials (CH View Book I, 27, 29); and repaired extensively in 1680, after being condemned as 'very defective' (GL MS 13475). The Inn appears on Ogilby and Morgan's map of 1677 (b59); the back buildings seem to have been also partially remodelled from those shown in Treswell's survey of *c.* 1611.

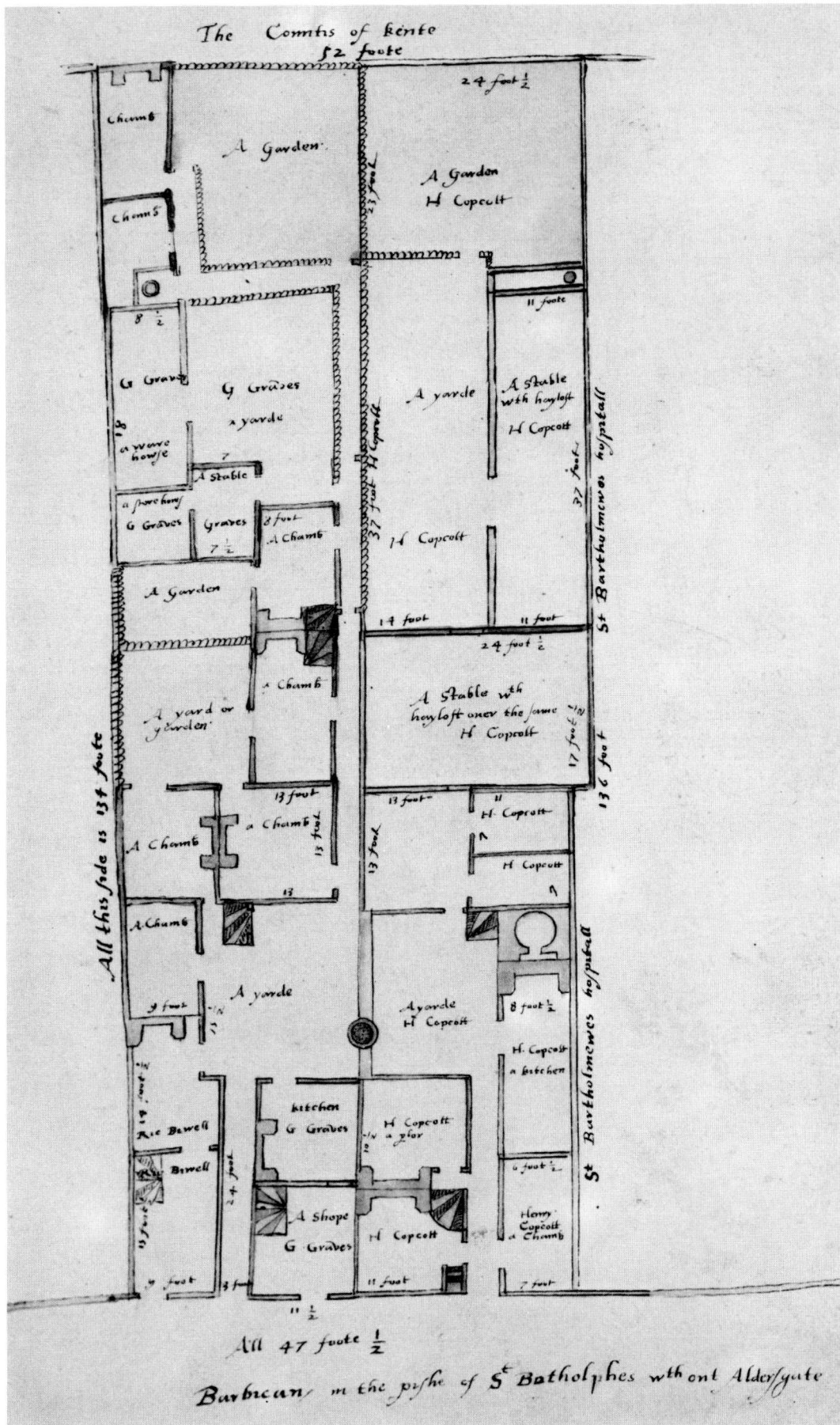

Figure 7. **4.** White Horse, Barbican Street (1:200). North is to the top of the plan.

5. 9, 10 Basing Lane

Plan Book, 24

Part of the bequest of John Watson to the Clothworkers' Company in 1555; two of these houses were ex-chantry property attached to St Andrew Baynard Castle (Hare 1860, 241; CD Box 54).

Two adjoining houses on the S side of the lane (Fig. 8) were of similar design, though with slight differences. They were of two-room plan with separate kitchens, and in each case a gallery led from the house over the yard at first-floor level – though to a room over the kitchen only in the case of Fuddes, the E of the pair. The function of the gallery in Fuller's tenancy is not clear. Fuddes' house rose to 4½ storeys, Fuller's to 3½.

Text of Reference, Plan Book (1612)

Thomas Fuddes: (2) A chamber next the street 18½' E–W with the stairs and passage, 18' 4" N–S with a chimney, a gallery leading out of the same over part of the yard into a chamber over the kitchen, which chamber is 17' E–W, 13' N–S with the chimney; (3) A chamber next the street with a chimney 18¼' E–W with the closet, stairs and a little chamber there × 19½' N–S; (4) Two chambers, one with a chimney, [both] 18¼' E–W × 19½' N–S; (5) A garret with a chimney 18¼' E–W × 19½' N–S; A cellar under part of the shop 14' E–W × 9' N–S.

Allen Fuller: (2) A chamber next the street 13½' E–W with the chimney × 14½' N–S, a chamber adjoining with a chimney 13½' E–W × 14¼' N–S, also a little room or gallery over part of the yard being 5' × 15'; (3) A chamber next the street 14½' E–W with the chimney × 15' N–S, another chamber adjoining 13½' E–W × 14½' N–S; (4) Two garrets over all, [both] 14½' E–W with the chimney, 29' N–S; A cellar under the shop 9' E–W × 17' N–S.

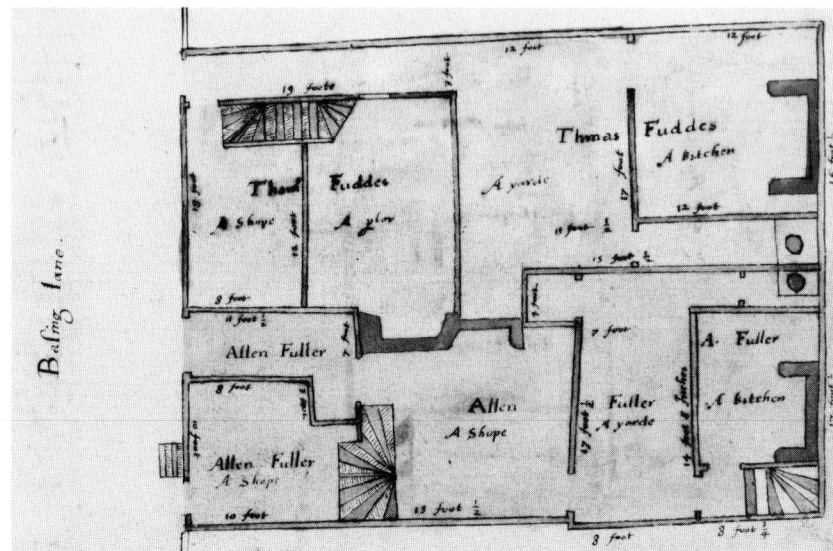

Figure 8. **5.** 9–10 Basing Lane (1:150). North is to the left of the plan.

6. 20 Basing Lane (later 25, Cannon Street West)

Plan Book, 24

This small property was part of the bequest of John Watson to the Clothworkers' Company in 1555 (Hare 1860, 142; CD Box 54). In 1560–1 the Company rebuilt it, at a cost of £27 15s. 8d. (RW Accts 1560–1, 9–11). No later modifications are mentioned in Company accounts, and it therefore seems likely that Treswell's survey of 1612 (Fig. 9) describes the property as rebuilt in 1560–1. The house rose to 4½ storeys. From its first-floor hall a small study hung over the street.

Text of reference, Plan Book (1612)

Dorothy Parsons: (2) A chamber or hall next the street 13½′ E–W with the chimney × 11½′ N–S besides the study hanging over into the street, a kitchen adjoining with a chimney 6′ E–W × 11½′ N–S; (3) A chamber with a chimney over the hall [no measurements], another little chamber adjoining 8′ E–W, 13′ N–S with the stairs and house of office; (4) Two chambers over the two chambers aforesaid; (5) Two garrets over all, 19½′ E–W, 14′ N–S; A cellar under the shop 8′ square.

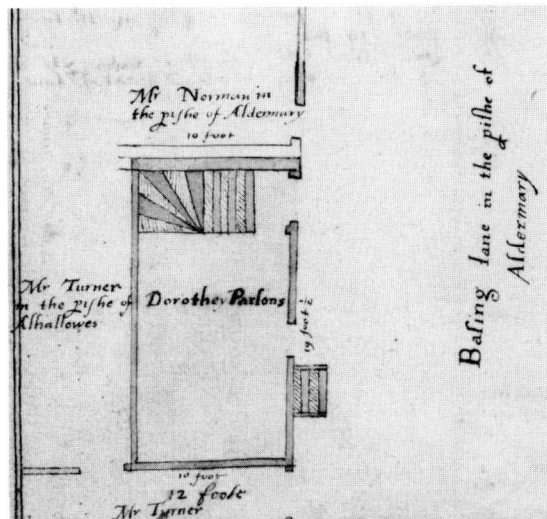

Figure 9. **6.** 20 Basing Lane (1:150). North is to the left of the plan.

7. 36–9 (later 37–40), now 182–4, Bishopsgate

Evidence Book, 22

Three houses and a large garden, part of the bequest of Sir Martin Bowes to Christ's Hospital in 1565 (GL MS 12949). The properties originally belonged to the hospital of St Mary Spital; in 1533 the hospital leased the southernmost to Richard Garnett, tailor, with its garden for 81 years at 20*s*. p.a. (GL MS 12949A). In 1595 the property was leased by Christ's Hospital to John (*sic*: Luke on the plan) Clapham for 60 years at the same rent. He died intestate, but his widow Anne, as Lady Anne Darrell, secured the remainder of the lease in 1642 (GL MS 12949B). The property was then the Three Tuns Tavern. In 1652 the property passed to Gilbert East, who laid out £100 on repairs; certainly the property had been greatly rebuilt in comparison to that shown in the present plan by 1693, when East added a further brick building at the rear (GL MS 12949B, M and N).

The plan shown here (Fig. 10) is one of the earliest datable in the Christ's Hospital collection, at 1607. In that year the hospital leased the middle building (Nos. 37–8) to Richard Plowman for 21 years at £4 p.a., paying a fine of £25. The lease mentions a 'plott hereunto annexed' i.e. a lease-plan. The plan is not present, but was reused in the next surviving lease of the property in 1661 (GL MS 12949E). It is clearly Treswell's plan which should have been attached to the lease

of 1607. In every detail except the colouring, which is a uniform brown for all walls, it resembles the plan in the Evidence Book.

All three houses were two rooms deep, though of different lengths; the middle property was of double width. They were of two storeys with garrets, except for the small tenancy of William Harrell which, the text on the lease-plan of 1607 adds, was only of two storeys.

Text of reference, Evidence Book (1607)

Luke Clapham, in the occupation of Peter la Catte: [2] A chamber next the street with a chimney 13½′ × 8½′, one other chamber adjoining the same 13½′ × 7½′, another chamber over the parlour with a chimney 16½′ × 14′, a chamber over part of the kitchen and the entry with a chimney 13′ × 10½′; [3] A garret over the same chamber 13′ × 10½′, also a garret next the street with a chimney 13½′ × 12½′.

Richard Plowman: [2] A chamber next the street 14½′ × 11′, another chamber next the yard 19½′ × 14½′ with a chimney; [3] A garret over the chamber aforementioned 19′ × 15½′.

Edward Walker: [2] A chamber next the street 13½′ × 8′, another little closet next the street adjoining to the same 13½′ × 4′, one other chamber next the yard with a chimney 11½′ × 11½′; [3] A garret next the street 14½′ × 12′.

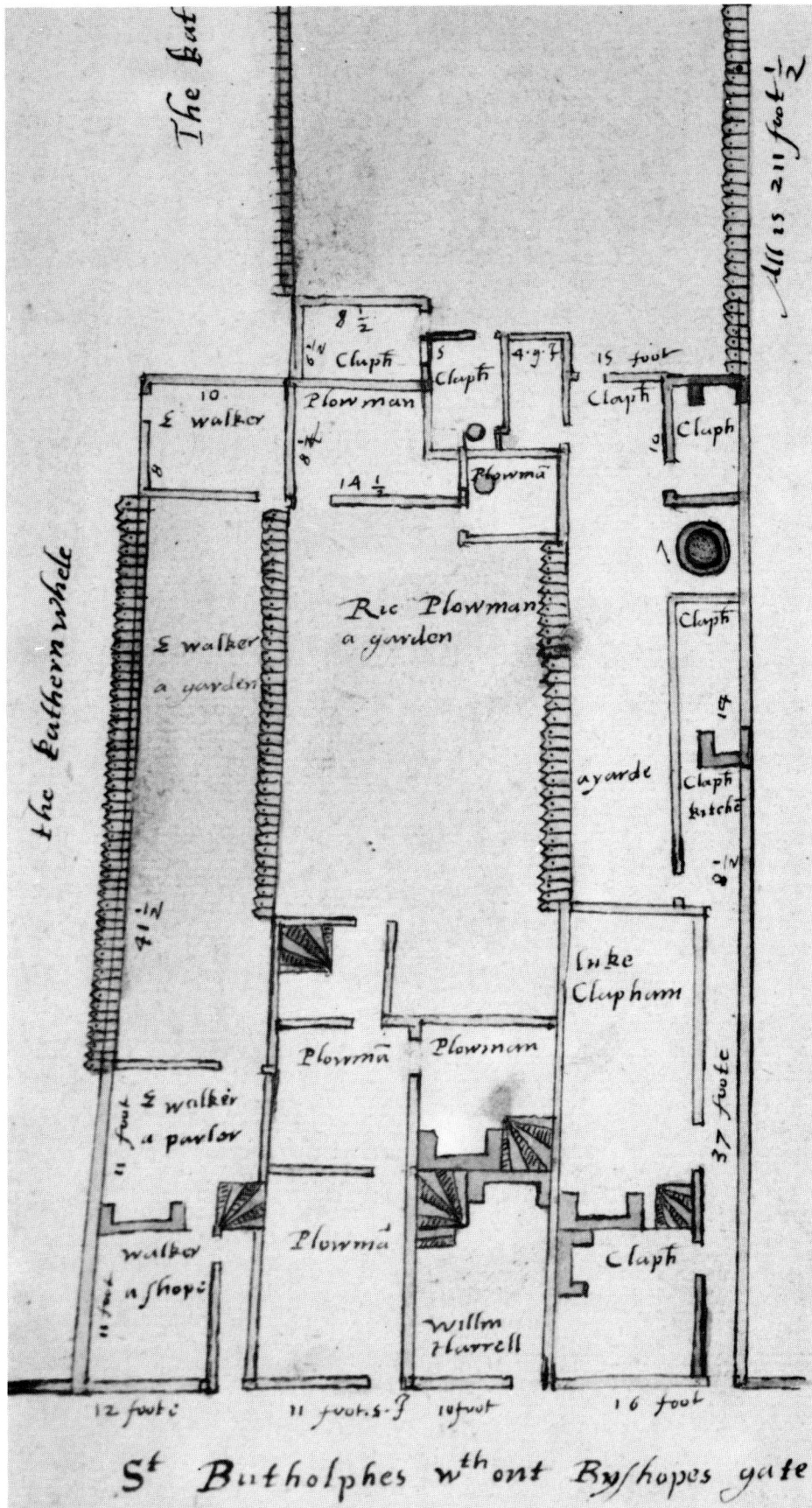

Figure 10. **7.** 36–9, later 37–40, now 182–4 Bishopsgate (1:150). North is to the left of the plan.

8. Garden in Katherine Wheel Alley, Bishopsgate (later the Cock public house and other houses in Cock Hill, Bishopsgate St)

Evidence Book, 13

This was a large garden to the E of Bishopsgate, at the end of Katherine Wheel Alley; part of the large bequest to Christ's Hospital by Sir Martin Bowes in 1565 (GL MS 12949). In 1574 the garden was leased by the hospital to Benedicte Spinola, who already occupied the gardens to the N and W (GL MS 12949B). Presumably this was part of Spinola's enclosure of that year of eight acres of land to form twenty tenteryards and certain gardens (Stow ii, 288). The plan of the garden by Treswell (Fig. 11) shows it fenced around, with a small two-room building in the SE corner. A stair leads to an upper storey, but no text of reference is attached.

Later deeds identify this garden as the site of 1–7 Cock Hill and 28 New Street (GL MS 12949I).

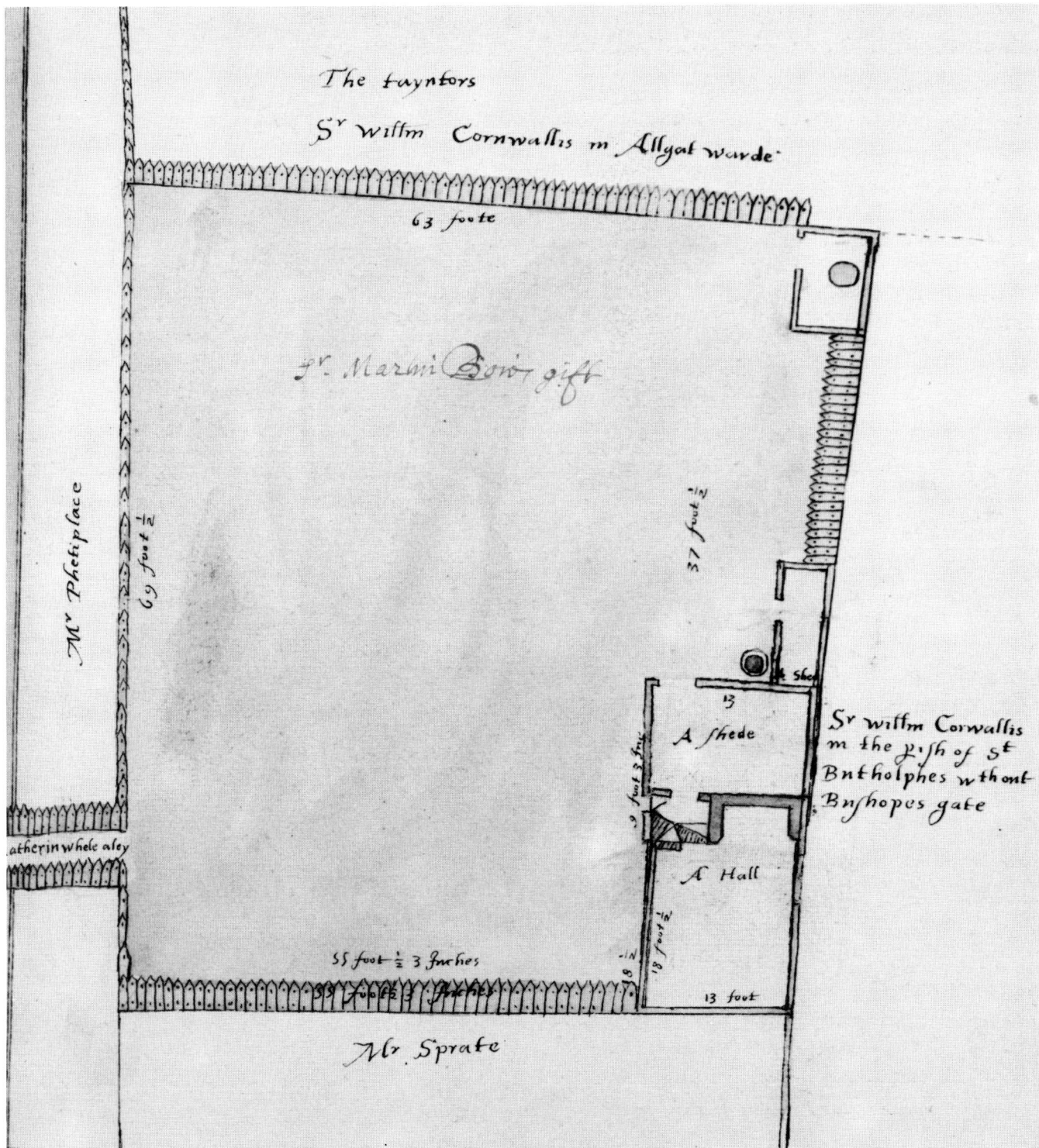

Figure 11. **8.** Garden in Katherine Wheel Alley, later 1–7 Cock Hill, 28 New Street, Bishopsgate (1:150).
North is to the top of the plan.

9. 34 Bow Lane, 1–3 St Thomas Apostle

Plan Book, 23

A corner property, known in 1612 as the Black Lion, fronted W onto Cordwayner Street (the S part of the present Bow Lane) and N on Turnbase alias Backe Lane. John Watson bequeathed the property, with the others nearby in Basing Lane (**5**) to the Clothworkers' Company in 1555 (CD Box 54).

The property, when surveyed by Treswell in 1612 (Fig. 12), comprised a 3½ storey block on the N side of an entry from Bow Lane. The substantial wall forming the N side of the Black Lion at ground level was of stone, with three internal buttresses or wall-stubs. The hall was at the front at first-floor level, overlooking Cordwayner Street (Bow Lane) and sailing over the entry; the principal stair to the first-floor chambers rose from the entry directly behind the shop, and a backstairs communicated between the first floor and the ground-floor kitchen. A larger second kitchen, with access only to the alley, was presumably related to the trade, perhaps in food, carried out in the shop.

Text of reference, Plan book (1612)

John Hodgkins: (2) A hall next the street 17½' E–W with the chimney, 23½' N–S, one other chamber adjoining 18' E–W with the chimney, 21' N–S with the stairs, passage and buttery, another chamber over the shop and kitchen next Turnbase Lane 16½' E–W with chimney and buttery × 16½' N–S with the stairs and the closet, also a garret over the back room by the kitchen; (3) A chamber next the street 18' E–W × 12' N–S, another chamber adjoining 18½' E–W with the chimney × 14' N–S, another chamber adjoining 19½' with the chimney × 21½' N–S, another room adjoining 6' E–W, 11½' N–S with a house of office in it, one garret next Turnbase Lane 15' E–W × 15½' N–S with a house of office in it; (4) Three garrets over the building next the street; one cellar 8' N–S × 8½' E–W, another cellar 13½' E–W × 14½' N–S, a little cellar under part of the shop next Turnbase Lane.

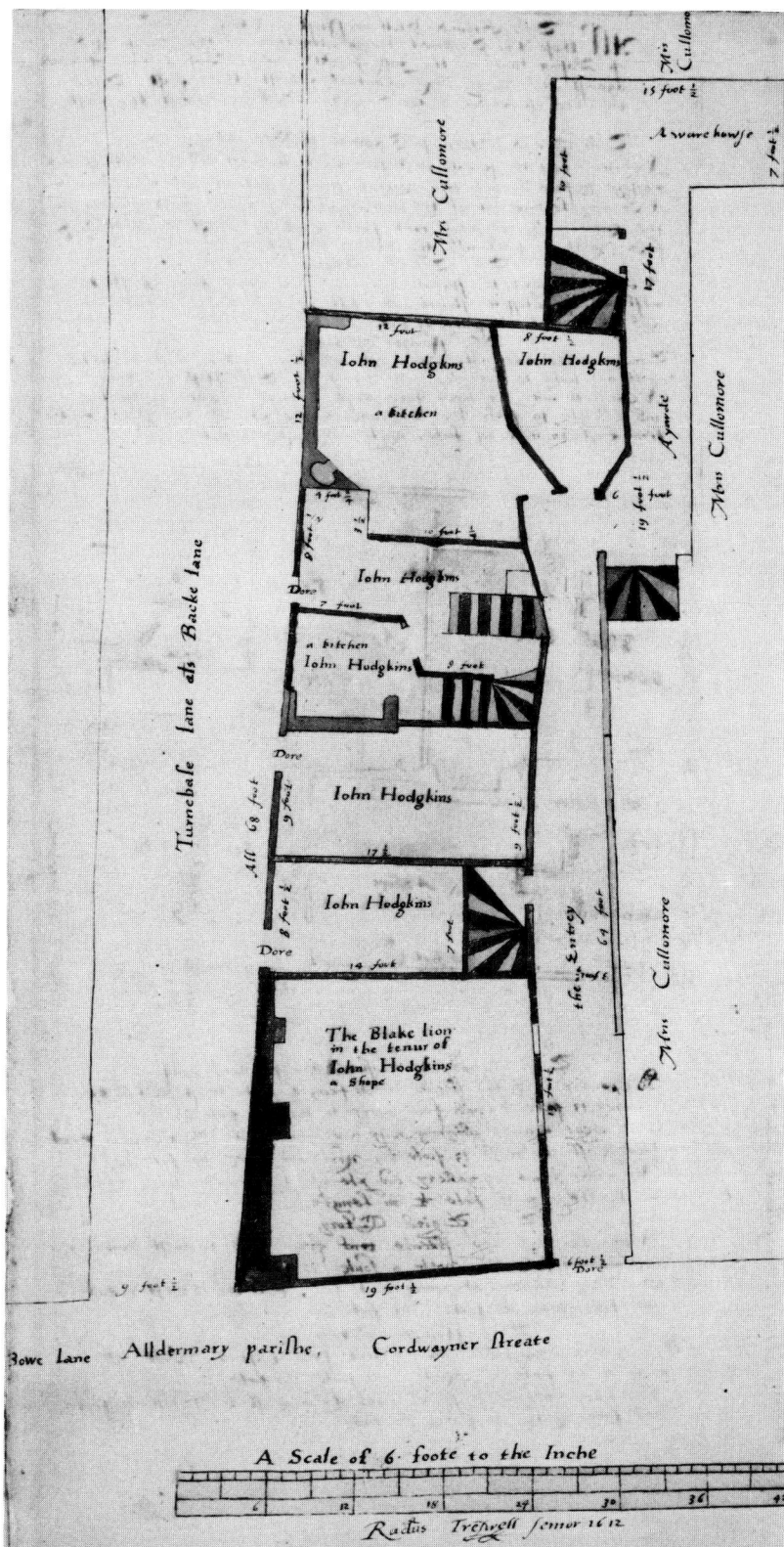

Figure 12. **9.** 34 Bow Lane, 1–3 St Thomas Apostle (1:150). North is to the left of the plan. *See also Plate 11.*

10. 36 Bread Street

Evidence Book, 8

On 24 July 1582 the treasurer of Christ's Hospital took possession of a tenement called The Ship, under the will of Thomas Hall, salter, late treasurer of the hospital (*Charity Comm*, 97). The house (Fig. 13) was of 3½ storeys, the hall and kitchen on the first floor.

Text of reference, Evidence Book (1611)

Mr Stephen Woodford: [2] A hall with a chimney 15½′ × 15′; A little chamber next the hall 9½′ × 6′; Also a kitchen with a chimney and oven 18½′ × 8½′ at the W end and × 5′ 10″ at the E end; [3] One other chamber over the hall next the street 16½′ × 15½′ with a chimney; One other chamber next the same 11′; [4] A garret over all with a privy 30′ × 13½′; A cellar under the shop of the same measure.

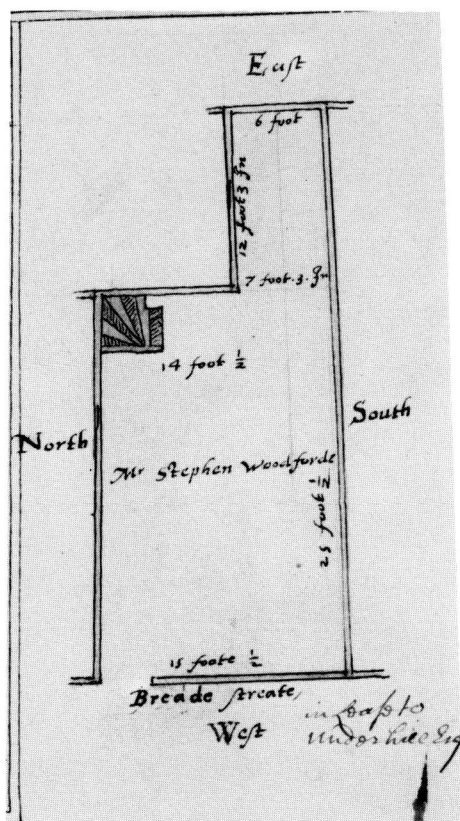

Figure 13. **10.** 36 Bread Street (1:150).
North is to the left of the plan.

11. 31 Catteaton Street, now part of site of Gresham College, Gresham Street

Plan Book, 43

This single house, on the N side of Catteaton Street and facing down Ironmonger Lane, passed to the Clothworkers' Company by the will of John Lute in 1585 (CD Box 58); it was called The Leadenporch at that date and in 1612. The plan (Fig. 14) is one of only two examples (cf. **43**) in the surveys where a building appears to have had intact stone walls on *both* long sides at ground level (in all cases the nature of walls at first-floor level and higher is not known). The dimensions of the cellar, reaching back from the street 31′, coincide with the start of a return shown in the W wall on the ground-floor plan, strongly suggesting that the structure was originally a stone house on a basement storey, with an internal area of 30½′ × 30½′ (though the basement was only half this size in 1612). In size and proportion this house would be similar to the Norman house recorded at Corbet Court, off Gracechurch Street, in the nineteenth century (Loftus-Brock 1872). It is also possible that the house was one of the many early medieval stone houses in this locality, the Jewry, based upon Old Jewry in the SE; a

Norman town house is said by Stow (i, 286–7) to be the core of the medieval Blackwell Hall, just to the N of this site in Basinghall Street.

Treswell's description of the interior in 1612 includes the most frequent use in these surveys of the word 'fair'; evidently it was in 1612, also, an impressive house. It was then of 3½ storeys on a cellar.

Text of reference, Plan Book (1612)

Thomas Inche: (2) A chamber next the street, one other fair chamber over the shop with a chimney, a fair hall over part of the shop with a chimney in it, a fair passage into the kitchen having a chimney and oven in the said kitchen, another chamber over the warehouse with a chimney, all 29′ E–W with the passages [no N–S measurement]; (3) A chamber over the kitchen with a chimney, another chamber with a chimney, two garrets over the same chambers aforesaid, a garret chamber next the street, another chamber adjoining to the same, two other fair chambers with two chimneys, 29′ E–W × 33½′ N–S; (4) A garret chamber next the yard 14½′ E–W with the chimney × 19′ N–S besides the house of office; A cellar under part of the shop 14½′ E–W × 31′ N–S.

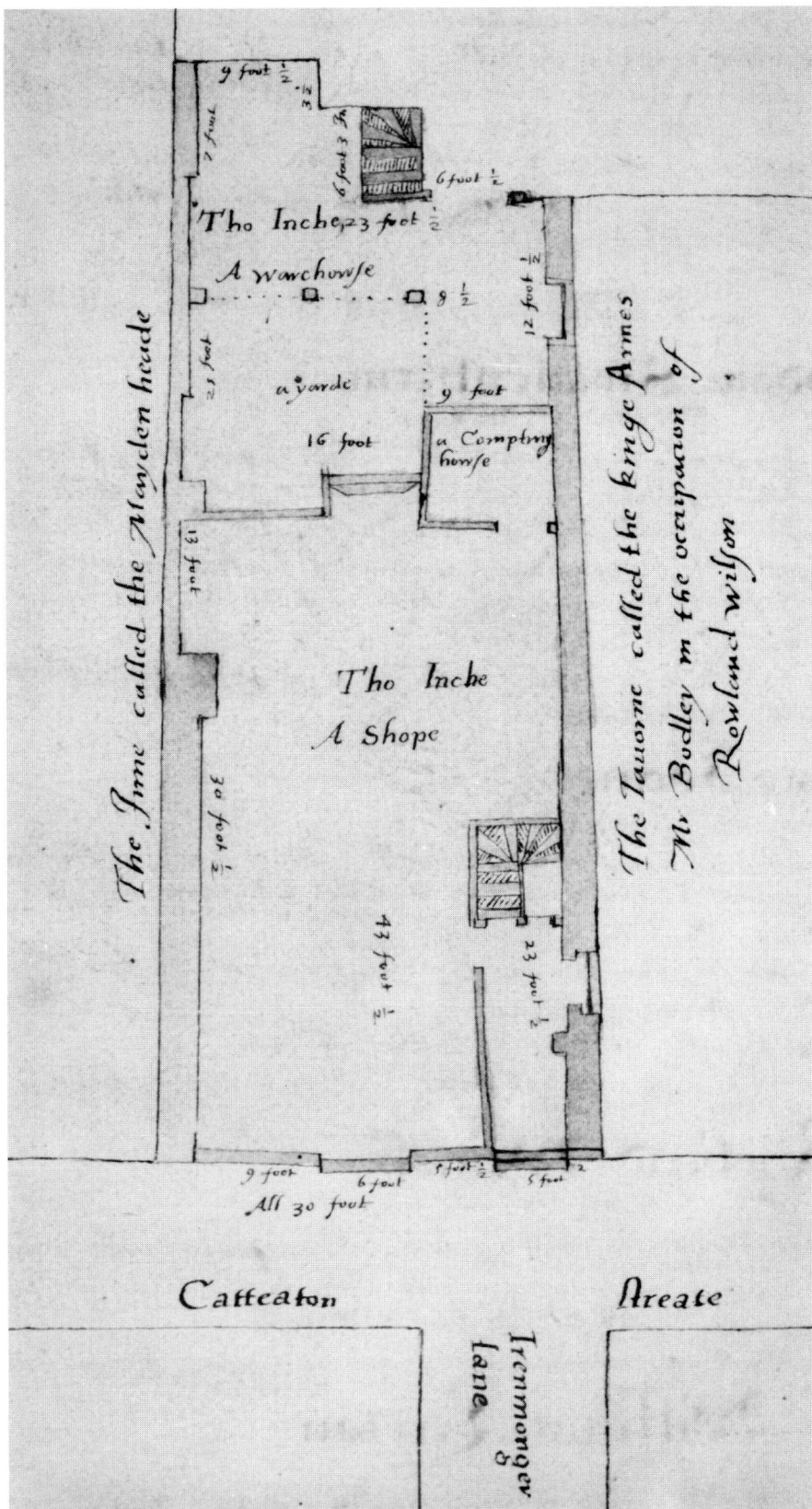

The Inne called the Mayden heade

9 foot ½
3½
7 foot
6 foot 3 ¼
6 foot ½

Tho Inche, 23 foot ½

A warehowse

9 ½

½ foot
12 foot

23 foot

a yarde

9 foot

16 foot

a Comptyng howse

13 foot

Tho Inche
A Shope

30 foot ½

43 foot ½

23 foot ½

The Tauorne called the kinge Armes
Mr Bodley in the occupacion of
Rowland wilson

9 foot   6 foot   5 foot ½   5 foot

All 30 foot

Catteaton

Areate

Irenmonger lane

Figure 14. **11.** 31 Catteaton Street (1:150). North is to the top of the plan.

5

12. St Michael le Querne, Cheapside

BM Crace Collection 1880–11–13–3516

This drawing, signed by Treswell and dated 1585 (Fig. 15), shows the parish church of St Michael le Querne at the W end of Cheapside and the Little Conduit at the E end of the church. The houses on both sides of the street are shown in simple form without differentiation; the openings of Foster Lane and Old Change are shown and named, and there is a simple representation of the gateway into St Paul's Churchyard.

There is at present no documentary context for this drawing. Its subject presumably relates to the detailed measurements given in its central area, evidently concerning the water-pipes leading to and from the conduit; they pass in front of the S door of the church, and through a reserved area (in which the pipes are expressly not shown)

33′ × 4′ in front of the church. This blanking out of the pipes is not explained.

In 1430 the church was enlarged, half on the common soil (*Cal L B L*, 106). At the same time the City undertook to keep the new conduit at the E end of the church in repair, granting 1000 marks for its completion (*Cal L B K*, 110, 243, 249, 253; cf. Stow i, 77).

If the enlargement of the church, partly on common soil, refers to the S aisle shown by Treswell, then the drawing might refer to the City's rights in its land through which the pipes had been laid during the fifteenth century. There is nothing in the City's records or those of the parish to suggest why or for whom Treswell drew the survey in 1585.

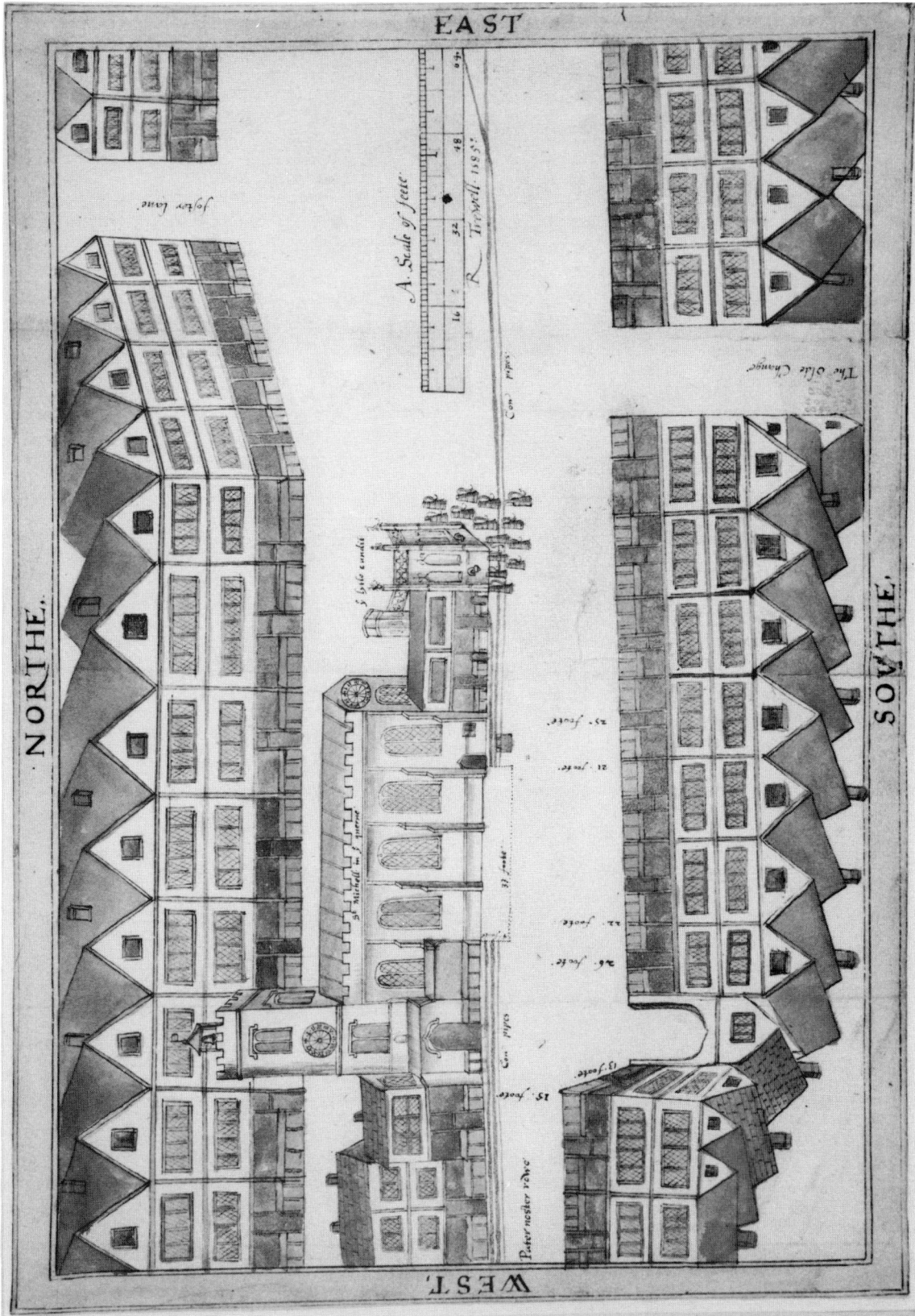

Figure 15. **12.** St Michael le Querne, Cheapside. See also Plate 1.

13–15. Bell (Gough's) Alley, Swan Alley and White's Alley, Coleman Street

Plan Book, 49–50; Weinstein 1980, Fig. 1

The survey in 1612 of these three blocks of property by Treswell for the Clothworkers' Company has been published and discussed (Weinstein 1980, 61–80). The property belonged to Rewley Abbey, a Cistercian house in Oxford. In 1528 the Abbott leased three gardens in White's Alley to Thomas Abraham the elder, leather-seller. By March 1543 the lands were in the possession of William Lambe (d. 1580); he left these, with much other property (e.g. **30**) to the Clothworkers' Company.

The Company Renter Warden's Accounts show that houses had been built on the gardens by 1594–5, though it is not clear when or in what order; there are no building accounts in Company records, implying that the tenants were responsible. One of the properties on White's Alley had a house on it in 1570 (CDW, 296–8).

The lands fall into three blocks: (**13**) between Swan Alley and White's Alley, now 4–5 Copthall Buildings (and probably part of the present property to the W); (**14**) Bell or Gough's Alley, now 1–2 Copthall Buildings; and (**15**) Bell or Gough's Alley, now 8–10 Telegraph Street. Their relationship is shown in Fig. 16, and the individual blocks are shown at a larger scale in Figs 17–19.

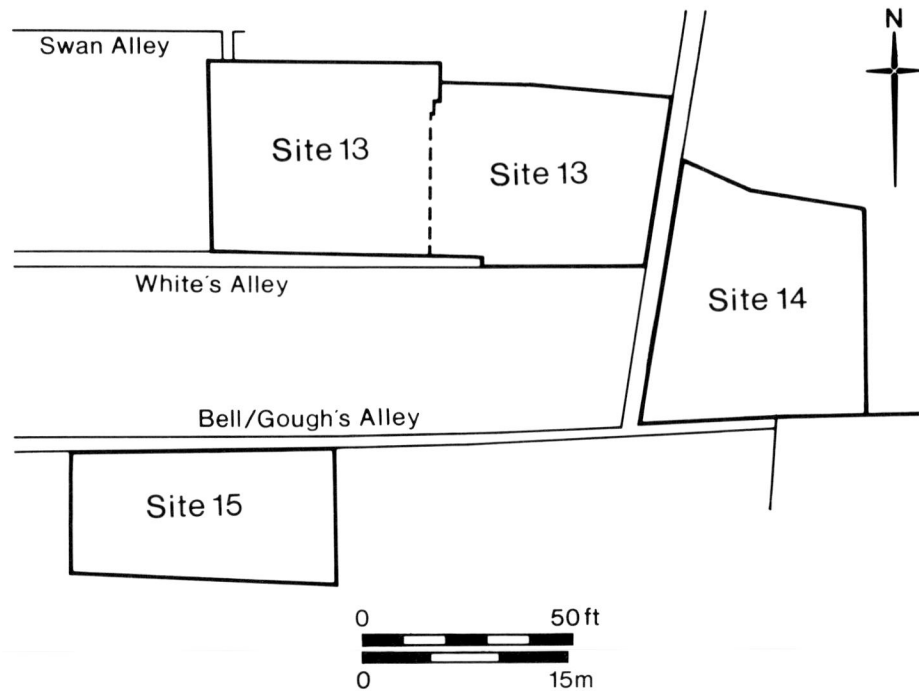

Figure 16. **13–15.** Location plan

13. Swan Alley/White's Alley, now 4–5 Copthall Buildings

Plan Book, 49–50; Weinstein 1980, Fig. 1

Here were two gardens with houses built on their N sides, let to two principal tenants (Mrs Butler and John Burdges) (Fig. 17). Mrs Butler's house was of 2½ storeys, but its parlour had a semi-octagonal bay window taking up much of the end of the building. The setting enabled the house to be entered in its long side, and thus this is a rare example of the lobby-entrance house in London. A bowling alley occupied a strip along the S edge of the garden, entered from White's Alley. The E of the two gardens had the house tenanted by Rawse, an undertenant of John Burduge or Burdges. This was also a lobby-entrance house, of 2½ storeys, with two studies on first and second floors, each 10½' by 10', looking into the garden.

Text of reference, Plan Book (1612)

Mrs Butler, now in the tenure of Thomas Stevenson: (2) A chamber over the parlour 16' × 11½' beside the chimney, another chamber adjoining with the stairs 16½' × 11½'; (3) A garret 16½' × 11½', another garret adjoining with a study in it 16½' × 11½'.

John Burduge alias Burdges now in the tenure of William Rawse: (2) A study over into the garden supported upon two posts 10½' × 10', a chamber over the kitchen with a chimney in it with the passage 18½' × 14½', another chamber adjoining to the same 14½' × 7', a chamber over the parlour with the stairs and chimney 22' × 14½'; (3) A study over the study aforesaid of the like bigness, two garrets over all in each with a chimney and both 19' × 14½', which two garrets are over the E part of the building aforesaid; A cellar under the parlour 17½' × 12'.

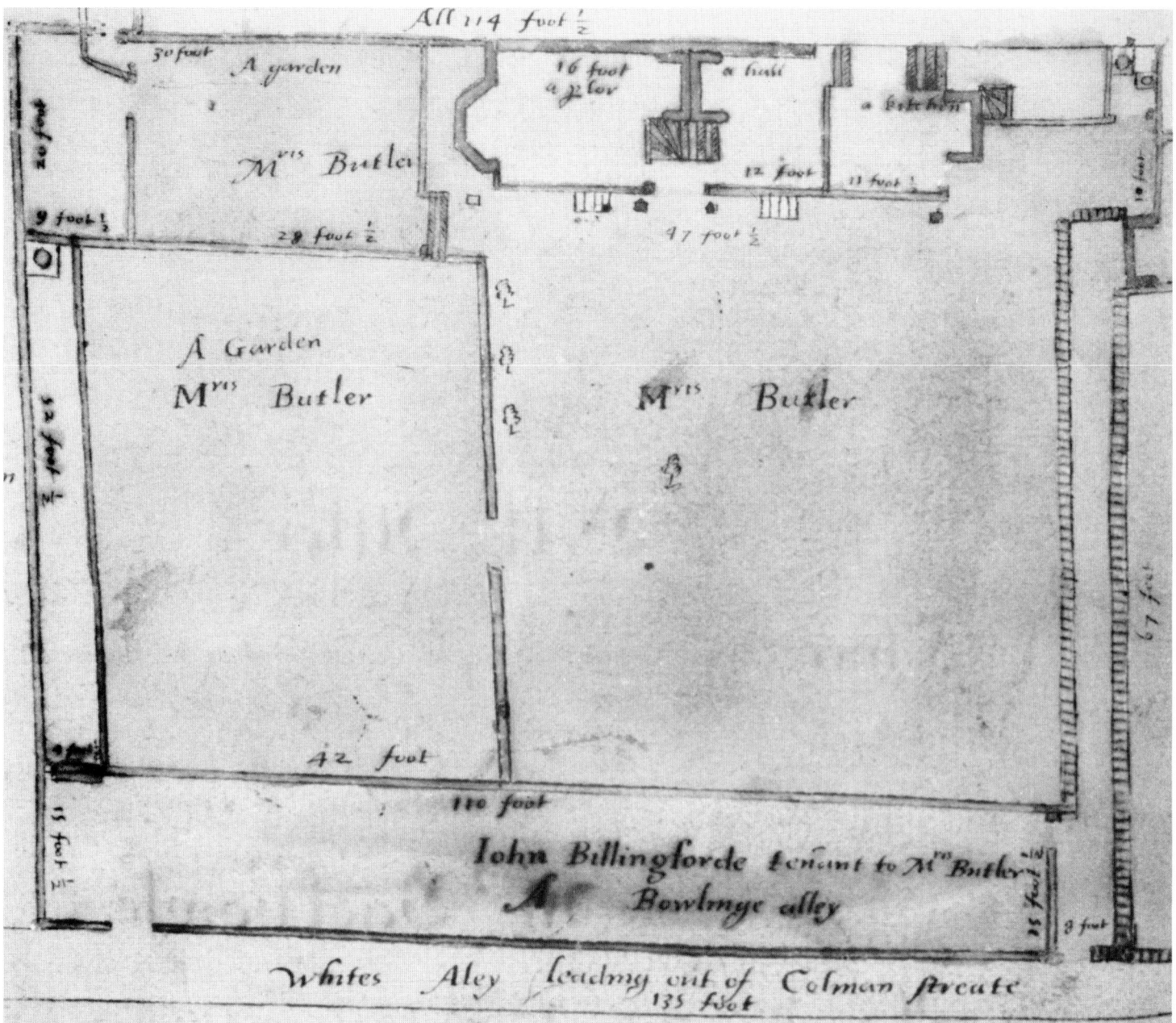

Figure 17. **13.** Swan Alley / White's Alley, Coleman Street, now 4–5 Copthall
Buildings (1:200). North is to the top of the plan.

23 foot

7 foot

9 foot 1/2

42 foot 1/2

a hall

12 foot 1/2

7 foot

42 foot 1/2

17 foot

a shede

a wash howse

17 foot 1/2

kitchen

Buttry

47 foot 1/2

7 foot

26 foot 1/2

8 foot

8 foot

A Garden

Iohn Burges

85 foot 1/2

45 foot

7 foot 1/2

26 foot 1/2

80 foot 1/2

26 foot

16 foot

90 foot

14. Bell or Gough's Alley, now 1–2 Copthall Buildings

Plan Book, 49–50; Weinstein 1980, Fig. 1

This pair of gardens (Fig. 18) were also bordered by buildings at one end; on the N side in the W garden, and on the S side in the E of the pair.

The W house, tenanted in 1612 by Peter Doby, undertenant of Joseph Samways, was on a platform raised above the garden by a low wall and steps. It comprised a haphazard arrangement of ground-floor rooms in an L-shape, with two rooms on the first floor and a garret over one of them. The E house, held by Edward Colley (on the plan) or Dolly (in the text of reference), undertenant of Mr Street, was a lobby-entrance house on two floors without garrets, with the unusual feature of the stair to the first floor being in the porch and not attached to the chimney-stack.

Text of reference, Plan Book (1612)

Joseph Samways now in a tenure of Peter Dobey: (2) A chamber with chimney 15¼′ × 12¾′, one other chamber over the workhouse with a chimney in it 16½′ × 15′ with the stairs; (3) A garret over the first chamber of the same bigness.

Mr Street, now in the tenure of Edward Dolly (Colley on plan): (2) A chamber over the parlour with a chimney in it 14½′ × 11½′, another chamber adjoining with a chimney in it 24½′ × 11′.

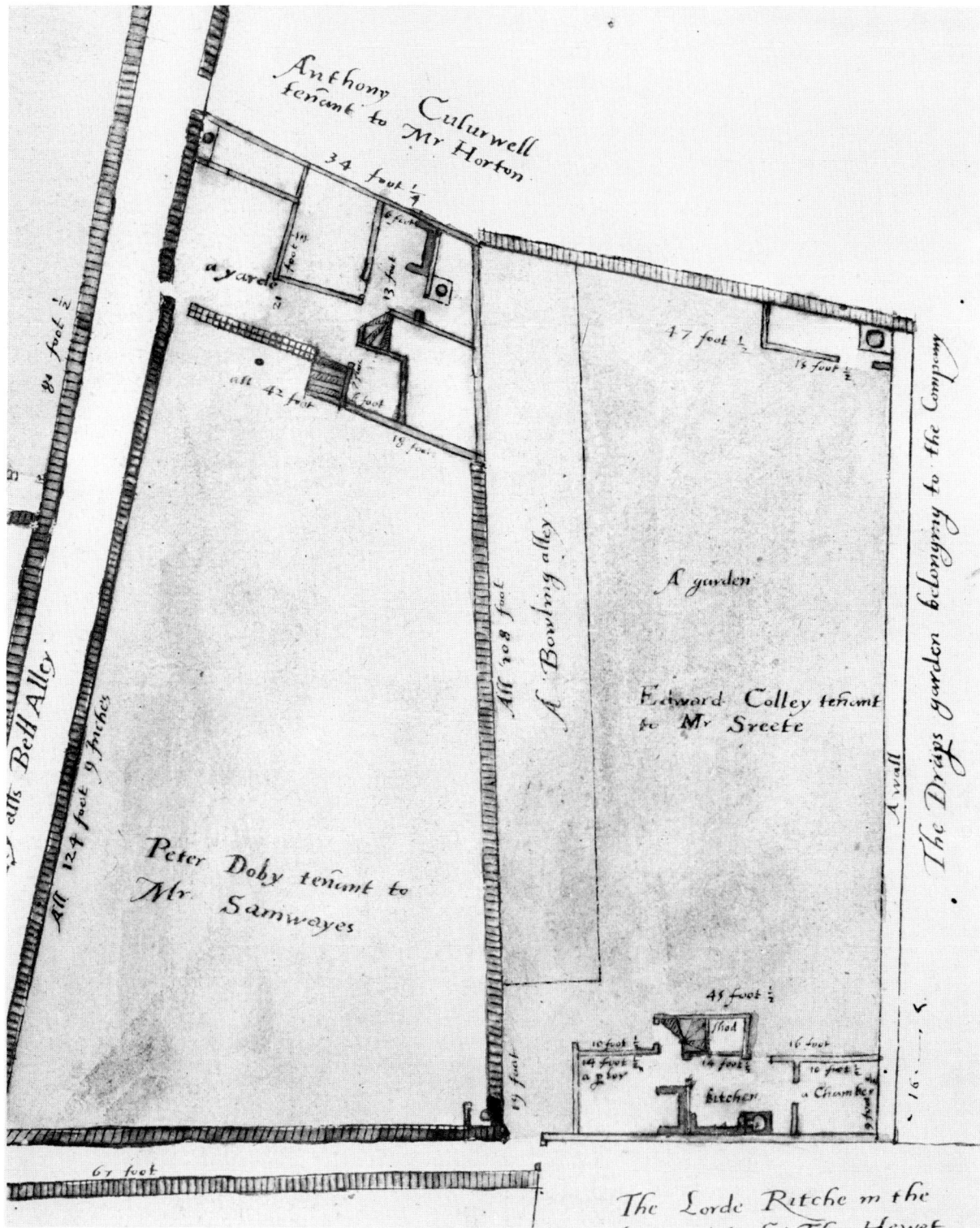

Figure 18. **14.** Bell or Gough's Alley, Coleman Street, now 1–2 Copthall Buildings (1:200). North is to the top of the plan.

15. Bell or Gough's Alley, now 8–10 Telegraph Street

Plan Book, 49–50; Weinstein 1980, Fig. 1

This rambling complex of rooms (Fig. 19) was divided among three undertenants (Myles, Fizardett, and Mary Ramsey or Remys) of a principal tenant, Mr Backhouse, who did not occupy the site. The largest of the three tenancies, of Mrs Ramsey, rose to 3½ storeys at the back of a small yard entered from Bell Alley on the N. The two smaller tenancies, of Fizardett and Myles, occupied the buildings fronting the Alley to the N, rising to 2½ storeys in both cases and probably joining over the entry. It is not clear who had rights to the garden, as the entrances were either to the alley or to the yard, which must have been common.

Text of reference, Plan Book (1612)

Mr Backhouse, a tenement now in the tenure of Sam Fizardett: (2) A chamber next the alley with the stairs and buttery 19½′ × 13′, a chamber over the gate there adjoining in Mrs Ramsey's house 13′ × 11½′, another chamber over part of Mrs Ramsey's house aforementioned 14′ × 12½′; (3) A garret over the first mentioned chamber 19′ × 13′, another garret adjoining 15′ × 12½′.

Mr Backhouse, another tenement now in the tenure of Mary Remys: (2) A chamber with chimney in 1. besides the chimney and the study 18′ × 11′, a chamber over the parlour beside the entry 18′ × 17′ with a chimney in it, a little room adjoining the same 8′ × 7′, a buttery with a kitchen in the middle hanging over into the yard 18½′ × 19½′, also a room over the kitchen with the stairs 14½′ × 11½′; (3) A chamber on the W side of the building 15¼′ × 10½′, one other chamber adjoining the same, some time parcel of it, with the chimney; (4) A garret over first mentioned chamber 20½′ × 15′; A little cellar under the same house 12½′ × 10′.

Mr Backhouse, one other tenement now in the tenure of Harman Myles: (2) A kitchen with chimney 12½′ × 10½′, a chamber adjoining over a part of the tenement aforesaid with the chimney 16½′ × 11½′; A chamber 13½′ × 13′ with a house of office in it, a garret chamber adjoining with chimney 17′ × 13′.

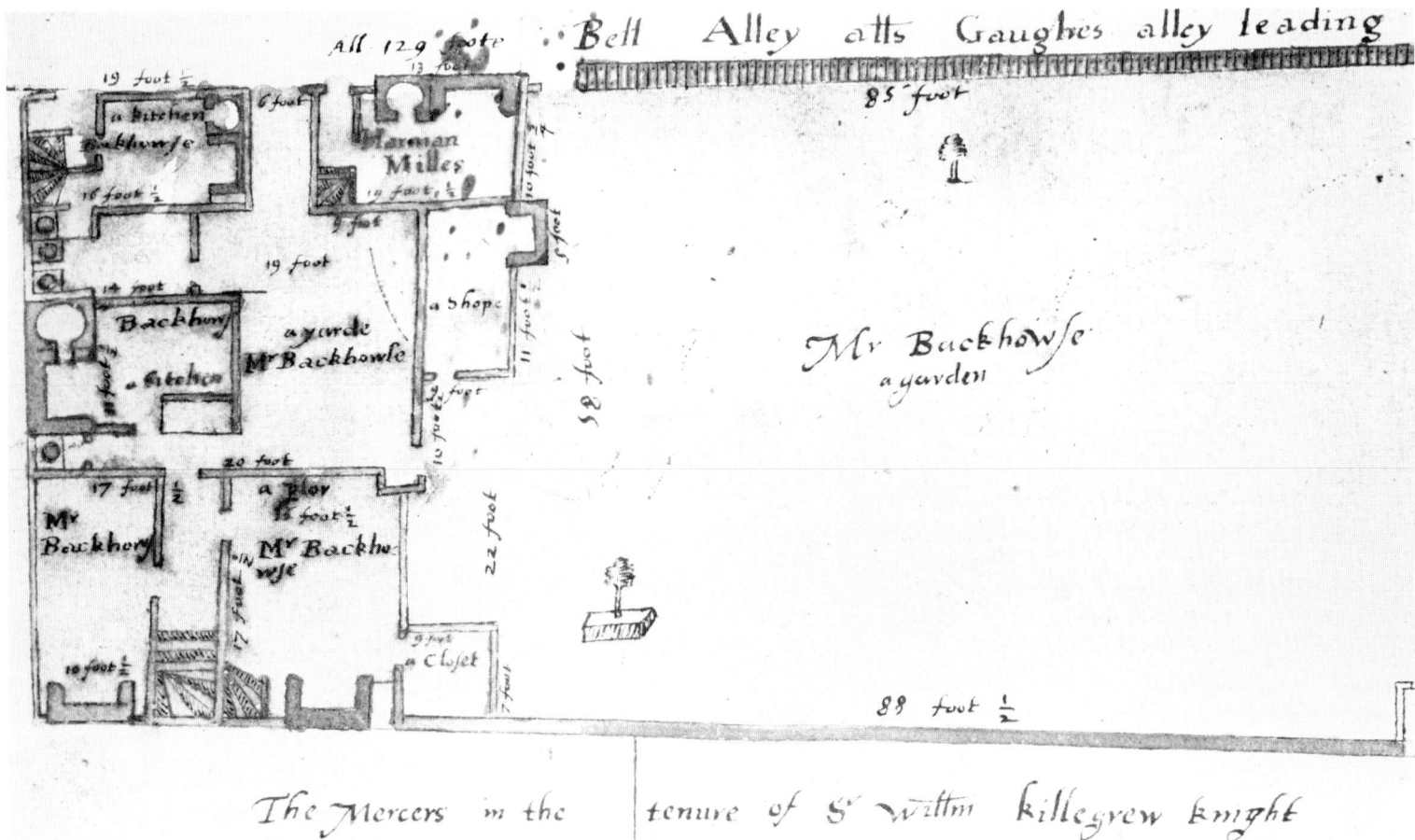

Figure 19. **15.** Bell or Gough's Alley, Coleman Street, now 8–10 Telegraph Street (1:200). North is to the top of the plan.

16. 16 Cornhill

Plan Book, 21

A property on the S side of Cornhill opposite the Royal Exchange, backing onto part of 'the stone house in Lumberd Street' in 1612. In 1445 William Chadworth and Laurence Sprynges, executors of Alice Boydnell, granted it to John Stocker (CD Box 58). The property appears to have stayed with the Stocker family until 1565, when Henry Stocker sold it to John Lute, who bequeathed it with the other property (see **11**) to the Clothworkers' Company in 1586 (*ibid.*). When surveyed in 1612 it was 4½ storeys high; a gallery led to a 'new building' on the first floor, and part of the roof was a flat lead.

Text of reference, Plan Book (1612)

Richard Bill: (2) A hall next the street 19¼' E–W with the stairs × 20' N–S with the chimney, another chamber adjoining 18½' E–W with the entry and stairs × 16½' N–S with the chimney, also a little gallery from the same over the yard into the new building, a chamber over the kitchen 20½' E–W with the chimney, 11' N–S, a compting house over the stairs and well; (3) A chamber next the street with a chimney, another chamber adjoining with a chimney, an entry over the comptinghouse leading into a chamber in the new building, all 62' N–S, 19½' E–W; (4) A chamber next the street with a chimney, closet, an entry into the house of office, a chamber adjoining with a door out into the leads to two little garrets over the new building, all 64½' N–S × 19½' E–W; (5) A fair garret over the old building 18½' E–W × 43' N–S; two cellars under the shop and warehouse 17½' E–W at the S, 16½' at the N, × 32' N–S.

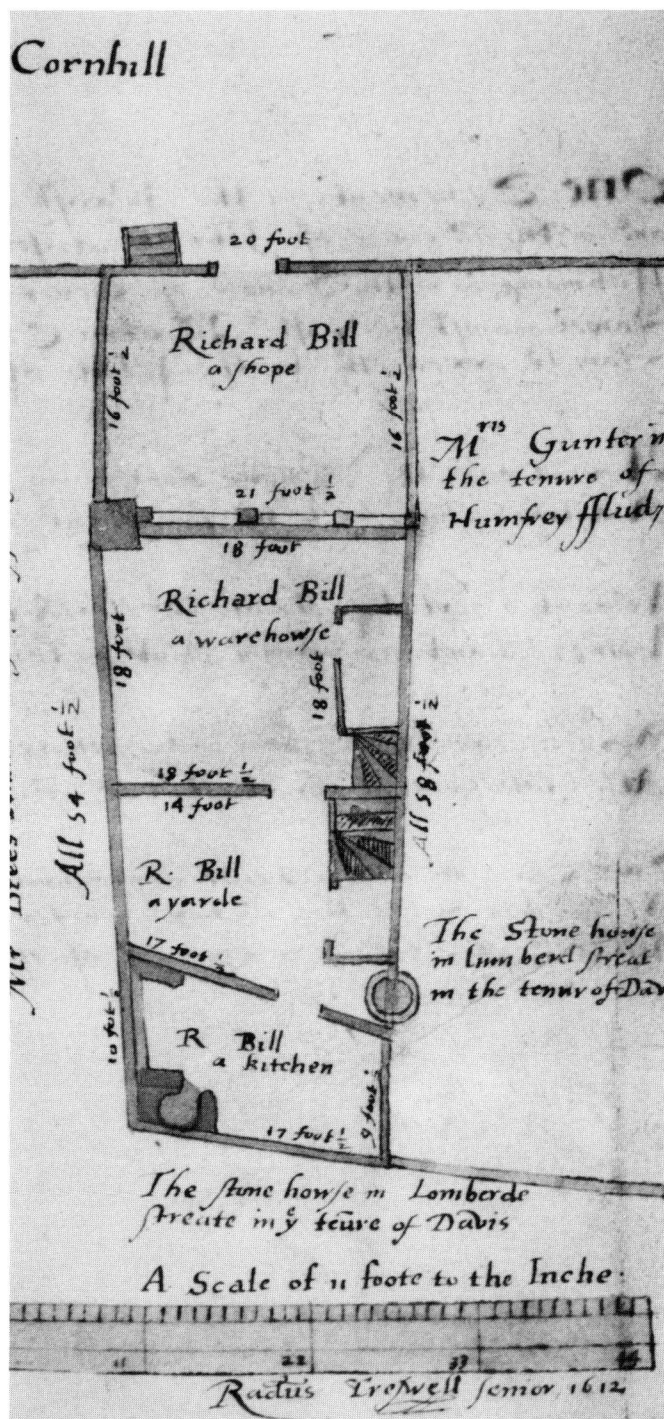

Figure 20. **16.** 16 Cornhill (1:150). North is to the top of the plan.

17. Wildman, Cornhill and Threadneedle Street

Plan Book, 21

This house, the Wildman in Cornhill, first appears in the records of the Clothworkers' Company in 1549–50 as the tenancy of Mrs Thorowgood, who paid a quarter's rent (RW Accts, 1549–50). This suggests that the property was acquired during that year, and possibly that Mrs Thorowgood, a widow, was the sitting tenant. But otherwise there is no documentation at Clothworkers' Hall which explains how the house came into the Company's possession.

The house is said to be in the parish of St Christopher; and the cumulative N–S measure of about 63′ would place the site, on Ogilby and Morgan's map (1677), in the narrow tongue of housing between the Royal Exchange and the end of Poultry (now the forecourt of the present Royal Exchange), about five houses from the end and directly opposite the church of St Christopher on the N side of Threadneedle Street. In 1612 (Fig. 21) the house was 5½ storeys high on cellars.

Text of reference, Plan Book (1612)

The Wildman Cornhill, in the tenure of George Harwood: (2) A hall 15′ E–W with the chimney, 37′ N–S with the passage, stairs, study and leads; (3) A chamber with a chimney 14½′ E–W × 35′ N–S; with the stairs; (4) Two chambers, one with a chimney, [both] 14½′ E–W × 35′ N–S (5) Two chambers with two chimneys, and a little room [together] of the same bigness; (6) A garret and a leade next the street 35′ N–S × 15½′ E–W; Two cellars, one under the shop, one under the warehouse, 32′ × 13′ with the vault.

Thomas Collins: (2) A hall next the street and a kitchen adjoining with two chimneys in them 12′ E–W × 25′ N–S; (3) Two chambers with two chimneys 12′ E–W × 27¼′ N–S; (4) Two other chambers, one with a chimney 12′ E–W × 27½′ N–S; (5) A garret over all 12½′ E–W × 28′ N–S; A cellar under his house and Mr Harwood's yard and buttery, 10′ E–W × 38′ N–S.

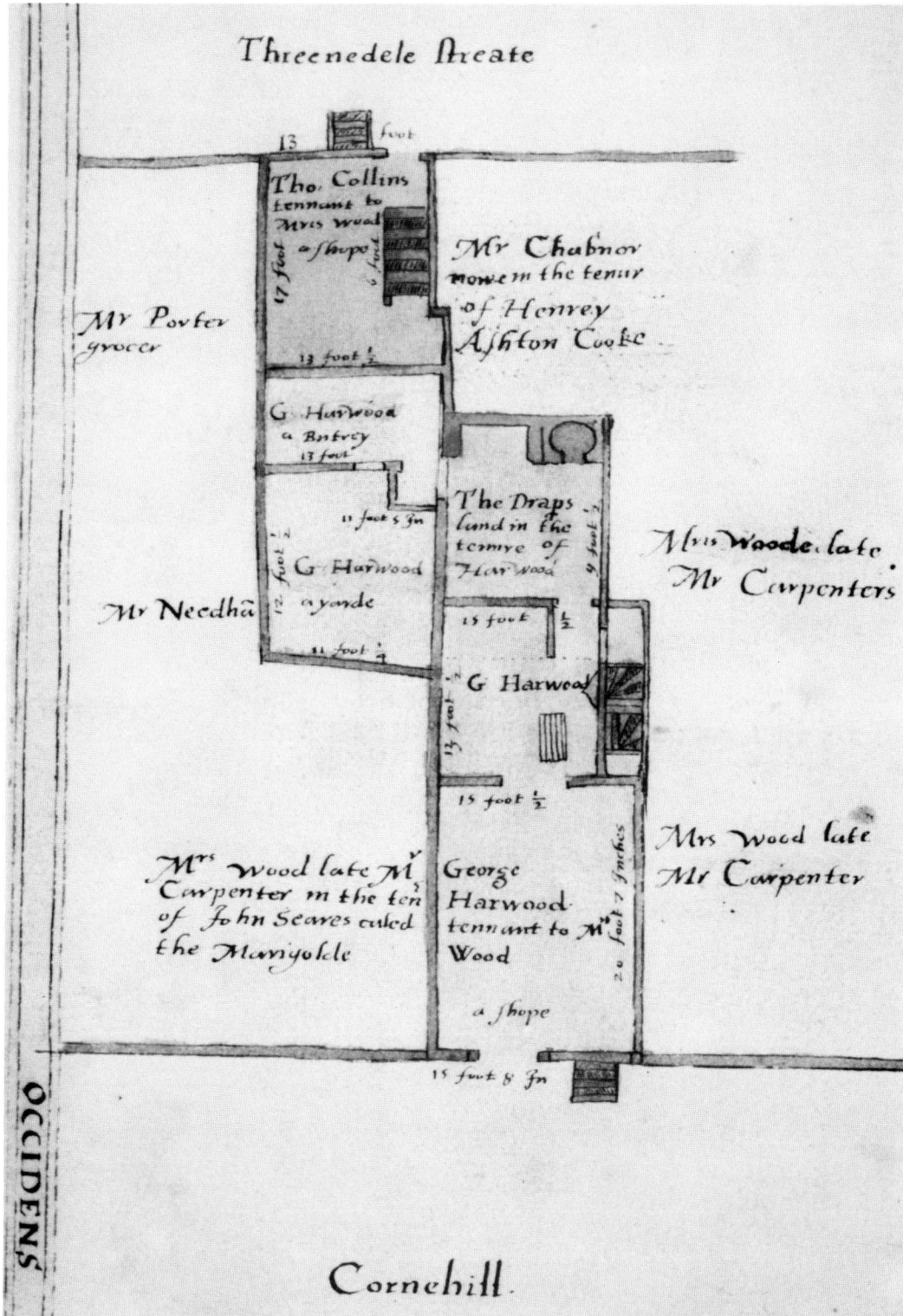

Threenedele streate

13 foot

Tho. Collins
tennant to
Mris Woad
a shope

Mr Chabnor
nowe in the tenur
of Henrey
Ashton Cooke

Mr Porter
grocer

17 foot

13 foot ½

G. Harwood
a Buttrey
13 foot

Mr Needhā

12 foot ½

G. Harwood
a yarde

11 foot 5 in

11 foot ½

The Draps
land in the
tenure of
Harwood

15 foot

Mrs Woode late
Mr Carpenters

G Harwood

13 foot

15 foot ½

Mrs wood late M.
Carpenter in the ten
of John Seares culed
the Marygolde

George
Harwood
tennant to Mrs
Wood

Mrs wood late
Mr Carpenter

20 foot 7 inches

a shope

15 foot 8 in

OCCIDENS

Cornehill.

Figure 21. **17.** Wildman, Cornhill (1:150). North is to the top of the plan.

18. Houses on N side Hart Street, later Crutched Friars

Plan Book, 17

By her will of 1596 Thomasine Evans bequeathed six properties in Crutched Friars to the Clothworkers' Company (CD Box 51). These lay on a wedge-shaped piece of land on the N side of Hart Street, immediately W of the S end of Northumberland Alley. In 1612 (Fig. 22) the buildings were generally of two rooms on each floor with yards behind. The tenancy of Hethersall, formerly two buildings, still retained its two street doors, and the juxtaposition of the entry to the adjacent tenancy of Hickes brought all three doors together. Hickes had a parlour alongside the street, an unusual position. His tenancy rose to 4½ storeys, whereas its neighbours were 3½ or 2½ storeys all on cellars. The text of reference is lacking for one tenancy, that of Lady Ashley.

Text of reference, Plan Book (1612)

John Dale: (2) A chamber next the street 15½' with the chimney × 14', one other chamber adjoining 15½' × 10' with the chimney; (3) A garret chamber next the street 15½' with the chimney × 14', one other garrett chamber adjoining 15½' × 9½' with the stairs; A little cellar under the chamber at the end of the yard 8½' × 5½', a cellar adjoining, only the passage between 10' × 6½', a cellar next the street 15' × 14'.

Mr Osborne, two tenements 'sometymes but one': [a] in tenure of William Wilcockes, (2) A chamber next the street 15' × 8½' with the chimney another chamber over the kitchen 8½ square; (3) A garret next the street 13½' × 8½' [b] In the tenure of Nicholas Stevens, (2) A Chamber next the street 15½' × 9½' with the chimney, one other chamber adjoining 8½' square; also a garret next the street in the third storey.

Mr Hickes: (2) A chamber or hall next the street 19' with the chimney × 16' with the entry, a little buttery next the street 12' with the stairs × 7' 3"; (3) A chamber next the street 20½' × 10½' with the chimney, one other chamber adjoining being next the street 20½' × 9½' with the chimney; (4) A chamber next the street 20½' × 9½' with the chimney, one other chamber adjoining 20½' × 10½' with the chimney; (5) A garret over all with a chimney; A cellar under all 19½' × 10'.

Mr Heathersall: two tenements 'sometymes but one': [a] (2) A chamber next the street 22'3" × 16½' with the chimney; (3) A chamber with a chimney being divided into the Chambers [*sic*.] 24½' × 16½'; (4) Two garrets over all 26' × 16½' with the chimney; A cellar under the same house 15½' square. [b] (2) A chamber over the kitchen and buttery 18' with the chimney × 10½', also a little room adjoining to the stairs; (3) A chamber over the chamber aforesaid 18' with the chimney × 11½'; (4) A chamber over the same chamber of the like bigness; A cellar under the same building.

Lady Ashley: [text missing].

The kinges lande in the tenure of Mr Ayms

A plot
A kitchen
Sr Andrew Ashley in the right of his Wiffe
A yarde

Sr Andrew Ashley

Mr Christopher Gaillor

Hare Streate at Crutchet Friers

A kitchen
A yarde
A yarde
Mr Hetherfall
Mr Hetherfall
A Butry
Hetherfall
Hetherfall
Dore
Dore the entrey
Dore
Hetherfall
A kitchen

Mr Hickes
Mr Hickes
Mr Hickes
A yarde
A plot
A kitchen
A plot
Dore

Mr Olborne
A kitchen
A yarde
A kitchen
A yarde
Thomas Haydon tenant to Mr Gaylor
Mr Olborne
Dore A shope

Iohn Dale
a shope
A kitchen
A Chamb
A Chamb
Dale
Iohn Dale
Iohn Dale
Dore

All 90 foot
All 36 foot

A Scale of 6 foot to the Inche
Radus Treswell senor 1612

Northumblande aleye
Northumbland Alley
Mr Gaylor

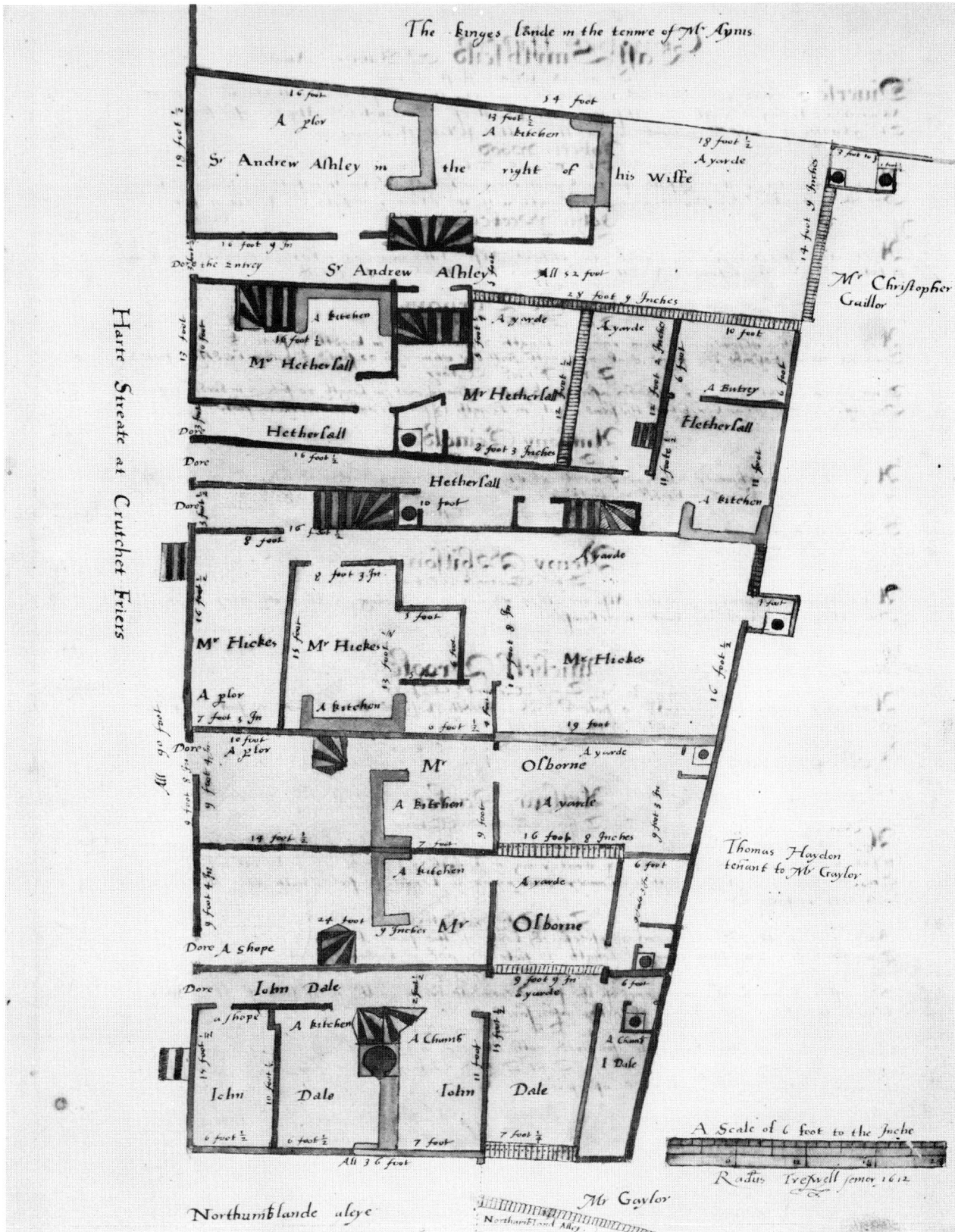

Figure 22. **18.** Crutched Friars (1:150). North is to the right of the plan.

19. 11–12 Fenchurch Street

Plan Book, 5

This block of property on the corner of Fenchurch Street and Philpot Lane was acquired by John Lute in 1541 and bequeathed with other property (see **11**) to the Clothworkers' Company by his will of 1585 (CD Box 1).

Three tenancies are shown in Treswell's survey of 1612 (Fig. 23); all three tenants, Cotton, Chauncey and Richardson, had a shop on the Fenchurch Street frontage. The largest was that of Richardson on the corner with Philpot Lane; as it had two doors to Fenchurch Street and two fireplaces, this was probably originally two shops. Cotton's shop was a lock-up, for the entry next door led to his chambers on the upper floors; his kitchen was on the third storey. Richardson's kitchen was on the ground floor and included a large oven. Chauncey's and Richardson's tenancies were 4½ storeys high, but Cotton's was apparently only 2½. Behind was a yard and further buildings of Chauncey.

The cellar stairs in Fenchurch Street led to to a large cellar on the corner under Richardson's building.

Text of reference, Plan Book (1612)

Hugh Richardson: (2) A chamber next the street 20′ 9″ E–W, 20½′ N–S with the chimney and stairs, one other chamber adjoining 20′ E–W, 8½′ N–S besides the stairs; (3) A chamber next the street 21′ E–W, 21′ N–S with the chimney and the stairs, one other chamber adjoining 8½′ N–S besides the chimney, 21′ E–W; (4) Two chambers next the street with two chimneys, [together] 21½′ N–S with the stairs and chimney, one other chamber adjoining 8½′ N–S besides the chimney, 21½′ E–W; (5) A fair garret over all 22′ 3″ E–W, 30′ N–S; Two cellars under all 17′ 8″ E–W, 26′ N–S.

Humphrey Chauncey: (2) A chamber next the street 9½′ E–W, 15½′ N–S, one other chamber adjoining 8½′ E–W with the chimney, 16½′ N–S, a gallery over part of the yard 16½′ × 6′, a chamber over part of the little yard backward 16½′ N–S × 14½′ E–W, one other chamber over the kitchen 12½′ E–W × 18½′ N–S with the chimney; (3) Two garrets, one next the street, the other adjoining [no measurements], a chamber at the S end of the yard 14′ × 8′, one other chamber adjoining to the same 15′ × 16½′ with a stoole of ease in it; (4) A chamber over the last mentioned chamber 16½′ N–S × 13′ E–W with a little study at the S end; (5) A garret over the chamber aforesaid 16½′ × 13½′ besides the passage into the same.

Edward Cotton: (2) A chamber next the street 18½′ with the chimney × 9′ 8″, a chamber over Mr Chaucey's parlour 16′ × 13½′; (3) A garret over the chamber last mentioned 17′ × 19½′, a little chamber next the street and a kitchen adjoining with a chimney both 23′ × 10½′ backwards, 9′ 2″ next the street; A cellar under the shop and entry 16′ 2″ × 9′.

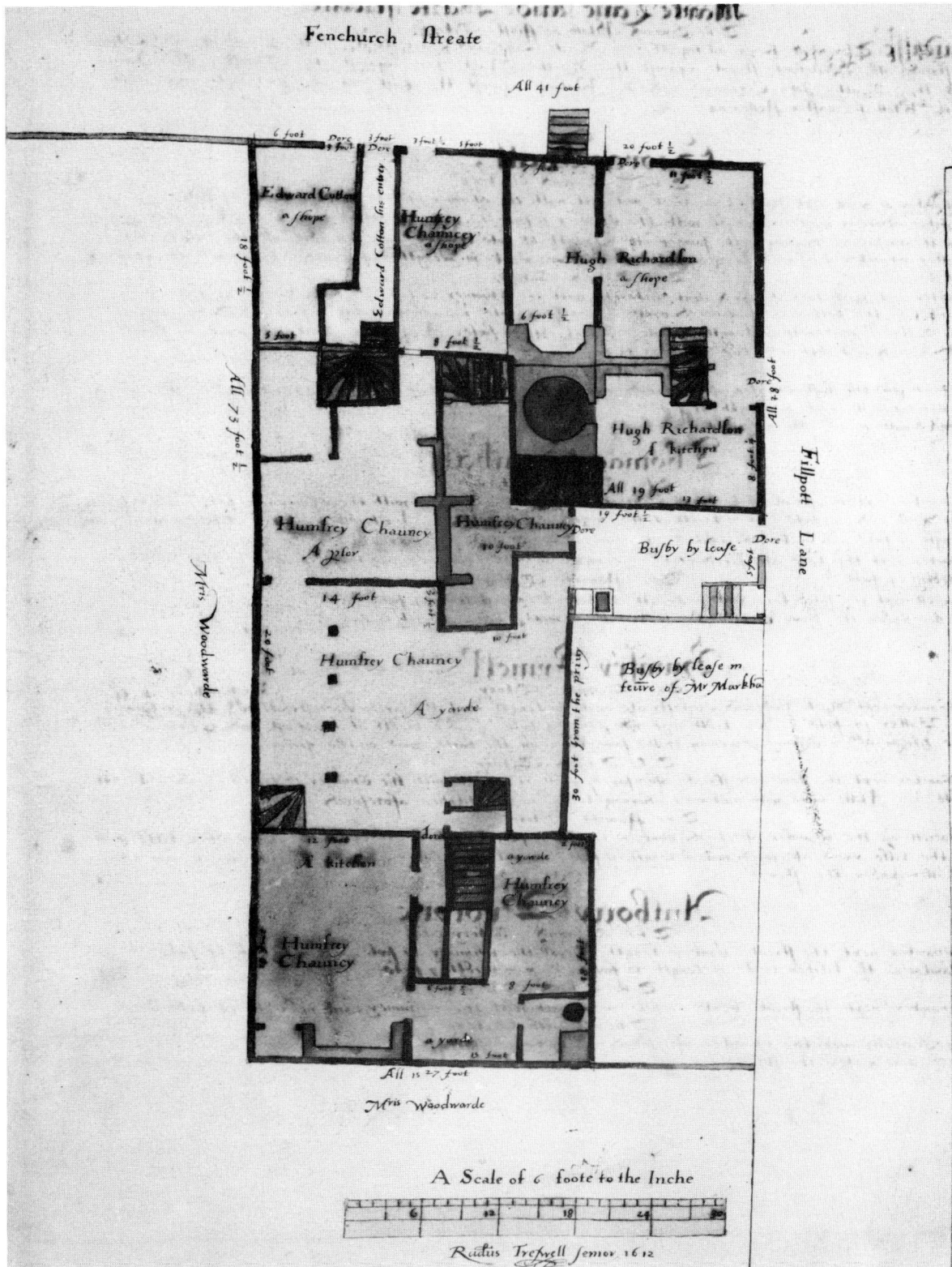

Fenchurch Streate

All 41 foot

6 foot   Dore   3 foot   7 foot ½   5 foot   20 foot ½
       9 foot   Dore   7 foot   Dore   11 foot ½

Edward Cotten
a shope

Edward Cotten his entrey

Humfrey
Chauncey
a shope

Hugh Richardson
a shope

18 foot ½

All 73 foot ½

5 foot

6 foot ½

8 foot ½

Hugh Richardson
A kitchen

Dore   8 foot
All

8 foot ½

All 19 foot   12 foot

19 foot ½

Mris Woodwarde

Humfrey Chauncey
A ploer

Humfrey Chauncey Dore
40 foot

14 foot

Busby by lease   Dore
5 foot

26 foot

10 foot

Humfrey Chauncey

A yarde

Busby by lease in
feure of Mr Markha

30 foot from the priuy

Fillpott Lane

12 foot

A kitchen

Humfrey
Chauncey

a yarde

Humfrey
Chauncey

Humfrey
Chauncey

6 foot ½   8 foot

a yarde   13 foot

All 15 ½ 7 foot

Mris Woodwarde

A Scale of 6 foote to the Inche

6   12   18   24   30

Raūlus Treswell senior 1612

Figure 23. **19.** 11–12 Fenchurch Street (1:150). North is to the top of the plan.

6

20. 47–8 Fenchurch Street

Plan Book, 3; LTS Pubn 72 (i) (1938)

This block of four houses was bequeathed by Roger Gardiner to the Shearmen's Company in 1520, when it was described as six tenements (CD Box 5; CDW, 47–50). The three houses forming the W half of the block (Jennynges, Robertson and Yeoman) in 1612 were of two-room plan; the outer ones rose to 3½ storeys, the middle ones to 2½ (Fig. 24). All had kitchens on the ground floor behind the shop, though one (Yeoman) had a shed in the yard which had a prominent chimney, possibly a former separate kitchen. All three had a room called a hall on the first floor over the shop, though in each case unheated; the stack from the kitchen passed up through the rear rooms, heating them instead.

The E half of the block was occupied by a larger house, with two smaller tenancies taking up most of the street range. The layout of the major tenancy (de Bees) suggests the adaptation of a medieval hall along the side of the property, with its kitchen to the S.

Tex of reference, Plan Book (1612)

William Jennyngs: (2) A hall over the warehouse being next the street from N to S 12½′ besides the stairs coming up × 12′ from E to W, a chamber over the kitchen from E to W with the chimney 14½′ × 16½′ from N to S with the passage and stairs besides a little closet on the S side hanging over into the yard; (3) A chamber next the street from E to W 12′ × 12½′ from N to S, one other chamber adjoining to the same from N to S with the stairs and passage 18′9″ × 13′ from E to W with the chimney; (4) A garret next the yard from N to S 19′ × 12½′ from E to W; A cellar under the warehouse 17′ × 12′ 2″.

Anne Robertson: (2) A hall over the shop and entry being next the street from E to W 11′ × 19′ from N to S, one other chamber adjoining to the same from N to S 10′ × 10′ from E to W besides the thickness of the chimney; (3) A garret over all from E to W 11′ × 31′ from N to S.

John Yeoman: (2) A hall over the shop 14½′ × 8¼′, a chamber over the kitchen with a chimney in it 14½′ × 9′, also a little chamber over part of the yard besides the stairs 12½′ × 8′; (3) A chamber next the street from N to S 19′ × 8½′ from E to W, another chamber adjoining from N to S besides the passage 12½′ × 10′ from E to W; (4) A garret chamber next the yard from E to W 9′ × 12′ N and S, one other garret next the street from E to W 9′ × 20½′ N and S; A cellar under the shop from N to S 21′ × 7′ from E to W another little cellar backward from N to S 9½′ × 6½′ from E to W.

Jaquis de Bees: (2) A chamber over the shop with the chimney 17½′ × 17′ one other chamber adjoining to the same being over the entry from E to W 7½′ × 15½′ from N to S, one other chamber over the parlour from E to W 16′ × 18½′ from N to S, one other little chamber over part of the entry from E to W 7′ × 7′ N and S, another chamber over the kitchen from E to W 15½′ × 12½′ from N to S with the chimney, a workhouse or garret adjoining to the same 23′ × 8¼′; (3) A garret room over all the said building except the last mentioned workhouse; A cellar under the shop from E to W 13¾′ × 12½′ from N to S, one other cellar under the kitchen from N to S 9′ × 13′ from E to W.

James Sutton: (2) A hall over the parlour and kitchen from E to W with the chimney 13′ × 23′ from N to S, at the S end of this hall is a buttery and a study; (3) Two chambers over the aforesaid hall, one with a chimney, both 25½′ × 13½′; (4) A garret next the street from N to S 16′ × 14′ with the chimney, one other garret adjoining 13′ × 10′; A cellar under the same building 19½′ × 12½′.

Iohn Saunders

Wittm Hallwood

17 foot

a Shope

Iames Dyer
a kitchen

Iaques de Bees

14 foot

21 foot

A wash house

dore

12 ½

A Hall

A kitchen

18 foot ½

23 foot 8 in

3 foot

24 foot

entry

12 foot ½

the Entrey

7 foot

dore

Iames
a glov

Sutton
a kitchen

A Garden
Iaques de Bees

A Shed

20 foot

Fenchurch streete

dore

18 foot ½

16 foot ½

Iohn yeoman
a Shope

19 foot

the entrey

Iohn
a Kitchen

Yeoman
A yard

Iohn Yeoman

69 foot

7 foot ½

21 foot ½

10 foot

A Shope

Butry

Anne Robinson
a kitchen

a yarde

38 foot

A shed

Wittm Iennigs

12 ½

16 foot ½

8 foot

dore

A Shope

Iennigs
a kitchen

Wittm Iennigs
A yard

a shed

16 foot ½

10 foot ½

36 foot ½

The kinges Lande

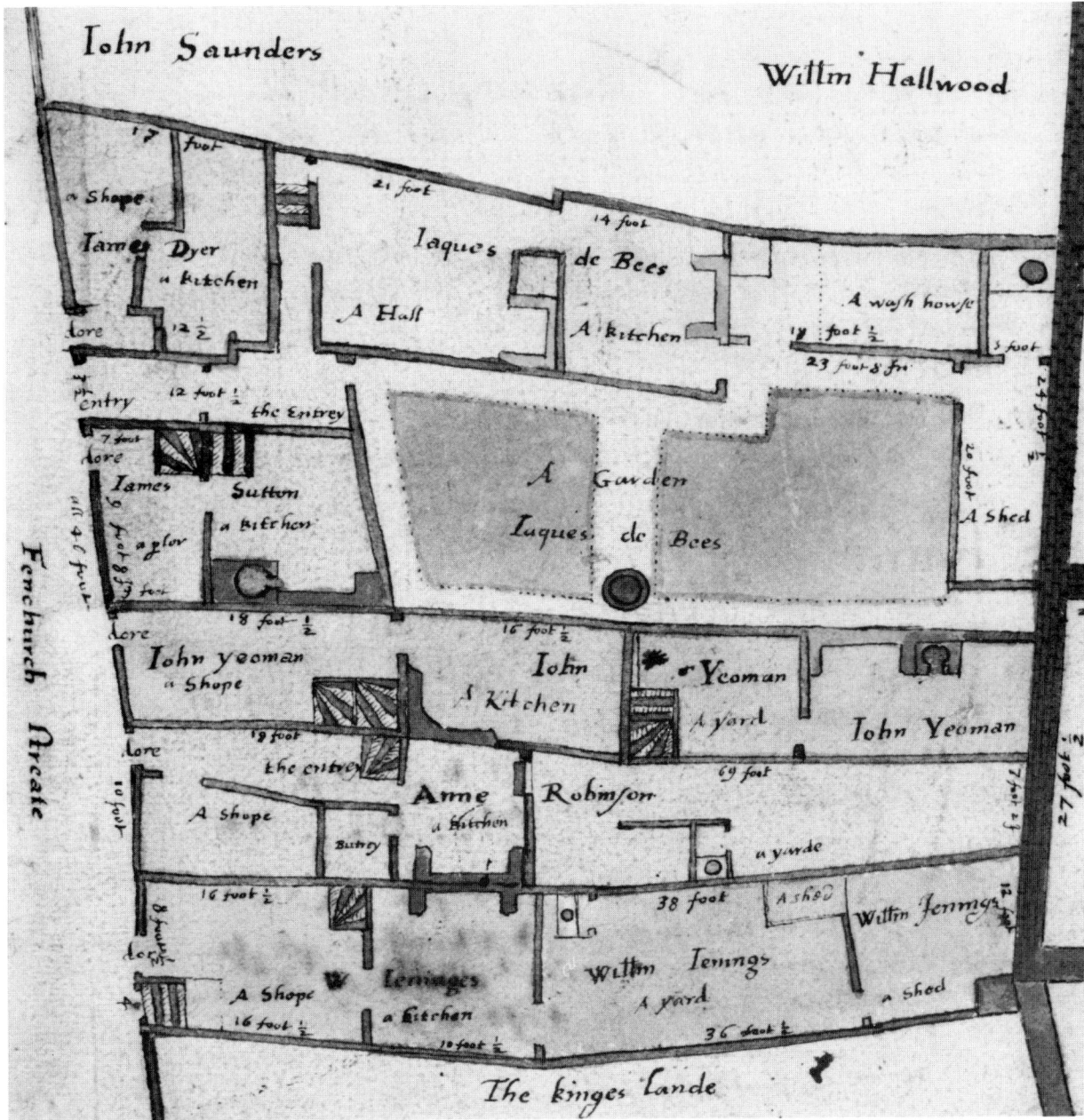

Figure 24. **20.** 47–8 Fenchurch Street (1:150). North is to the left of the plan. *See also Plate 4.*

21. 115 and 118 Fenchurch Street, 12–14 Billiter Street

Plan Book, 10–11; LTS Pubn 75 (viii) (1941)

This block of property on the W corner of Billiter Lane (later Street) as it met Fenchurch Street comprised, in 1612, two separate parts: the grand house and associated tenements to the N and E of Ironmongers' Hall, and the Tennis Place, a separate bequest to the W of the Hall (Fig. 25).

In 1314 Sir John Perry granted to the hospital of St Mary Spital, Bishopsgate, the tenement he had by gift of John son of John Rogemonde in the parishes of All Hallows Staining and St Katherine Cree, between the tenement of Gilbert and two others on the W and the tenement already of the hospital on the E, from the way from Alegate to Garscherche in the S and the tenement of Matthew le Chaundler to the N (CD Box 15). As the parish boundaries in 1677 passed through the site of the main building of the large house as shown by Treswell, Perry's grant probably refers to the principal part of the property. In 1520 the amalgamated property, now including the frontage to Billiter Lane, was sold by the hospital to the Wardens of the Fullers' Company (*ibid.*); it is likely to have functioned as their hall until the amalgamation with the Shearmen to form the Clothworkers' Company in 1528, and the consequent move to the new Clothworkers' Hall (**29**) (Girtin 1958, 13; CCO 1605–23, 224 (1619–20)).

The house and tenements can be described in three parts: (a) the great house behind both frontages, (b) the range astride the main gatehouse of the former to Fenchurch Street, and (c) the small houses forming the facade to Billiter Lane, including a subsidiary gate to the large house.

(a) the great house

In 1612 this comprised an entry from Fenchurch Street which passed into a courtyard, at the back of which lay the hall with a semi-octagonal bay window. A first-floor gallery around three sides of the yard led to chambers on two of the sides; there was a second storey over the buttery and kitchen, but only partly over the hall, which appears to have had no rooms over it. From

the hall a three-storey range, including a gallery, led at right angles along one side of the larger of two gardens. In the second garden, by the kitchen, was a brick tower (first mentioned, as 'insufficient', in 1593 (CCO 1581–1605, 142)).

Text of reference, Plan Book (1612)

Sir Edward Darcy: (2) a chamber over the little room at the N end of the Longe Seller 14½' × 7¼', another chamber adjoining to the same with a chimney on the E side 19½' × 18' within the walls with a little house of office behind the chamber aforesaid, a fair parlour adjoining to the chamber aforesaid with a chimney in it 31' besides the passage up out of the hall into the same × 19', a chamber over the buttery and entry 20½' next the garden × 15½' besides the chimney, one other chamber adjoining 26' × 12½' with a little closet in it, one other chamber adjoining to the same 13' × 8', a chamber once part of the hall with a fair passage into it 9½' × 9½', one other chamber adjoining 14' × 12', a chamber on the W side the court 30' with the chimney × 11½' besides the gallery which serveth for passage into the other chambers, one other chamber adjoining with a chimney in it 22' × 22', also two chambers over the gate and on the S side of the same court, (3) also a garret over one of the same chambers, also a gallery on the E side the same court leading into a chamber next Billiter Lane being over the gate 16' × 55' with the chimney, one other chamber next Billiter Lane of the like bigness; (3) a long gallery over the building on the E side the garden 68' within the walls × 15½'.

(b) the gatehouse range to Fenchurch Street

In 1556–7 the Company, noting that the houses at Billiter Lane end were about to fall down, assigned moneys to their rebuilding, and appointed one Revell to be carpenter (CCO 1536–58, 275v, 278). It is possible this was either Nicholas Revell (*fl. c.* 1520) (Harvey 1954, 222) or a relation. Three tenements were rebuilt in 1557–8 (RW Accts); the rent rose from 58*s.* p.a. to £8 (the great house behind rented at £4 p.a. at this time). It seems likely that this is the prominent block shown in this position on the copperplate map of *c.* 1559–60 and the woodcut map based upon it; in 1612 the corner block rose to 4½ storeys on cellars.

John Jenings: (2) A chamber next the street with a chimney 17' × 14'; (3) Another chamber 19' with the house of office × 14' with the chimney; (4) Two garrets

20′ × 16½′; A cellar under the same house 14′ 6″ square.

Arthur Harrison: (2) A chamber over the shop on the W side of the entrance into the messuage in the tenure of Darcy 17′ × 13½′ with a chimney, another chamber adjoining and over the said entry or passage 18′ × 8½′, another chamber next the street with a chimney 15½′ square, another chamber behind the same and next Billiter Lane with a chimney 15½′ with the passage × 11½′, another chamber over the kitchen with a chimney 14½′ to the back of the chimney × 12′; (3) A fair room over the three first mentioned chambers next the street with two chimneys in it 40′ × 14½′ at the E end and 19′ at the W end, a chamber next Billiter Lane 16½′ with the passage × 11½′ with the chimney, another chamber next Billiter Lane and adjoining to the chamber aforesaid with a chimney 15½′ × 11½′; (4) A garret chamber next the street 18½′ × 18′ with the chimney, a garret adjoining 19½′ × 16′, a chamber with a chimney over the last mentioned chamber in the 3rd storey 16½′ × 11½′, another chamber adjoining 18′ × 9′; (5) A garret next Billiter Lane with diverse partitions in it 28′ with the house of office at the N end × 17½′; A long vault or cellar under his own and under diverse other tenements in Billiter Lane unto the gate leading out of the lane into Darcy's messuage, 83½′ within the walls × 12′, another vault under the passage out of Fenchurch Street 25′ × 7′ at the S end, 6′ at the N end.

(c) the remaining small houses along Billiter Lane

This row of one-room plan houses, comprising eight houses and the subsidiary gatehouse of Darcy's great tenancy, was composed in 1612 of houses of differing dates; they rose to between 2½ and 3½ storeys. Two sub-groups can be distinguished. In 1536–7 the Company bargained with Thomas Delyke, carpenter, for two new houses, paying £12 (CCO 1536–58, 69); and with Walter Coper, probably a mason, for making foundations and chimneys and for tiling, paying £19. The frame was viewed at Croydon by men of the Company, and the rents fixed at 26s. 8d. The building accounts for the new houses indicate three houses (RW Accts, 1537: three cellar windows, three privy seats, mention of the 'middle house'), but subsequent accounts indicate four houses at the new rent. Three of the new houses seem to be the three forming the N end of the row, backing onto the gallery range of the large house; despite the same rents, they were of differing sizes.

In 1571–2 the tenant of the Great House took tenancy of one of the houses in Billiter Lane and may then have made it into a subsidiary gate; in 1603–4 this and two houses to the S were converted into a gatehouse by rebuilding into two storeys and a garret (RW Accts). The other houses in the row have no individual histories in the period 1528–1612, and each may have been built before 1528.

[From S to N] Widow Kinricke: (2) A chamber next the lane 15½′ with the stairs and chimney × 13½′; (3) A garret over the chamber aforesaid 16′ × 12′.

Arthur Harrison: [tenant to Darcy; the stair must have communicated with chambers over the inner gatehouse of Darcy] (2) A chamber next the street over the entry and kitchen 15½′ with the chimney × 12′; (3) A chamber with a chimney 16½′ × 12′; (4) A chamber 18′ × 12′ with a chimney; (5) A garret overall 18′ × 12′.

Brian Wilson: (2) A chamber next the lane 15½′ × 12′ with a chimney; (3) A garret 15½′ × 12′.

[for chambers over the gate see (a)]

Richard Harris: (2) A chamber with a chimney and closet 18′ × 12′; (3) A chamber with a chimney 20′ × 14′; (4) A garret 20′ × 14½′.

John Dickman: (2) A chamber next Billiter Lane 20′ × 12′ with a chimney and buttery in it; (3) A chamber over the chamber aforesaid 20′ × 13½′ with a chimney and closet; (4) Two garrets sometimes one with a chimney 20′ × 14½′; A cellar under 14′ × 9′.

Widow Smith: (2) A chamber next Billiter Lane with a chimney 18′ × 13½′; (3) A garret over the aforesaid chamber; A cellar under the building 16½′ × 15½′.

Thomas Gall: (2) A chamber next the lane 19½′ × 16½′ with the chimney; (3) Another chamber 21′ × 16½′ with a chimney; (4) A garret over all 22′ × 16½′ with the chimney; A cellar under the house 15½ square.

Widow Halliwell: (2) A chamber next Billiter Lane 19½′ × 9′, another chamber adjoining being next the lane 19½′ × 12′ with a chimney; (3) A garret over all 21½′ × 20½′, A cellar under the house 16′ × 14′.

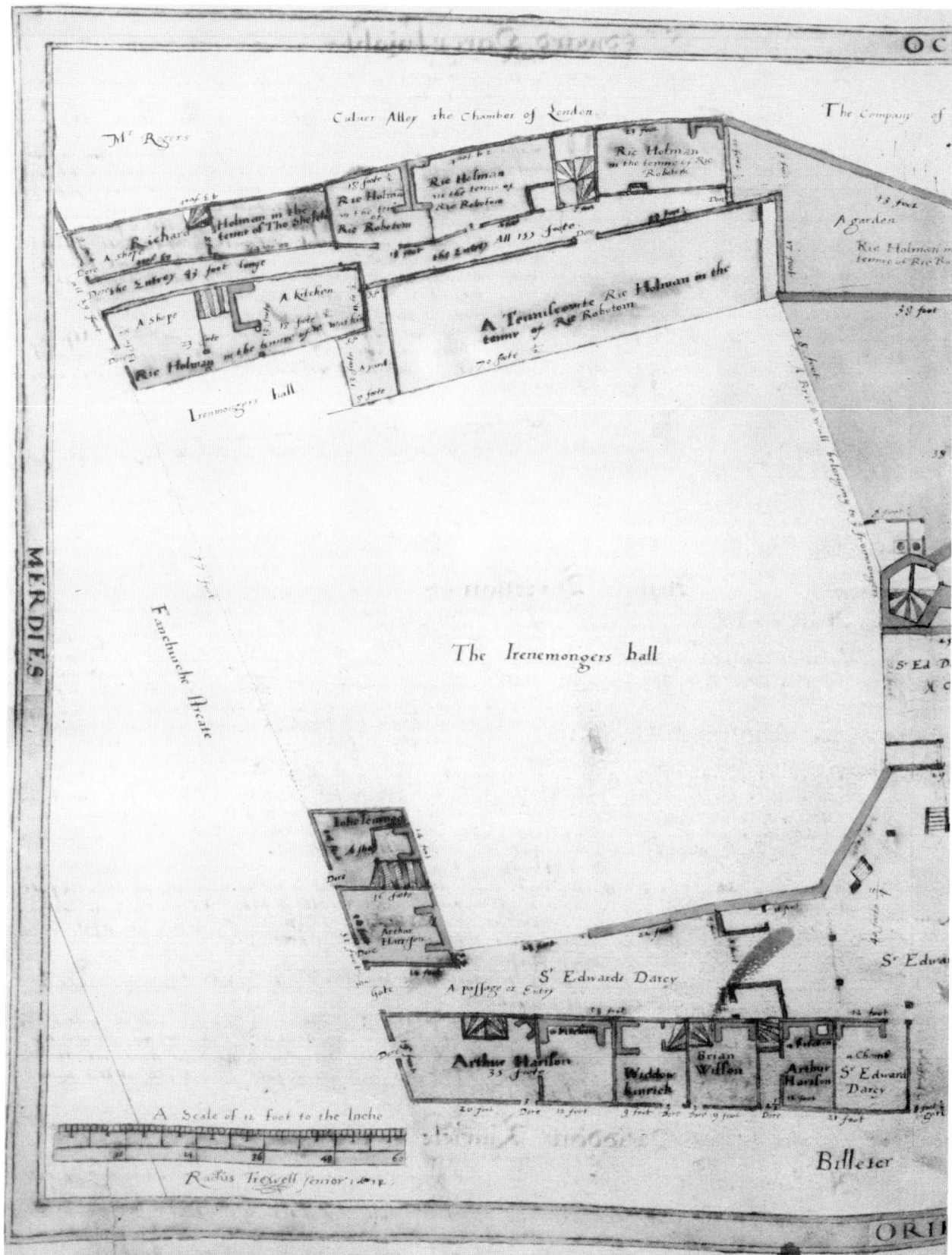

Figure 25. **21.** 115 and 118 Fenchurch Street, 12–14 Billiter Street (1:300). North is to the right of the plan. *See also Plate 6.*

Fishmongers Lande

The Fishmongers Land

41 foot

A Garden

Sr Edwarde Darcy

Sr Ed   Darcy

Akitchen

A Garden

Sr Ewarde Darcy

a Buter

Dore

Sr Edward Darcy

Botery

A walke 70 foot   Sr Edwarde Darcy

A Seller

Sr Edwarde Darcy

The Hall

Sr Edward Darcy

yarde

de Darcy

Dore

A plor

A kitchen

Sr Edwarde

Darcy

Sr Edward Darcy

14 foot

A rock place

A rock place

Aesate place

satcher

The fishmongers

lande

A Chuck

Sr Edw

Darcy

The Aldrige

a shope

Ro. Harris

a butcher

John Dickman

a butcher

Aloe Smith

Widdowe

Widd Goall

The Ha

Widdowe

Hallywell

A Shope

A Shope

16 foot

17 foot

lane

SEPTENTRIO

16 Dykes

Tennis Place, later 118 Fenchurch Street

Plan Book, 10–11; LTS Pubn 75 (viii) (1941)

A property in the parish of All Hallows Staining called the Tennyspley was owned by John Yonge, tailor, in 1481 (*Comm Ct 1374–1488*, 207). The present property, in the same parish, is first called the Tennisplace in the Clothworkers' Company records in 1535 (CDW, 223–4). In 1533 John Dale had sold the property to Margaret, Countess of Kent, who entrusted it with other property (see **44**) to the Company in 1538 (confirmed in her will of 1540 (CD Box 21)).

In Treswell's survey of 1612 (Fig. 25) a main tenant, Richard Holman, and three sub-tenants are named. The frontage, 2½ storeys high, was divided between Sheffield, who only had a ground floor tenancy, and Watkin, who had large rooms above. Robotham held chambers along the rear of the property, also 2½ storeys high.

Text of reference, Plan Book (1612)

Richerd Robotham, tenant to Mr Holman: (2) A chamber next the tennis court in 1. with the chimney, entry and counting house 31′ × 15′, two chambers adjoining to the same 23′ × 14½′ with a chimney; (3) Two garrets besides the passage up 24½′ × 15½′, which garrets are over the two chambers aforesaid; A little cellar 13′ × 11½′.

William Watkin, tenant to Mr Holman: (2) A chamber next the street with a chimney 20′ × 13′, one other chamber adjoining to the same with a chimney in it besides the chimney 18½′ × 12½′; (3) A garret next the street 20′ × 13′.

22. 1–6 Fleet Lane, 16–21 Farringdon Street, Modern Court

Plan Book, 47; LTS pubn 73 (iv) (1939)

By his will of 1538 Walter Wilcockke bequeathed property in Seecollane or Fletelane to Thomas Bonyfaunte; the same property was bequeathed later in 1538 to the Clothworkers' Company by Robert Peele, vicar of Chilham in Kent (CD Box 66). There is no indication how large this bequest was, but by the time of Treswell's survey in 1612 (Fig. 26) property which is at least in part, and probably all of, the bequest is shown on both sides of Fleet Lane as it met the Fleet. Nos 16 Farringdon Street and 1 Fleet Lane were created after the Great Fire by straightening up the S corner of the lane; the Fleet ditch became Farringdon Street.

The property shown in Treswell's survey can be divided into three parts: (a) the great house, (b) the other buildings N of the lane (left on the plan, Fig. 26); and (c) buildings S of the lane, backing onto the Fleet Prison.

(a) Lady Wood's house

There is no text of reference in Treswell's survey, and information about all the floors but the ground floor shown on the plan is therefore lacking. The great place in Fleet Lane was extensively repaired in 1560, including the use of Caen stone and 'hard stone ready wrought' (RW Accts, 1560–1); though none of the walls shown by Treswell is of his usual thicker 'stone' type. The house shown in 1612 comprised hall, parlour and kitchen with other chambers at the back of a small yard entered from Fleet Lane; on the E side was a large garden with a 'grasse plotte'.

(b) the buildings on the N side of Fleet Lane

These divide into a row of one-room plan houses to the E, and those to the W of the great house, including Blacksmith's Court or Flowerdeluse Alley. Treswell specifies in the text of reference that the majority of these tenants (in both sub-groups) were tenants to Lady Wood. The seven tenancies forming a row along the Lane, backing onto the garden or the house itself, were of 2½ to 3½ storeys, and showed some differences in their internal arrangements on the ground floor. Only one (Scott) had a cellar. The buildings W of the gate into the great house comprised two sections, two

tenancies fronting the lane (Stevenson, Taster) of 3½ and 2½ storeys respectively; and Blacksmith's Court, which bordered the Fleet Ditch. At the street end, Richard Taster held a 2½ storey house in his own name, but sublet it to Henry Potton. Behind, the alley comprised five small tenancies and an even smaller kitchen let to a sixth (Brookes). The buildings were 2½ storeys high, and there was clearly a certain amount of multi-occupation. Although two tenants (Devonshire and Goodman) on the E side of the court had 2½ storey houses to themselves, those on the W side were split onto one-room tenancies on the ground floor (Owin, Rice, Johnson) with two-room (chamber and garret) tenancies over them (Hall, Wood, Priest respectively). Brookes had a similar pair of chambers over his tiny kitchen. Hall, Wood and Priest all had houses of office overhanging the Fleet Ditch, as did three of the ground floor tenants.

Text of reference, Plan Book (1612)

Fleet Lane [N side]

John Carrington, tenant to the Lady Wood: (2) A chamber with a chimney 15′ × 11′; (3) A chamber over the chamber aforesaid 15′ × 11′; (4) A garret over all.

Christopher Bowe, tenant to the Lady Wood: (2) A chamber with a chimney 15′ × 11½′; (3) A chamber over the chamber aforesaid 15′ × 11½′ with a chimney in it; (4) A garret over all.

Widow Honor, tenant to Lady Wood: (2) A chamber with a chimney in it 14½′ × 11½′ (3) A garret over the chamber aforesaid with a chimney in it.

Thomas Austyn, tenant to the Lady Wood: (2) A chamber with a chimney in it 14½′ × 11½′; (3) A chamber over the chamber aforesaid of the like bigness; (4) A garret over all.

Thomas Scott, tenant to the Lady Wood: (2) A chamber with a chimney in it 14½′ × 11½′; (3) A chamber over the chamber aforesaid; (4) A garret over all; A cellar under the same house.

Thomas Atherton, tenant to the Lady Wood: (2) A chamber with chimney in it 14½′ × 11½′; (3) A chamber over the chamber aforesaid 15½′ × 11½′.

Richard Bullman, tenant to the Lady Wood: (2) A chamber 14½′ × 11′; (3) A chamber with a chimney and little closet over into Fleet Lane 15½′ × 11½′; (4) A garret chamber over the same.

The great house in the tenure of Lady Wood: [text lacking]

Widow Stevenson, tenant to the Lady Wood: (2) A chamber over the gate leading into the Great House 21′ 2″ × 8′ 4″ with a chimney on the W side and a little room on the E side behind Bulman's house, another chamber adjoining with the chimney 15½′ × 11′, one chamber behind the same 15½′ × 9½′ besides the chimney; (3) Two garrets over the two last chambers aforesaid, two chambers over the first mentioned chamber over the gate 22½′ × 8′ 2″; (4) A fair garret over the same; Also a cellar under the same tenement.

Richard Taster, tenant to the Lady Wood: (2) A chamber with a chimney 10½′ × 12′, one other chamber behind the same with the chimney 19′ × 11′ 7″, also an entry leading out of the same chamber to a house of office being over Fleet ditch 13½′ × 2½′; (3) Two garrets over the two chambers aforesaid.

Richard Taster, a tenement next the Fleet ditch and in the tenure of Henry Potton: (2) A chamber over the shop and kitchen, with the chimney 19′ × 13½′; (3) Two garrets over the same chamber.

Blacksmiths Court alias Flower de luce Alley, in the tenure of Lady Wood:

W side: (2) A chamber over Widow Johnson's chamber, with the chimney 15½′ × 14½ with a little house of office over the Fleet ditch, in which chamber dwelleth George Priest; (3) A garret over the same.

(2) A chamber adjoining to the aforementioned chamber and in a little tenement wherein dwelleth one Thomas Brookes 14′ × 9½′ with the chimney; (3) A garret over the same.

(2) A chamber over the chamber in the tenure of Thomas Rice wherein now dwelleth George Wood 14½′ × 13′ with a chimney at the N end and a stool of ease over Fleet ditch; (3) A garret over the same.

(2) A chamber with a chimney wherein dwelleth John Hall which chamber is at the N end of the building on the W side of Blacksmiths Court aforesaid 15′ besides the stairs coming up × 14′ with the chimney, also a little stool of ease over the Fleet ditch, one other chamber adjoining to the same being over part of the Lady Wood's mansion house 14½′ × 11½′ with the chimney.

E side: William Goodman (2) A chamber with a chimney in it 13½′ × 10½′; (3) A garret with a chimney in it over the same.

William Devonshire : (2) A chamber with a chimney in it 13½′ × 12′.

(c) South of Fleet Lane, the irregular shape of the available space probably contributed to the mixed shapes and sizes of the seven tenancies surveyed in 1612. The street frontage was uniformly 4½ storeys high except for the house of Widow Swettenham, which was only 2½ storeys. Features of interest include the position of the well in the yard to the E; Hearne's cellar, entered from the inner yard and not from the street; and two instances of ovens separate from kitchen fireplaces, in the tenancies of Scafe and Tyrry, though in each case a chimney (the source of heat for the ovens) was not far distant.

Text of reference, Plan Book (1612)

Fleet Lane [S side]

Richard Tyrry, tenant to the Company, which tenement was late in the tenure of Widow Hodson: (2) A chamber next Fleet Lane aforesaid 26′ × 12½′ with a chimney in it, one other chamber adjoining being over the kitchen with the stairs and passage 16½′ × 11½′ with a chimney; (3) A chamber next the lane aforesaid 26′ × 13½′ with a chimney made within the Fleet wall, one other chamber backward and adjoining to the chamber aforesaid; (4) A chamber with a chimney in it and a garret adjoining being over the chambers over the kitchen; (5) A garret with a partition in the middle being next Fleet Lane aforesaid; A cellar under the same house 21½′ × 11½′.

Richard Skafe, tenant to the Company: (2) A chamber next the lane aforesaid with a chimney in it 13½′ × 9½′, another chamber adjoining 24½′ × 8½′; (3) A chamber next the lane aforesaid 18′ × 16½′, one other chamber adjoining to the same with a chimney in it 12′ × 8½′; (4) A chamber 28½′ × 9½′, one other chamber adjoining to the same 15½′ × 9′ with a chimney at the S end; (5) Two garrets over all of the like bigness; Also a cellar under part of the same house 19½′ × 10½′.

Widow Swettenham: (2) A chamber next the lane aforesaid 11½′ × 9½′, one other chamber adjoining on the E side 15½′ × 8′ 4″, a chamber over the parlour and entry besides the chimney 14½′ × 14′, one other little room adjoining 8′ × 4′ 9″, a chamber over the kitchen 15½′ × 12½′ (3) A garret over the first mentioned chamber, and garrets over all the rest, also a chamber next the yard 14½′ × 10½′.

Davy Joanes: (2) A chamber next the lane aforesaid with a chimney at the W end 15½′ × 10½′, a kitchen

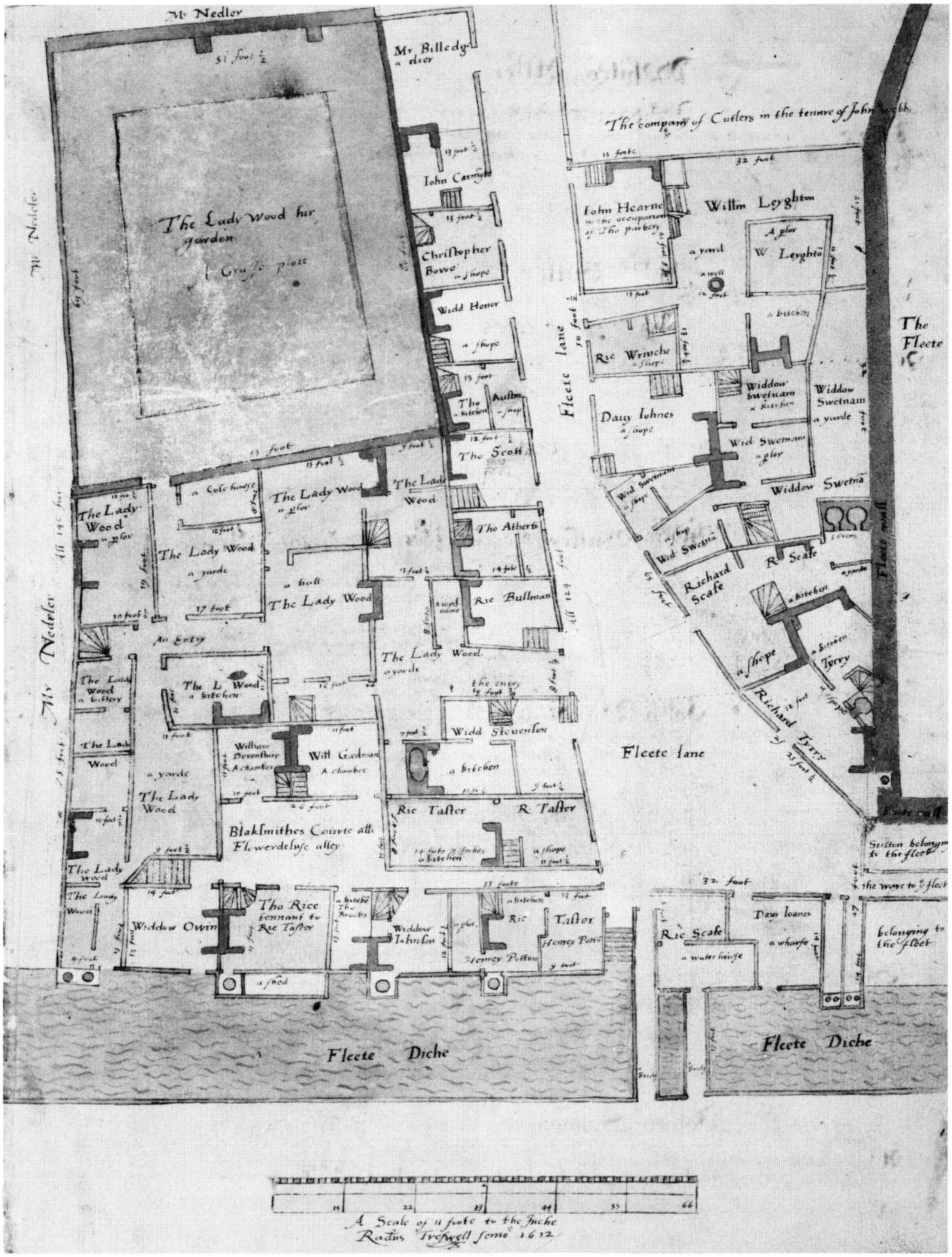

Figure 26. **22.** 1–6 Fleet Lane, 16–21 Farringdon Street, Modern Court (1:300). North is to the left of the plan. *See also Plate 10.*

adjoining to the same with the chimney 14½′ × 9½′; (3) Two chambers, the one with a chimney, 22½′ × 16½′; (4) A garret over all being of the like bigness with a chimney in it; A cellar under the same house 16′ × 13½′.

Richard Wrinch: (2) A chamber next Fleet Lane being over the shop 17′ × 13′ with a chimney, a kitchen adjoining being over William Layton's work-house within the walls 12½′ × 9½′ with the chimney; (3) Two garrets over the chamber and kitchen aforesaid of the same bigness; Also a cellar under the shop.

William Layton: (2) Two chambers, the one over the parlour, the other over the kitchen, and a little room newly built with a chimney.

John Hearne: (2) A chamber with a chimney 21′ × 16½′; (3) A chamber over the chamber aforesaid with a chimney in it; (4) Diverse chambers over the chamber aforesaid with a chimney and a house of office; (5) One garret over all with diverse partitions in it; There is also a cellar under the same house.

23. 36 Friday Street

Plan Book, 22

In 1599 Peter Blundell gave £150 to the Clothworkers' Company; out of this they purchased this house on the E side of Friday Street (CD Box 74; Hare 1860, 11–12). The house was of 4½ storeys on cellars (Fig. 27).

Text of reference, Plan Book (1612)

John Harrison, scrivener: (2) A hall over the shop 13½' × 12' with the chimney, a kitchen adjoining 18' × 9 9" at the W end with the chimney, 5' 3" at the E end; (3) A chamber next the street 16' × 12¼' with the chimney and stairs, another chamber adjoining 18' with the closet × 9' 9" 'in breadth as the kitchen'; (4) A long room 28' 5" × 12½' at the W end, 10½' at the E end, a little room at the E end of the same; (5) Two garrets and a lead 24½' besides the lead × 12' with the chimney and stairs; A cellar under the shop 10' 3" × 9½', a cellar under the E end of the house 17½' with the passage × 6' at the E end.

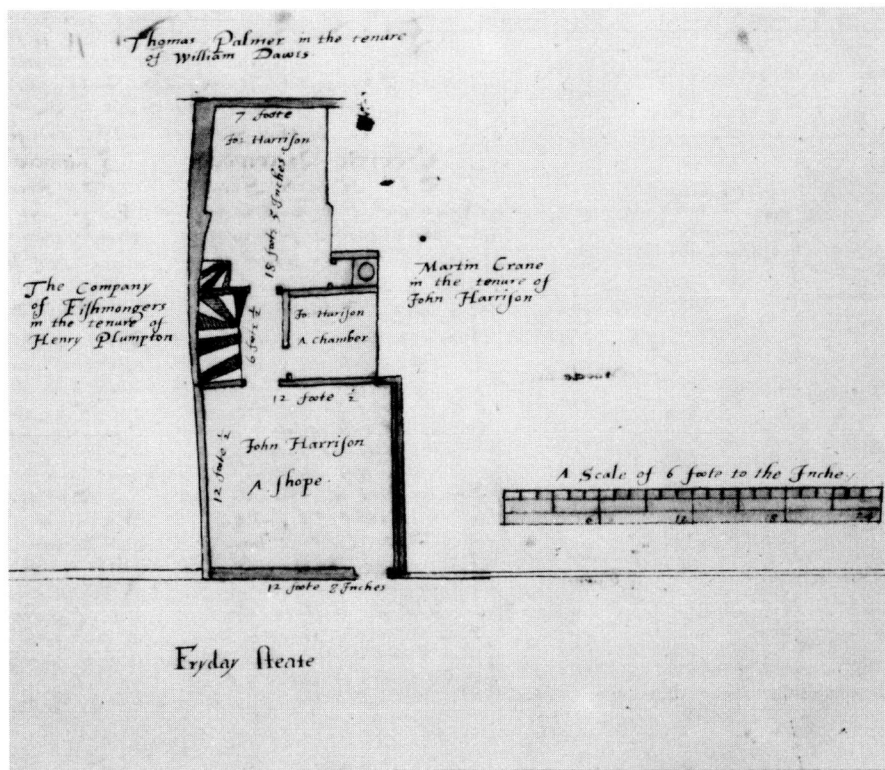

Figure 27. **23.** 36 Friday Street (1:150). North is to the left of the plan.

24. House on Garlick Hill

Plan Book, 25

By his will of October 1603 Michael Parlor, clothworker, bequeathed a house in Garlick Hill to the Clothworkers' Company (CDW, 147–8; RW Accts 1603–4). It lay on the E side of the street, in the parish of St James Garlickhithe; but the precise location is not known.

When surveyed by Treswell in 1612 (Fig. 28) the house was of 2½ storeys, apparently without cellars.

Text of reference, Plan Book (1612)

Thomas Storkey, tailor: (2) A chamber next the street 17½′ E–W with the stairs × 13½′ N–S with the chimney, also a little kitchen adjoining to the same; (3) A garret 17′ E–W × 13½′ N–S, one other garret adjoining 12½′ E–W × 13½′ N–S.

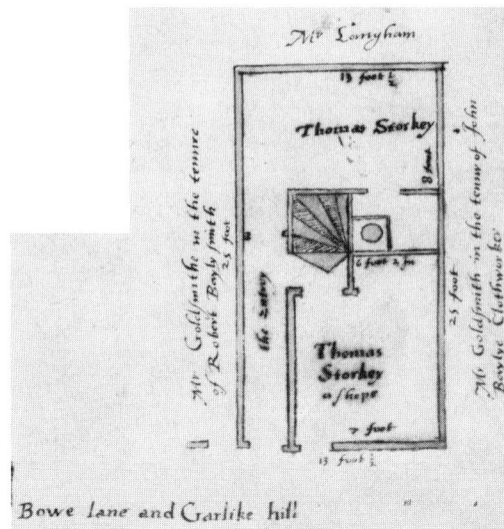

Figure 28. **24.** House on Garlick Hill (1:150). North is to the left of the plan.

25. Giltspur Street and Cock Lane

Evidence Book, 17

Henry Suckley or Suckliffe, merchant tailor, granted four messuages at Pie Corner, Smithfield, to a trust in 1558 (*Inq PM*, ii, 17–19); they passed by his will to Christ's Hospital in 1586, presumably on the death of his wife Agnes (*Charity Comm*, 98). The Hospital was however drawing rent from the property from 1568–9 (CH Treas Accts 2, *s.a.*). The survey by Treswell (Fig. 29) dates from before 1611, when the tenancy of John Welles on the plan was granted to Thomas Hartley (CHMB 3, 121v). The plan is unusual in having no text of reference but a certain amount of text written on the individual tenancies. Comparison with a view of the main block in 1624 (CH View Book I, 16–20) adds further details of rooms, such as cellars, which probably existed in 1611, and tells of recent internal changes ascribable to the period *c*. 1611–24.

The rectangular block of property divided into two parts: (a) a row of four tenancies facing Giltspur Street to the E (bottom of the plan) with small yards behind, and (b) a court entered from Cock Lane, in which were smaller dwellings.

(a) the four tenancies on the W side of Giltspur Street were part of the row or street called Pye Corner. Stow (ii, 22) derived the name from an inn sign; in 1677 Ogilby and Morgan gave the name to Giltspur Street between Cock Lane and Hosier Lane. The large ovens shown by Treswell suggest that these houses were involved in the food trade. The houses were of 2½ or 3½ storeys. In the front room of Robert Hollier's main tenancy, against the back wall, were two square brick pillars supporting a 'range'.

Text written on plan (before 1611) with details from view of 1624 (in square brackets)

William Parret [in 1624 in the occupation of Thomas Swallow, cook]: [2] A chamber with a chimney over the shop [16′ × 12′ part whereof is over Hartley's house], a chamber to the rear [9′ square, a little room behind that 13′ × 11′]; [3] Two garrets over the other chamber and this [a garret over the previous room 13′ × 11′, another garret 18′ × 4′, all very much decayed]; A cellar under the shop.

John Welles [in 1624 in the occupation of Thomas Hartley, harnessmaker for coach-horses]: [[2] A room over the shop 15½′ × 14′, a little room 6′ × 9′; [3] A chamber over the room next the street 11½′ × 17′ with the staircase; [4] A garret of the same l, and b. all very much decayed.]

Robert Hollier [baker, in occupation also in 1624]: [2] Over the main shop, a chamber 21′ on the S, 19½′ on the N, 15′ on the W, 13½′ on the E, a chamber over the back room 15′ 3″ E–W and 16½′ N–S, a little chamber over the well 8′ [× 16′], a chamber over the ovens 11½′ [× 16½′, a place for bavins (brushwood) 14′ × 12′ over the ovens, a room at the end of the Cooke Roome 20′ × 17½′]; [3] Three garrets all 38½′ × 15′ 8″, two little garrets at the W end of Hurste's garret both in l. 18½′, b. 13′ 8″ and 11′ respectively; [A cellar much decayed 18′ × 14′]. Hollier was also tenant of two rooms alongside Cock Lane, entered from within his house: on the Treswell plan these have [2] a chamber with chimney, 18½′ N–S × 15′ 3″ at the E and 14½′ at the W ends. By 1624 these rooms had evidently been rebuilt. The ground floor partitions had been re-arranged to give two small rooms each 13′ × 5′, in the W of which Hollier stored his meal. On the second storey were two chambers each 12′ × 10′ and a 'little hovel' 14′ × 4′. A cellar under the meal house (i.e. this building) 20′ × 12′ was then recorded.

Edward Hurste [in 1624 'the victualling house at Cock Laine end sometyme Fraunces Coltmans now in the tenure of Robert Hollyer']: [2] A hall 13½′ on the E side, 11′ to the chimney on the N, 17½′ on the S, [16′ × 18½′]; [3] Two garrets, one over the hall the other over part of Hollier's chamber [a room over the previous 17′ × 10½′, a study at the N side of the said room 7′ × 3½′, a room backward over a room in the possession of the baker (i.e. Hollier) between the kitchen and this room, 10′ × 15′].

(b) the court on the S side of Cock Lane. Five of the seven small tenancies shown on the plan have some added text. Thomas Cobb and Margaret Gryffin both had '3 rooms one over the other' which probably indicates three storeys, i.e. two upper chambers; but the stair to the upper chambers of Cobb was not within his ground-floor room. The ground floor of the range to

West

St Barthlmewes hospitall

willm Norris

Tho Cobb 3 romes one ouer the other

Maryret Gryffin 3 romes one ouer the other

Androw one Chamb ouer this pte

Davy Charles Bell a Chamb ouer this rome

Charles Bell a Chamb ouer this

Denis A Chamb ouer this and 2 foot ½ Charles Bell

Comon privy

A Courte or yarde

willm Parret a yarde

Jo welles

Callaway

A yarde

Callaway

Ouens

Robert Hollier

Robert Hollier a yarde

well

Ouens

kitchen willm Parret a Chamb ouer this

Robert Hollier A Chamb ouer this bacbe rome east and west 15 foot 3 fnth sonth and north 16 foote ½ Ouer the well a litle Chamb 8 foot ouer the Ouens a thamb 11 foote ½

Robert Hollier Ouer this rome is a Chamb with a Chimney, at the east ende 13 foote 3 Inches at the weste end 14 foot sonth and north 19 foot

Sout St Bartholmewes hospitall

W Parret a Chamber ouer this

John welles

R Hollier

Ouens

R Hollier

willm Parret A Shopp A Chamb wth a Cham ouer this shupp and 2 yardes ouer the other Chamber and this, and a seller vnder this shupp

A Shopp John welles

this pte to ½ Ouens is excepted out of Holliers Lease

Robert Hollier a shope Ouer this shopp is a chamb sonth 21 foot north 19 foot West 15 foote East 13 foot ½ and ouer Robt Holliers Chambers is 3 yarete in length 38 foot ½ In bredth 13 foote 8 Inches more a litle yarret at the west end of the yarret both in length 18 foot ½ bredth 13 foot 8 In

Edward Hurphis kitchen

Ouens

Edward Hurste a shope Ouer this shope and kitchen a hall at the east ende is foot ½ the north side 11 foot to the Chimny on the sonth side 17 foot ½ and a 2 yarret one ouer his hall the other ouer pte of Holliers Chamb 13 foot ½

Cock Lane

North

East   The howses at Pye corner

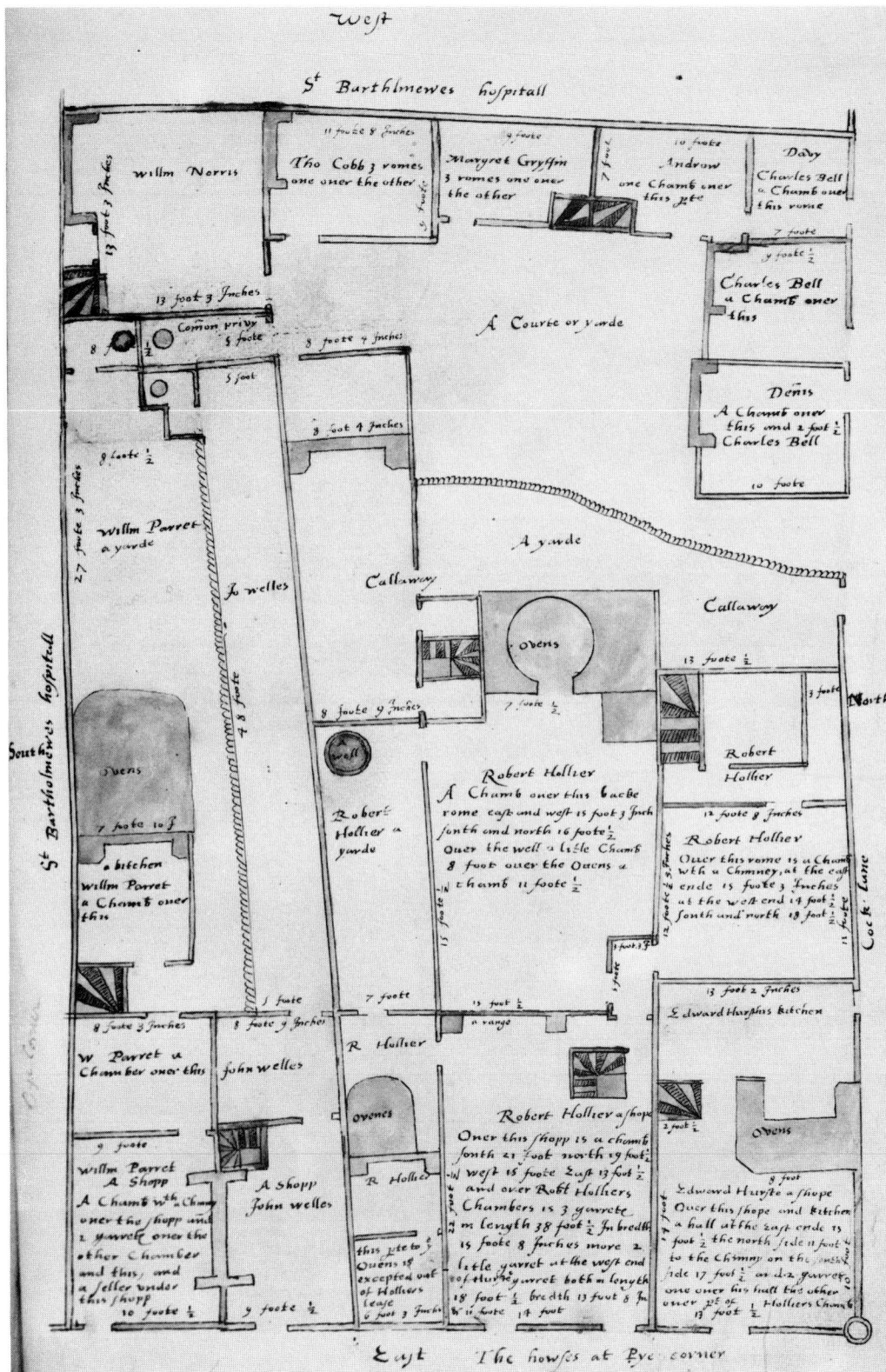

Figure 29. **25.** Giltspur Street and Cock Lane (1:150). North is to the right of the plan.
See also Plate 7.

Cock Lane comprised three small rooms in the tenancies of Andrew Davy, Charles Bell and ? Dennis. Davy had two chambers behind in the court, one over the other; Bell had a chamber over Davy's ground floor, and the tenancy of Dennis seems to have incroached into that of Bell at first floor or higher. The access to these upper chambers must have been from the court behind.

26. 140–1, Houndsditch

Evidence Book, 15

These two houses on the E side of Houndsditch were confirmed by Thomas Browne and Robert Wilson to John Arnold in 1562/3. Arnold granted them to John Warreyn in 1564; Warreyn granted them to his son George Warren, leatherseller, in 1576. Lawrence Ponder was one of Warren's tenants in 1583, and his widow Anne is seen to occupy the southern of the two properties in Treswell's plan. Warren meanwhile sold the two properties to John Wriothesley, haberdasher, in 1586, and he sold them to Thomas Lawrence, goldsmith, in 1588 (GL MS 13442). Lawrence is recorded as the donor of the properties to Christ's Hospital in 1593, but no deed or will is preserved (*Charity Comm*, 101).

Both houses (Fig. 30) were of 2½ storeys, and of identical plan on the ground floor. They differed however on the first and garret floors, jettying different distances into the street. Neither had a cellar. A copy of the Treswell plan, signed and dated 1607, survives with a lease of 1712 (GL MS 13443). The properties shown in the plan were rebuilt by 1667, when they were also planned.

Text of reference, Evidence Book (probably reflecting state in 1607)

Anne Ponder widow: [2] A chamber next the street 14½' × 11½' besides the stairs, one other chamber over the kitchen 11½' × 11¼'; [3] A garret over the chamber last mentioned 14' × 12'.

John Hinde: [2] A chamber next the street 15½' with the chimney × 12' with the stairs, a chamber next the yard 13' with the stairs × 12'; [3] A garret over the chamber last mentioned 12½' × 12'.

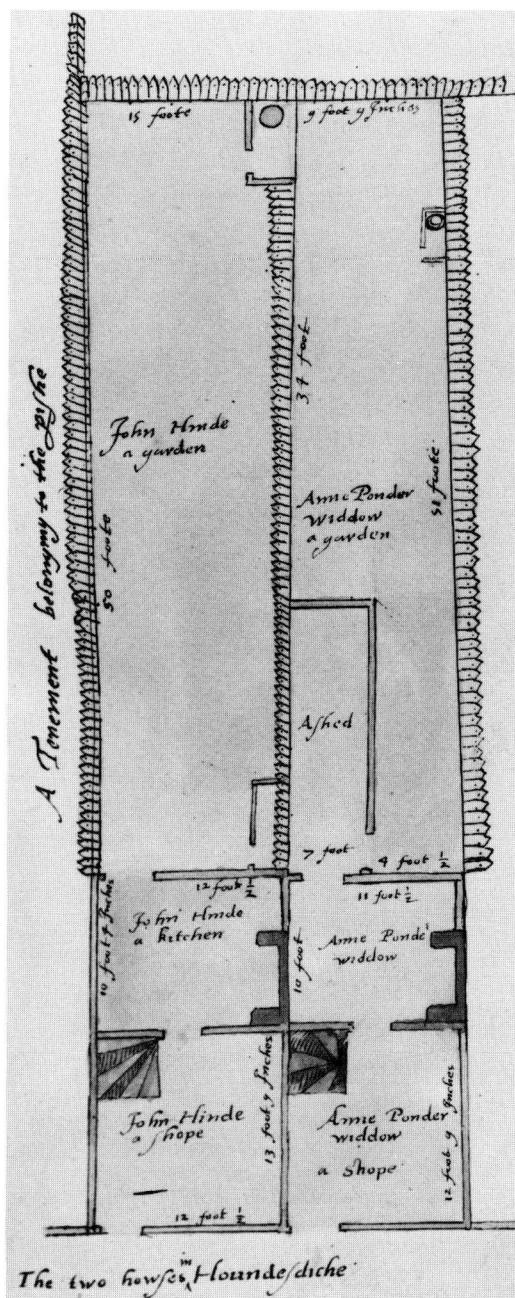

Figure 30. **26.** 140–1 Houndsditch (1:150).
North is to the left of the plan.

27. Old Leathersellers' Hall, 50–5, now 49 London Wall

Leathersellers' Company Archives

By 1477 the Leathersellers' Company possessed a hall in London Wall (Black 1871, 72). In 1543 the Company acquired part of the conventual buildings of St Helen's nunnery in Bishopsgate, and moved their hall there (*ibid.*). The hall site was then let out. In 1613 the Court resolved that The Old Hall should be divided into 'reasonable dwelling-houses'. Black, in his *History* of the Company, declared that the W part of the estate was divided off and divided into three shops, with kitchens, a parlour and a garden behind; and that this was surveyed by Robert [*sic*] Treswell the elder in 1614 (*ibid.*, 73).

A plan (Fig. 33) on vellum survives at the present Leathersellers' Hall. In general style it closely resembles Treswell's other surveys, but is not signed or dated. Slits towards the bottom indicate it was originally attached to another document.

It is not at present possible to verify Black's statements concerning the authorship or date of this plan. No trace of any payment to Treswell appears in the company records, which survive from 1608. An MS Schedule of Ancient Deeds, drawn up by Black *c.* 1834, does however speak of a larger plan, signed by Treswell and dated 1614, which Black copied in sketch form (p. 25, 59). This shows that the Leathersellers' estates comprised two blocks S of London Wall, separated by

a space. The inference must be that the present plan is a copy, presumably contemporary and quite possibly by Treswell, of part of this larger plan, which has not survived. The larger plan would presumably have resembled that of the fragmented Clothworkers' Company estate nearby (**13/15**).

The present plan shows a street-range of 2½ storeys, with an entry leading to a small yard surrounded by two kitchens and a parlour; behind lay a garden, its boundary formed by the covered course of the Walbrook stream. It is not clear whether the plan was drawn before or after any alterations to the Old Hall; the small dimensions of the chambers and the fact that no tenants are named on the plan seem to support the latter.

Text of reference, on the plan (?1614)

(2) A chamber over the kitchen next the garden, another chamber over the warehouse with a chimney in it, a fair chamber next the street with a chimney in it, and a fair round window on the S side, another chamber next the street adjoining to the same with a chimney in it, a little chamber over the kitchen and a fair chamber over the parlour and entry, a little house of office in the SE corner; (3) Two half garrets over the chambers next the street and other garrets, all the length of the Old Hall; One cellar under one of the shops, another cellar under the chamber next the street.

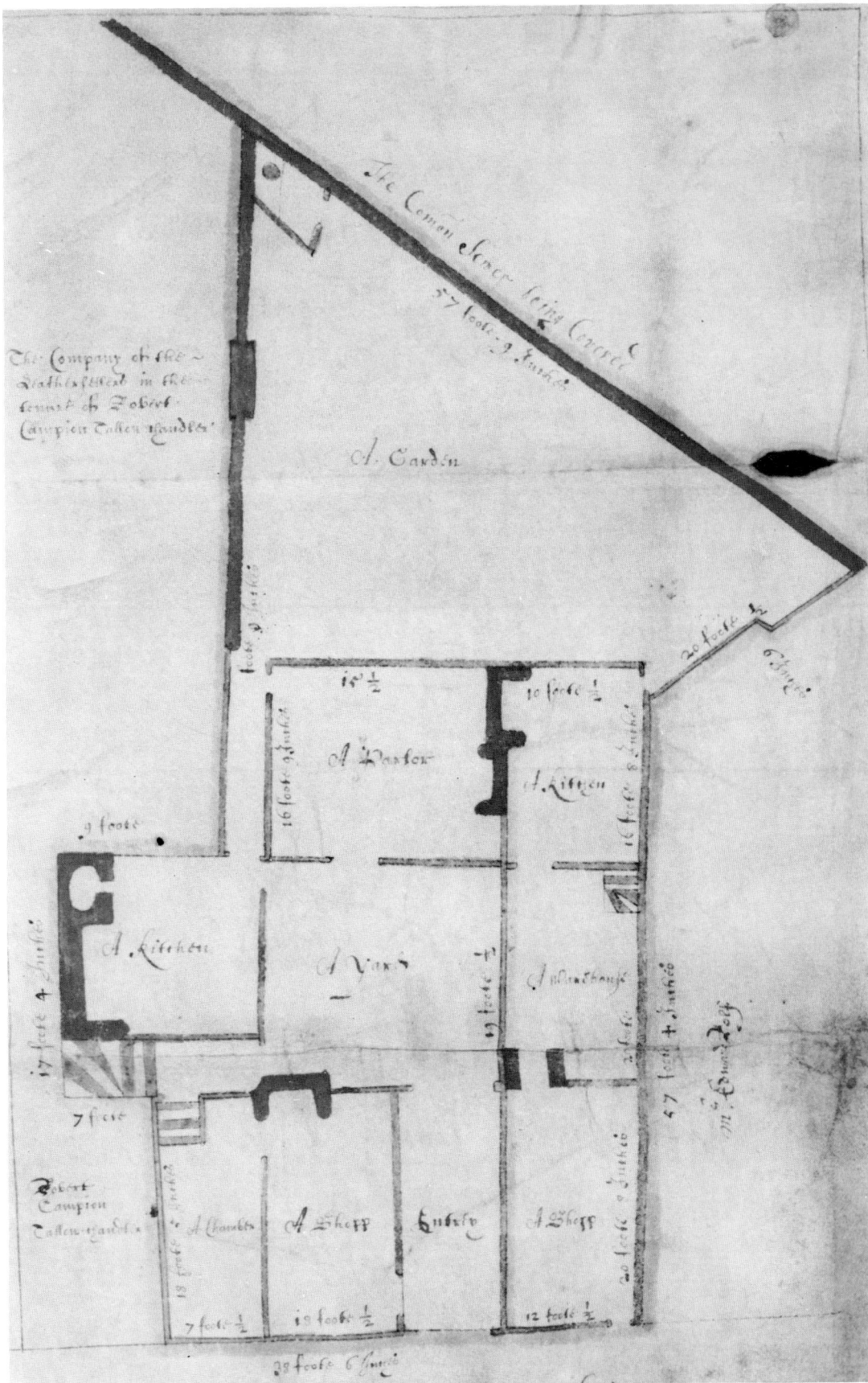

The Comon Sewer being Covered

57 foote 9 Jnches

The Company of the
Death is setled in the
tenant of Tobiet
Campion Tallow Candles

A Garden

The Company of the
Death is setled in the
tenant of Tobiet
Campion Tallow Candles

20 foote ½

6 Jnches

foote 9 Jnches

9 foote

15 ½

10 foote ½

16 foote 9 Jnches

A Parlor

A Kitchen

16 foote 8 Jnches

17 foote 4 Jnches

A Kitchen

A Yard

13 foote

A warehouse

47 foote 4 Jnches

Mr Edward Raffe

7 foote

20 foote 4 Jnches

Robert
Campion
Tallow Candles

18 foote 9 Jnches

A Chandlo

A Shopp

Entrie

A Shopp

20 foote 4 Jnches

7 foote ½

12 foote ½

12 foote ½

28 foote 6 Jnches

Figure 31. **27.** London Wall (1:150). North is to the bottom of the plan.

28. 62–3 Mark Lane

Plan Book, 6

Four houses forming the SE corner of the junction between Hart Street and Mark Lane; they were part of the bequest of Oliver Claymond (see also **31**), an early master of the Clothworkers' Company, by his will of 1540 (Hare 1860, 24–5). The houses were totally rebuilt by the Company in 1562–3, apparently with a single frame; the accounts (QW Accts 1562–3) described them as a 'great place' and three others. The larger house (Ivatt) included a yard, warehouse and larger cellar, which the others did not; but otherwise they were all similar 3½ storey buildings on cellars (Fig. 32). The dimensions for the first floor of the corner tenancy (Rymell) suggest that the first-floor jetty on the corner sailed 2′ into Mark Lane (the major street) and 1½′ into Hart (Whiteharte) Street.

Text of reference, Plan Book (1612)

George Ivatt: (2) A chamber or hall next Mark Lane 19′ with the chimney × 14′, a kitchen adjoining 15½′ with the chimney × 9½′, a buttery over part of the yard and adjoining to the same 14′ 2″ × 7′ with the entry, one other chamber backward over the Longe Room 20′ × 13½′ with the chimney; (3) A chamber next Mark Lane 20½′ with the chimney × 14½′, a chamber over the kitchen abovementioned 14½′ × 9½′, the closet, entry and stairs [together] 14½′ × 7′, a chamber backwards 19½′ × 13½′ with the chimney; (4) A garret over the last chamber aforementioned 20′ × 14′, one other garret with a chimney 31′ [no breadth given]; A long vault or cellar under all.

Thomas Gambell: (2) A chamber next the street Mark Lane 20′ with the chimney × 15½′ at the E end, 13½′ at the W end, a chamber over his kitchen 10′ × 9½′; (3) A chamber next the lane aforesaid 20½′ with the chimney and house of office × 14½′; (4) A garret next the lane 20½′ × 14½′; A cellar under the shop 13′4″ × 12½′.

Humphrey Rymell: (2) A chamber on Mark Lane and Hart Street 17½′ next Hart Street with the chimney and buttery × 14½′ next Mark Lane, breadth at the E end 15′ 9″, a little kitchen with a chimney adjoining over the back room; (3) A chamber next the lane and street aforesaid 18½′ with the chimney × 14½′, a little room with a chimney adjoining over the kitchen aforesaid; (4) A garret over the chamber aforesaid 18½′ × 14½′, one other little room over the last room aforesaid 11½′ × 6′ 9″, also a little garret over the same; A cellar under the shop.

Antony Browne: (2) A chamber next the street 17′ besides the chimney × 14½′, a chamber over the kitchen 12½′ × 7′; (3) A chamber next the street 20′ with the chimney × 14½′; (4) Two garrets over the chamber aforesaid with a house of office; A cellar under the shop.

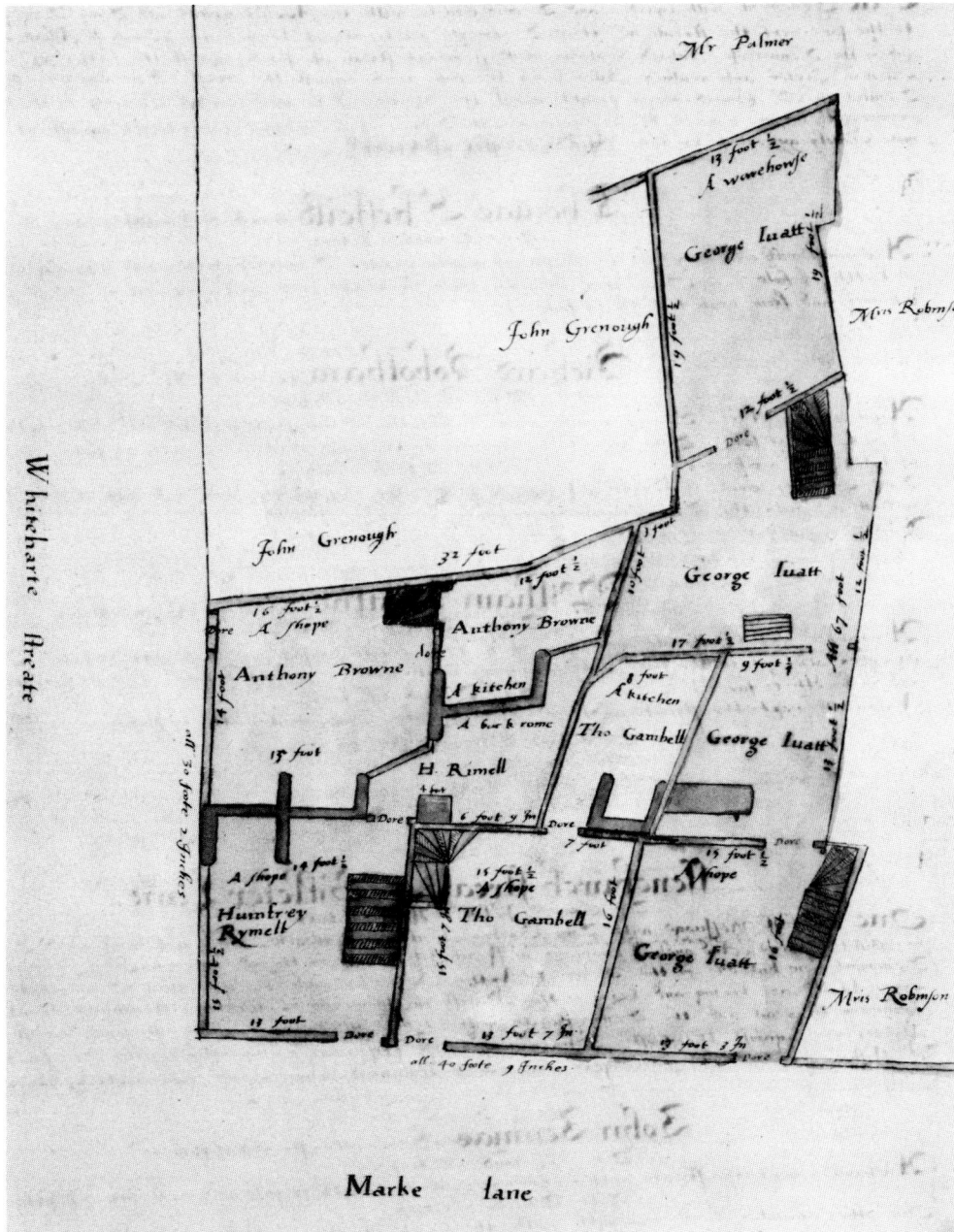

Figure 32. **28.** 62–3 Mark Lane (1:150). North is to the left of the plan.

29. Clothworkers' Hall, Mincing Lane

Plan Book, 3; LTS Pubn 72 (i) (1938)

In 1170–97 Stephen, prior of Holy Trinity Priory, Aldgate, granted property in the parish of St Dunstan in the East to Alfred the Roofer (*Cooperator*) which Pain the fishmonger, his brother, had held, for a rent of 1*s* 8*d*. p.a. (HTP, 202); this tenement was increased by the grant of another, presumably adjoining and presumably much larger, to Edeua daughter of Walter, in 1197–1221 (*ibid.*, 204). This second property was described as 25¼ ells long and 8½ ells wide. The joint quit rent of 5*s*. 8*d*. p.a. continued to be paid, and this with the coincidence of owners' names for the two parts confirms that this property eventually became Clothworkers' Hall. Deeds in the Company's possession survive from 1349 (CD Box 6); the property passed via William de Stanes, apothecary, to Sir Reginald de Grey and others, who released their claims to de Grey and wife in 1376. Letters Patent of Edward III of that year confirmed the grant to de Grey; the house extended from Mincing Lane to the churchyard of All Hallows Staining. In 1397, when de Grey's son Reginald sold the property, it was known as Grey's Inn. In 1399 William Marker, stockfishmonger, and Nicholas Glover were the owners; and the property continued to be passed between groups containing fishmongers in the early fifteenth century. One such group contained twenty-four names, including two aldermen.

In 1456 they sold it to a group of Shearmen, and the association with clothworkers began. The Shearmen united with the Fullers in 1528 to form the Clothworkers' Company. Repairs in 1539–40 suggest that the parlour was in a two-storey range (RW Accts 1539–40).

In 1548 the company decided to rebuild the hall. A 'new frame' was expected (CCO 1536–58, 202); but shortly afterwards a bricklayer, Henry Davyron, bargained to bring up and make the sides of the walls of the hall with brick, 18′ high. This may indicate a timber-framed wall infilled with brick. James Maylam of East Mallinge, in Kent, shipwright, brought timber for the hall by water (QW Accts 1548–9). The hall, with its parlour of 1594 (QW Accts 1594–5) and garden was surveyed by Treswell in 1612 (Fig. 33). The hall measured 45½′ × 27½′, open to the roof, with a single-step dais and two semi-octagonal oriel windows, one larger than the other, at high table end. The hall lay between a courtyard entered through a gatehouse (which contained the beadle's house) from Mincing Lane and the garden, in which were two knots. Beyond the screens passage, which gave access through to the parlour, lay buttery, pantry and kitchen, probably relics of the pre-1548 house. This S block had two floors over, including the Ladies' Chamber, Dry Larder, Plate Chamber, Little Comptinghouse, Armoury and the Pastry (above the kitchen ovens, approached by the little stair shown in the kitchen). Both parlour and hall were on undercrofts.

Text of reference, Plan Book (1612)

Clothworkers' Hall: (2) A chamber over part of the parlour called the Ladies' Chamber with a fair chimney on the S side 33′ E and W × 20′ 9″ N and S, in which chamber is a fair canted window at the E end on the N side 10′ × 7′, one other chamber adjoining to the same being over part of the chamber aforesaid from E to W 19½′ × 21′ N and S, wherein is on the N side a canted window 8′ 4″ × 7′ with a fair passage up, one other room called the Dry Larder E and W besides the passage 41′ × 16½′ N and S, there is at the E end within this room a chamber called Plate Chamber, and at the W end is a Little Countinghouse, one other room called the Armory house being over the kitchen 35′ 2″ E and W × at the E end 18′ 4″ and at the W end 17½′, also one room over the ovens called the Pastry; (3) A gallery and a countinghouse 53′ E and W × 16½′ N and S on the S side of which gallery is a chimney and two gunpowder houses, also on the N side is a door into a leads contain the l. of the gallery and the countinghouse × 3′ 9″ besides the two canted leads on the canted windows above mentioned, also one garret chamber at the W end of the gallery aforesaid with a

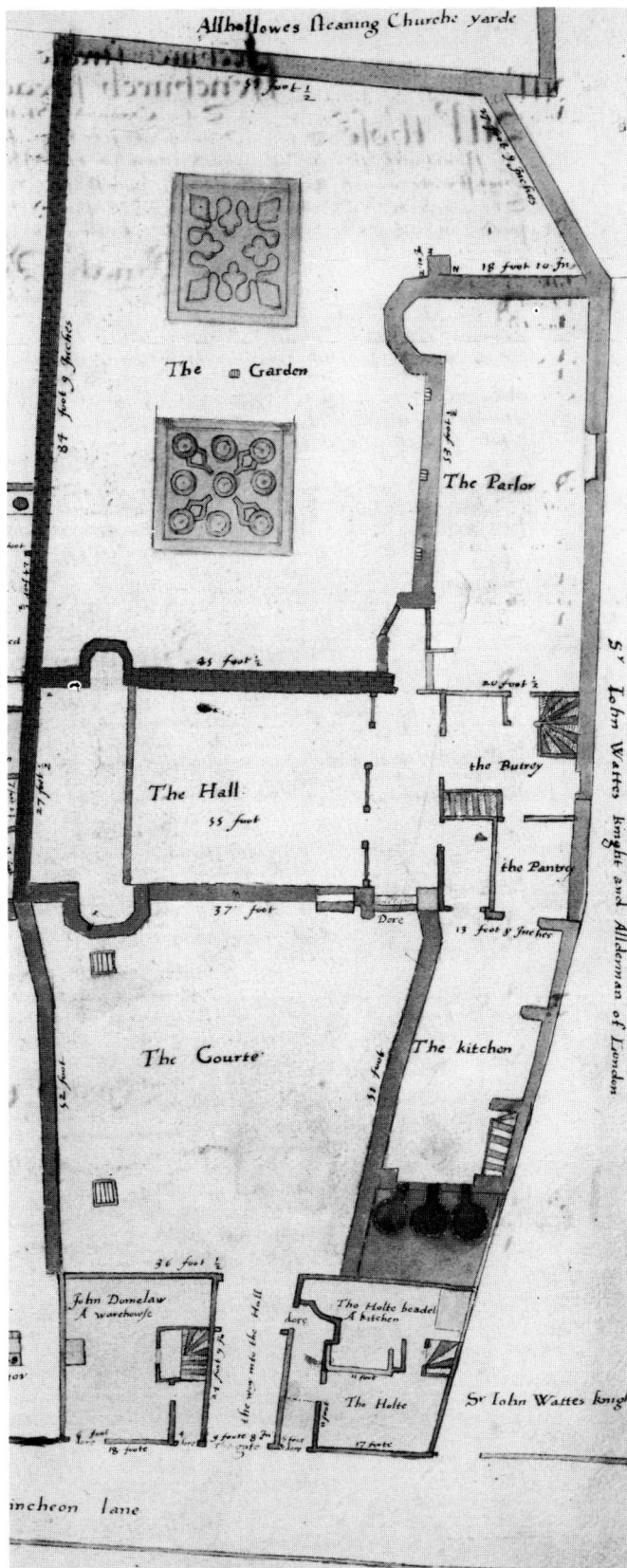

Figure 33. **29.** Clothworkers' Hall, Mincing Lane (1:300). North is to the left of the plan. *See also Plate 4.*

stool of ease in the S corner 16½′ S and N and 11½′ E and W with a door out into a gutter on the W side; A cellar with a pair of stairs out of the great court and another pair out of the buttery which cellar was sometime parcel of the cellar under the court and hall from E to W 13½′ × 18′ N and S, one other vault or cellar under the long parlour.

Thomas Holte Beadle being on the S side of the passage into the hall: (2) A chamber or hall next Minchin Lane 18′ from N to S × 14′ from E to W, with a chimney on the S side, one other chamber adjoining to the same 16½′ × 10′; (3) A chamber with a chimney from N to S 20½′ × 13½′, one other chamber adjoining to the same from E to W 13′ × 22½′ N and S with a stool of ease at the S end; (4) A garret over all the rooms aforesaid; A cellar under his shop and kitchen from E to W 20′ × 20½′ from N to S.

John Domelaw his house being on the N side the passage into the hall: (2) A chamber or hall next Minchin Lane being over his shop and the passage into the hall from E to W 10′ × 28′ from N to S with a chimney on the E side and a little closet hanging over into Minchin Lane being on the W side, one other chamber backward on the passage into the hall aforesaid from N to S 9½′ × 14′ from E to W, a kitchen adjoining to the chamber aforesaid from N to S 20′ × 11′ from E to W with the chimney, also a little buttery hanging over into the great court aforesaid; (3) A chamber over the kitchen aforesaid 20′ × 11½′ with a chimney on the W side and a hanging closet on the E side, one other little chamber adjoining to the same 16½′ × 10½′, two chambers, one with a chimney in it, in 1. next Minchin Lane aforesaid 28′ × 12′; (4) A garret next Minchin Lane aforesaid from E to W 18½′ × 12½′ from N to S, one other garret on the N side of the same from E to W 18½′ × 14′ from N to S, one other garret from N to S 30′ × 12′ from E to W, there is also over all a roof to lay fagotts in; A long vault or cellar under the said John Domelaw's house and under the Clothworkers' court from E to W 76′ × 20′ from N to S, with a pair of stairs out of Minchin Lane, one other cellar adjoining to the same being under the hall of the same Company in b. from E to W with the arch of brick 30′ × in1. from N to S 49′.

30. St James' Hermitage/Lambe's Chapel, Monkwell Street

Plan Book, 37; LTS Pubn 72 (ii) (1938); Schofield 1984, x

The hermitage of St James, situated on the city wall between Cripplegate and the NW corner of the city (marked by Bastion 12) was said, in 1255, to have been given by Richard I to his chaplain Warin in 1189 (*Cal P R 1247–58*, 402); but another record speaks of it as founded in the reign of John (Harben 1918, 319). By 1289, when it was extended by the incorporation of an adjacent lane (*Cal P R 1281–92*, 401), the Hermitage was a cell of the Cistercian house of Garendon (Leics.); at this time a hermit, Friar Robert, was mentioned. In 1338 William de Lyouns, 'heremite', of the Cripplegate hermitage, was restrained from repairing the wall of the hermitage by his neighbour, Thomas Sporon, goldsmith, but allowed to continue by the city (*Assize of Nuisance*, 333). The Countess of Pembroke founded a chantry in the Hermitage for the soul of her husband, Sir Aylmer de Valence (d. 1323) (*Memorials*, 553); and in 1364–5 it was used for ordinations (*Sudbury Register II*, xlv). In 1382 the Abbey leased a further garden 165′ long from the city (CD Box 19).

After the Dissolution, by 1539 the hermitage site was owned by Robert Draper of Camberwell, Surrey, and he leased it to William Lambe, clothworker (*ibid.*). The site was granted to Lambe in 1543 (*L & P H VIII*, XVIII(I), 201). A near-contemporary biography of Lambe asserts that he lived 'in the house next to St James chapel' (A Fleming, *Some Account of William Lambe*, c. 1580, repr. 1875). It passed to the Clothworkers' Company as part of Lambe's considerable bequest (see also **45**) in 1580.

The undercroft of the chapel (Schofield 1984, Fig. 41), datable on architectural grounds to *c*.1140, was removed during rebuilding in 1872 and partially re-erected by the Clothworkers' Company on the site of the nave of All Hallows Staining, Mark Lane.

When surveyed by Treswell in 1612 (Fig. 34) the estate was in two main parts, N and S of a long brick wall which divided the two entrances to Monkwell Street. In the absence of other evidence it seems likely that the medieval Hermitage was originally the land to the N, including the chapel, and the property to the S was an additional bequest by Lambe.

The larger, N part comprised a medium-sized house, presumably the house occupied by Lambe, of 2½ storeys (Bestney), with a garden and access into the adjacent Bastion 12. A second tenant (Hunte) had rooms adjacent to the chapel and access to the leads over it; a third tenant (Speght) ran a school in the highest buildings, of 3½ storeys, next to Monkwell Street. He was also tenant of the undercroft below the chapel, and used it as a cellar.

The S property comprised an alley going past a two-room building to a small court in which were five one-room plan houses of 2½ storeys each. The first-floor and garret dimensions agree to the extent that all five may have been a single construction.

Text of reference, Plan Book (1612)

Mugwell Street

George Moult: (2) A chamber next the street 15′ × 10½′, one other chamber adjoining to the same being over the entry 14½′ × 10½′, a chamber over the kitchen 16½′ with the chimney × 13½′; (3) A garret over the building next the street and a little room over the house of office at the end of the yard.

William Butler: (2) A chamber 12′ × 5¼ at the W end × 12½′ at the E end; (3) A garret over the same chamber of the like bigness.

Patrick Murffee: (2) A chamber with a chimney 13½′ × 13½′; (3) A garret over the same chamber of the same bigness.

John Rose: (2) A chamber 14′ × 16½′; (3) A garret over the same of the like bigness.

Hugh Cheyney: (2) A chamber with a chimney 14′ × 12½′; (3) A garret over the same of the like bigness.

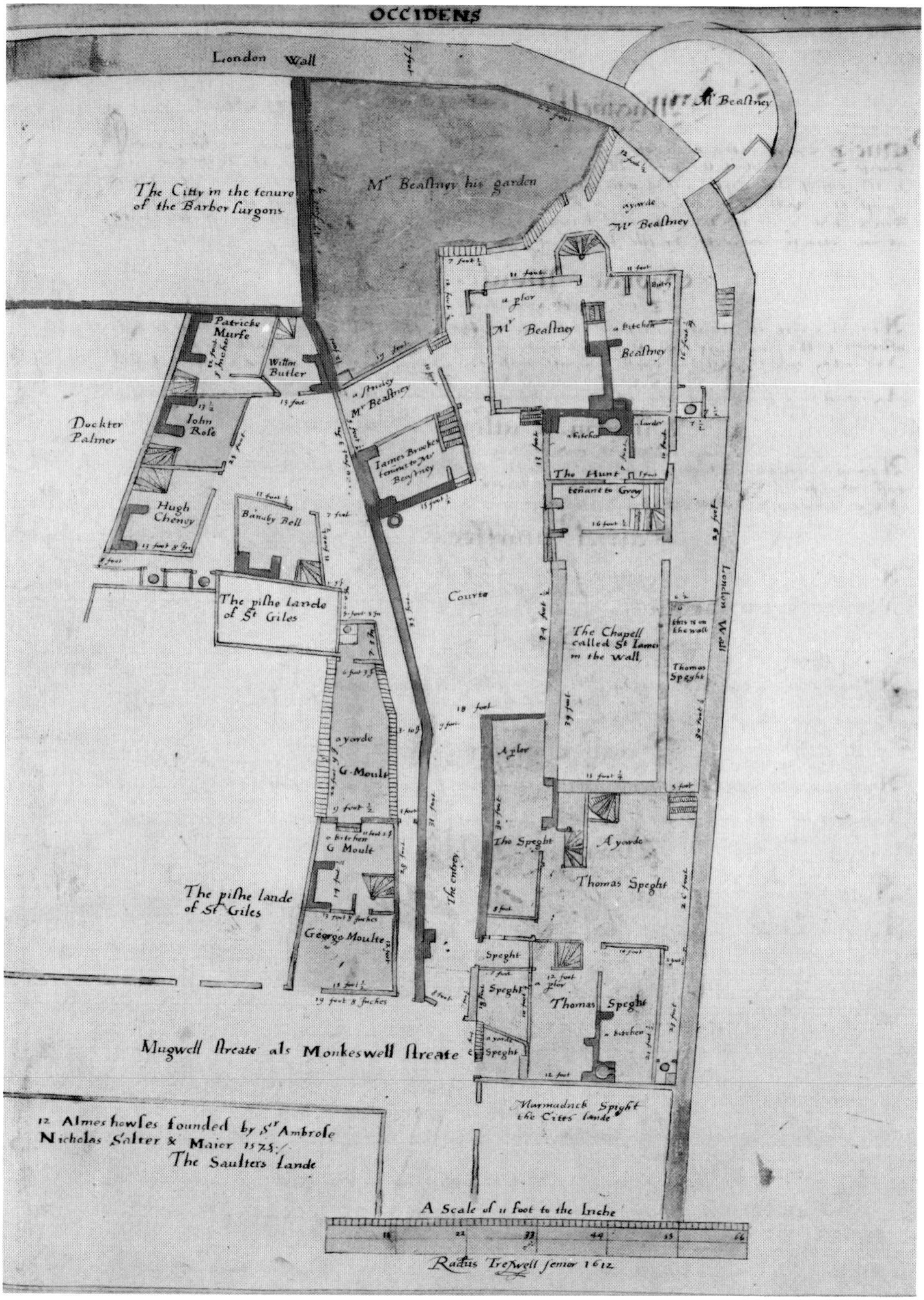

OCCIDENS

London Wall

Mr Beastney

The Citty in the tenure of the Barber Surgons

Mr Beastnyy his garden

Mr Beastney

a plor

Patricke Murfe

Willm Butler

Mr Beastney

Beastney

Ducktor Palmer

John Rose

a study Mr Beastney

James Brooker tenant to Mr Bentney

The Hunt tenant to Gray

London Wall

Hugh Cheney

Bandy Bell

The pishe lande of St Giles

Courte

The Chapell called St James in the Wall

Thomas Speght

a yarde

G. Moult

Ailor

G. Moult

The Speght

A yarde

The pishe lande of St Giles

The entrey

Thomas Speght

George Moulte

Speght

Speght

Thomas Speght

Mugwell streate als Monkeswell streate

Speght

Marmaduck Spyght the Cites lande

12 Almeshowses founded by Sr Ambrose Nicholas Salter & Maier 1578 / The Saulters lande

A Scale of 11 foot to the Inche

Radus Treswell senor 1612

Figure 34. **30.** St James' Hermitage / Lambe's Chapel, Monkwell Street (1:300). North is to the right of the plan. *See also Plate 9.*

St James in the Wall

Mr Bestney: (2) A chamber over the parlour 20½′ × 16½′ with a chimney, one other little chamber adjoining to the same 7′ × 7′, one other chamber adjoining being over the kitchen 20′ × 11′ with a chimney; (3) A garret chamber 20½′ × 16′, two garrets adjoining to the same 20½′ × 10′, a round turret over the staircase 10′ × 10′ [*sic*] with a door out into a lead; A cellar under the aforesaid parlour 18′ × 10½′.

James Brookes, tenant to Mr Bestney; (2) A chamber with the chimney and stairs 16′ × 12½′, one other chamber adjoining to the same 17′ × 9¾′; (3) Two garrets 17′ × 10′.

Mr Gray, in the tenure of Thomas Hunte: (2) A chamber with a chimney 16½′ × 16′, a buttery 12½′ × 4¼′, a chamber at the W end of the chapel 20¼′ × 11½′ with the chimney; (3) A garret chamber at the W end of the building 9¾′ × 9′, another chamber at the S end of the same with a chimney in it 11½′ × 9½′, one other chamber adjoining to the same 11½′ × 9½′, one other chamber 10′ × 9½′, a chamber next the lead with a passage out into the said lead 22¾′ × 21′, the lead over the roof of the chapel 32′ × 20½′; A cellar under part of the chapel 21′ 7″ × 7′ at the N end × 8′ at the S end.

Thomas Speght: (2) A schoolhouse 32′ × 19½′ at the W end × 16½′ at the E end, a chamber at the E end of the said school 12½′ × 11½′, a chamber over the parlour and adjoining to the chamber aforesaid 18′ × 14½ besides the chimney and stairs, a chamber adjoining being over the kitchen 22¼′ × 10′; (3) A chamber over the last mentioned chamber with a chimney in it 22′ × 9½′, another chamber adjoining 18′ besides the passage ×14′ besides the chimney, a chamber over the gate 12½′ × 12½′ besides the passage, also a garret over the school with a little room at the E end; (4) Two garrets over the two first mentioned chambers in the third storey 25′ × 25′; A cellar under the chapel 21¾′ × 20½′.

31. Foxe's Court, [St] Nicholas Lane/23–5 Abchurch Lane

Plan Book, 15; LTS Pubn 74 (vii) (1940)

In 1363 Elias Chaunceler granted back to Sir Edward Kendale the property he owned between St Nicholas Lane and Abchurch Lane (CD Box 59, 1). In 1377 the property had passed, perhaps by way of an Elizabeth Kendale in dowry, to William de Bughbrigge, clerk, who granted it to Sir John Cobham, three citizens and two other clerks (*ibid.*, 2). In 1382 this group quitclaimed to John de Bosham, one of their number (*ibid.*, 3); and in 1390 Bosham, a mercer, demised the property to three more clerics: John Turk, John Poydras and Robert Turk (*ibid.*, 4). This group then leased all 'illud magnum hospitium' which a Daniel Damar had held to John Basse *pannarius* (draper), together with nine shops and solars which Basse had recently built, for 60 years at a rent of 12 marks (*ibid.*, 8, 9). At the same time they leased two further shops in Abchurch Lane, between this block of property to the E and 'the entrance of the large gate of John Turk *et al.*', to Simon Ingram, 'lyndraper' (*ibid.*, 6, 7). In 1397 John, son of John Basse, sublet his property to John Attilburg, Prior of Bermondsey Abbey and Richard Forster of London (*ibid.*, 10); Attilburgh sublet it again to John Burford, 'belyeter' (*ibid.*, 12), who also held the Crown, Aldgate at this time (**3**).

Between 1397 and 1424 the freehold passed from Turk, Poydras and Turk to Richard Jepe, rector of All Hallows, Honey Lane. Robert Turk must have willed it to Thomas Trumpington to support a chantry in All Hallows for the Turk family, since Trumpington willed it in 1425 (proved 1428) to Jepe for this purpose (*Cal Wills* ii, 447). Jepe granted it to a large group of citizens, including John Carpenter; the three survivors, Clemens Lyfy, draper, John Chisehill and Thomas Mullyng, quitclaimed to Simon Eyre in 1448 (CD Box 59, 14–17). Eyre granted the property to his son Thomas and Elizabeth his wife, and Thomas granted it to Richard Heton, Richard Quatremayne and Richard Peverell in 1459

(*ibid.*, 18, 19). This group sublet to a physician, Matteo Dominico de (?) Serege in 1468, and to John Saunder, draper, in 1470 (*ibid.*, 20–2). Saunder or Saunders, called a 'sherman' in 1488, owned the property by the time of his death in 1504. One notable set of subtenants were Fernando de Castro and Diego de Castro, merchants of Burgos in Spain, who leased the property for £10 p.a. in 1488. In this lease Saunder undertook to 'make defensible [the property] and the sieges of the same do to be purged and the pavement of the same do to be repaired as ofte as nede shal be' (*ibid.*, 27). In 1491 Alphonse de Burgos was tenant at the same rent; and it was noted 'that there remayneth in the chamber over the parlor a standing close bedde of Estriche borde' belonging to Saunder (*ibid.*, 28). By his will of 1504 Saunder left the property to his wife, and on her death to his daughters Agnes, wife of Oliver Claymond, and Mary, wife of Richard Nicholl (*ibid.*, 31). Claymond was one of Saunder's executors; he had sole control of the property by 1520 (*ibid.*, 32–3). In 1533 Claymond, an early master of the new Clothworkers' Company, granted the property to a group of clothworkers; it was fully granted to the company by reversion after Claymond's widow's death, under the terms of his will in 1540 (*Cal Wills* ii, 646). In 1542–3 Claymond's son-in-law John Clerk also quitclaimed his interest, via Claymond's daughter Tomasin, to the Company (CD Box 59, 39). The Company then leased it to a succession of tenants. Notable among these was John Foxe, clothworker, who leased the property in 1585–6 for £80 p.a., whereas the rent in 1582–3 had been £24 (RW Accts); thereafter the main house on Nicholas Lane was called Foxe's Court.

The estate surveyed by Treswell in 1612 comprised two parts (Fig. 35; N is to the bottom of the plan). A great house lay on the N side of a court entered from Nicholas Lane through a three-storeyed street range. The house comprised a hall, perhaps originally 28½' × 20', entered by steps

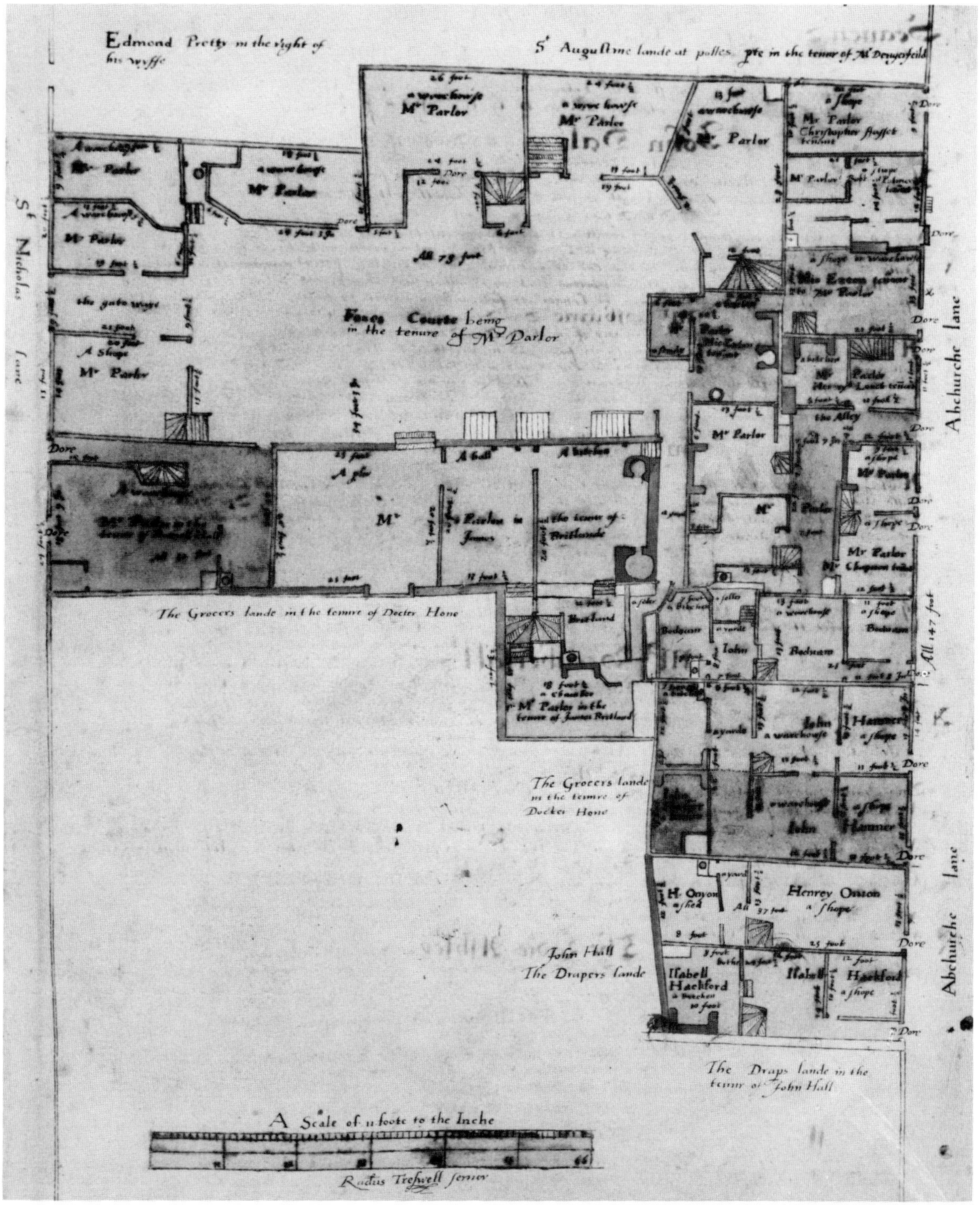

Figure 35. **31.** Foxe's Court, [St] Nicholas Lane, 23–5 Abchurch Lane (1:300). North is to the bottom of the plan. See also Figure 3.

and on a cellar. The hall had evidently been divided by 1612 into a smaller hall and parlour, the original door being blocked up and a new entrance made directly into the parlour which formed the upper two-thirds of the original hall. Beyond the screens was a kitchen with a large stack which occupied nearly all the end of the range. The gatehouse block to Nicholas Lane contained first- and second-floor galleries on the court side, with access down to the court; each floor had several rooms running the width of the range, as in galleried inns. The hall range was four storeys high, and a subtenancy on Nicholas Lane (occupied by Daniel Hall) rose to four storeys with garrets. Around the S and W sides of the courtyard were warehouses, three of two storeys and one of only one storey.

Text of reference, Plan Book (1612)

Foxe's Court, (St) Nicholas Lane

Mr Parler, the great capital messuage [in tenure of James Britland on plan]: (2) A chamber over the kitchen and hall with closet in it 29½' with the chimney × 24½' at the W end × 21¼ at the E end, one other chamber adjoining to the same being over part of the parlour with a chimney in it 25' × 14½', a staircase with a house of office on the N side 11½' × 8', one chamber with a chimney over parte of Daniell Hall's warehouse, a chamber over the gate at the E end of the court aforesaid 20½' × 14½' besides two little closets, one other chamber adjoining 20½' × 15½', also a gallery leading unto the same two chambers 44' × 4' with a house of office at the S end, a chamber with a chimney which chamber is on the S side of the court 24' × 19¼', a gallery on the same side 21' × 4' 9", one other chamber 20' × 12½', also one little study adjoining being in the staircase, one other room over a warehouse 25¼' × 19½', one other room hanging part over the yard or court being the W end of the said court 7' with the stairs and passage ×13½', a chamber next Abchurch Lane being once Fawcett's shop 23' × 11½', a chamber over Mr Exton's kitchen 21½' × 16½; (3) A chamber with a chimney and closet 26½' × 15½', one other little chamber 15½' with the entry and passage × 14½', one other chamber 15' × 11½', one other chamber adjoining with a chimney in it, the staircase with the house of office 11' × 9', a chamber over the gate 23½' × 14½' with the chimney, one other chamber on the S side the same 23½' × 14½' with the chimney, one other chamber

23½' × 14½', one long gallery serving for the three chambers aforesaid 44' × 3', a little chamber at the W end of the court 14' × 13', one other chamber 21½' × 15½' with the chimney; (4) A chamber on the N side the court 15½' × 15', one other chamber adjoining to the same being next the court 17½' with the chimney and closet × 12½', two other chambers adjoining one with a chimney 29' × 20', a chamber adjoining 28' × 14½' with the chimney, a gallery leading to all the said chambers 35' × 7½', a square turret over the staircase 12½' × 9½'; A chamber in the third storey over Daniell Hall 27' × 14' with the chimney.

Daniell Hall, tenant to Mr Parlor: (2) A hall next St Nicholas Lane with a chimney and a kitchen adjoining with a chimney both 26½' × 23'; (3) A chamber next the lane aforesaid with a chimney 24' × 15½', one other chamber adjoining 23' × 12½'; (4) Three chambers with two chimneys in them all 28' × 24'; (5) A garret over all 30' × 30'; Also a cellar under the same house 29' × 20'.

The second part of the estate (though probably inseparable from it from earliest times) comprised a frontage of eleven houses to Abchurch Lane (Fig. 35). The nine northern houses were on the site of nine built shortly before 1390 by John Basse (see above); it is possible that the arrangement of rooms and kitchen on the ground floor, and possibly some of the fabric, dated from his building.

The five houses to the N (towards the bottom of the plan) were of two-room plan with separate kitchens across a small yard; in one case the two ground-floor rooms had been thrown together, and in the same house the kitchen was replaced by a shed. The coincidence of alignment of partitions, stairs, and some correspondence in dimensions of upper chambers, together with a uniform height of 3½ storeys, suggests that all five were part of one frame and built as a unit. The houses also shared the feature of a heated chamber on the first floor next the street which probably functioned as a hall.

S of this group of five houses were more individual buildings; their construction may have been dictated by the presence of the adjacent great house; a gateway to Abchurch Lane is mentioned for instance in 1390, and was probably somewhere on this part of the site. The shops, two of one-room plan and four of mixed one- and two-room plan, were of 3½ storeys with one exception.

Text of reference, Plan Book (1612)

Robert Palmer, a tenement in Abchurch Lane: (2) A chamber next Abchurch Lane 22½′ × 12′ with the chimney; (3) Three chambers, one with a chimney, and a kitchen adjoining all 25′ × 23½′; (4) A garret 23½′ × 12½′; A cellar under the same house 12½′ × 8′ 9″.

Nicholas Exton: (2) A chamber next Abchurch Lane aforesaid 22½′ × 12½′ with the chimney; (3) A chamber with a chimney 23½′ × 12½′; (4) A garret over all 23½′ × 12½′; A cellar under the shop 16′ × 11′.

Henry Lovett, a tenement in Abchurch Lane: (2) A chamber over all 20′ 8″ × 10½′ with the chimney; A garret over the same; A cellar 9′ 9″ × 9′ 6″.

The Alley in Abchurch Lane

(2) A chamber over Christofer Fawcett's room 16′ × 8′ 7″; A garret over the same; A chamber over Edward Jones' room 14½′ × 13½′ with the chimney; Also a little garret over the same.

Mr Chapman, a tenement in Abchurch Lane: (2) A chamber next Abchurch Lane 17½′ × 14½′ with the chimney, another chamber and buttery adjoining 16′ × 11′ being next the said lane; (3) A chamber next the said lane 13′ 8″ × 11½′, one other chamber adjoining 16′ 4″ × 16′ 4″ with the chimney; (4) A garret over the chamber aforesaid 16′ 8″ × 14′ with the chimney; A cellar under the N part of the building 13½′ × 10½′.

Isabell Hackford, one tenement: (2) A chamber next Abchurch Lane with a chimney 14′ × 13½′, one other chamber adjoining 18½′ × 14′ with a house of office; (3) A chamber next the lane aforesaid with the chimney 15½′ × 14′, one other chamber adjoining to the same with a chimney in it; (4) Two garrets over all 39′ × 14′.

Henry Onyon, one tenement: (2) A chamber next the lane 13½′ × 13½′ with the chimney, one other chamber adjoining 13½′ × 13½′; (3) A chamber next the lane aforesaid 15′ × 13½′, one other chamber with a chimney adjoining 13′ × 13′; (4) A garret over all 28½′ × 13½′.

John Hanmer, one tenement: (2) A chamber next Abchurch Lane with the chimney 16½′ × 13′, one other chamber adjoining with the stairs 13′ × 10′; (3) A chamber next the aforesaid lane with the chimney 18½′ × 13′, another chamber adjoining 12½′ × 11′ 9″; (4) A garret over all 28′ × 12′, also a little garret over the E end of the same; A cellar under the shop 12½′ × 10′ 8″.

John Hanmer, one other tenement late David Jenkins: (2) A chamber next the aforesaid lane 13½′ × 13½′ with the chimney, one other chamber adjoining 13½′ × 13½′; (3) A chamber next the said lane 15′ × 14′, one other chamber adjoining 13′ 9″ × 13′ 4″; (4) A garret over all 29′ × 13′ 9″; A cellar under the shop 11′ × 10½′.

John Bodnam, one tenement in Abchurch Lane: (2) A chamber next the aforesaid lane with the chimney and closet 13½′ × 13′, one other chamber adjoining 13½′ × 13½′, a little room over the cellar 15½′ × 6′; (3) A chamber next the lane aforesaid 15′ × 13′, one other chamber adjoining 13½′ × 13′; (4) A garret over all 29′ × 13½′.

8

32. Lady Lucy's House, later Dean's Court, Old Bailey; later 38–40 Fleet Lane, 1–5 Dean's Court, 28–31 Seacoal Lane

Christ Church Oxford, MS Estates 45

In 1528 William Tymbigh, prior of Charterhouse, leased this property to Sir John Mordaunt, knight, for 90 years (Christ Church Oxford, MS Estates 45, 2). The property was purchased by Sir Edward North and sold by him to Henry VIII, who granted it to Christ Church in 1546 (Christ Church Book of Evidences 1, 464–6). The tenant in 1600 was Sir Edward Lucy; Lady Lucy appears as the tenant in 1610, when Treswell surveyed the property, presumably for the college (Fig. 36) (Christ Church Deeds, London St Sepulchre's, 1–9). The survey is not itself dated, but is endorsed '1610'. A draft for the same is also extant (Christ Church Deeds, London, St Sepulchre's, 4).

The plan, which is drawn on paper, shows a substantial house at the end of a long alley on the W side of Old Bailey (unnamed, but called Dean's Court by the time of Ogilby and Morgan's map in 1677). The house comprised a hall, kitchen and pantry, and two parlours; the high end of the hall and both parlours had large windows which are shown in section (an unusual feature for the Treswell plans: see also **33**). There is no text of reference, but four stairs are shown in the ground floor plan, of which two may have led to cellars and two probably led upwards (from the hall and the parlours). Around the garden were single-storeyed chambers and privies; a further set of steps, which because of the fall of the land must have led downwards, went into a stable yard which contained a building marked 'the stable and Coche howse'.

In 1866 the property was identified as nos. 38–40 Fleet Lane, 1–5 Dean's Court, and 28–31 Seacoal Lane (Christ Church Deeds, London St Sepulchre's, 19). In 1872 it was sold to the London, Chatham and Dover Railway Company.

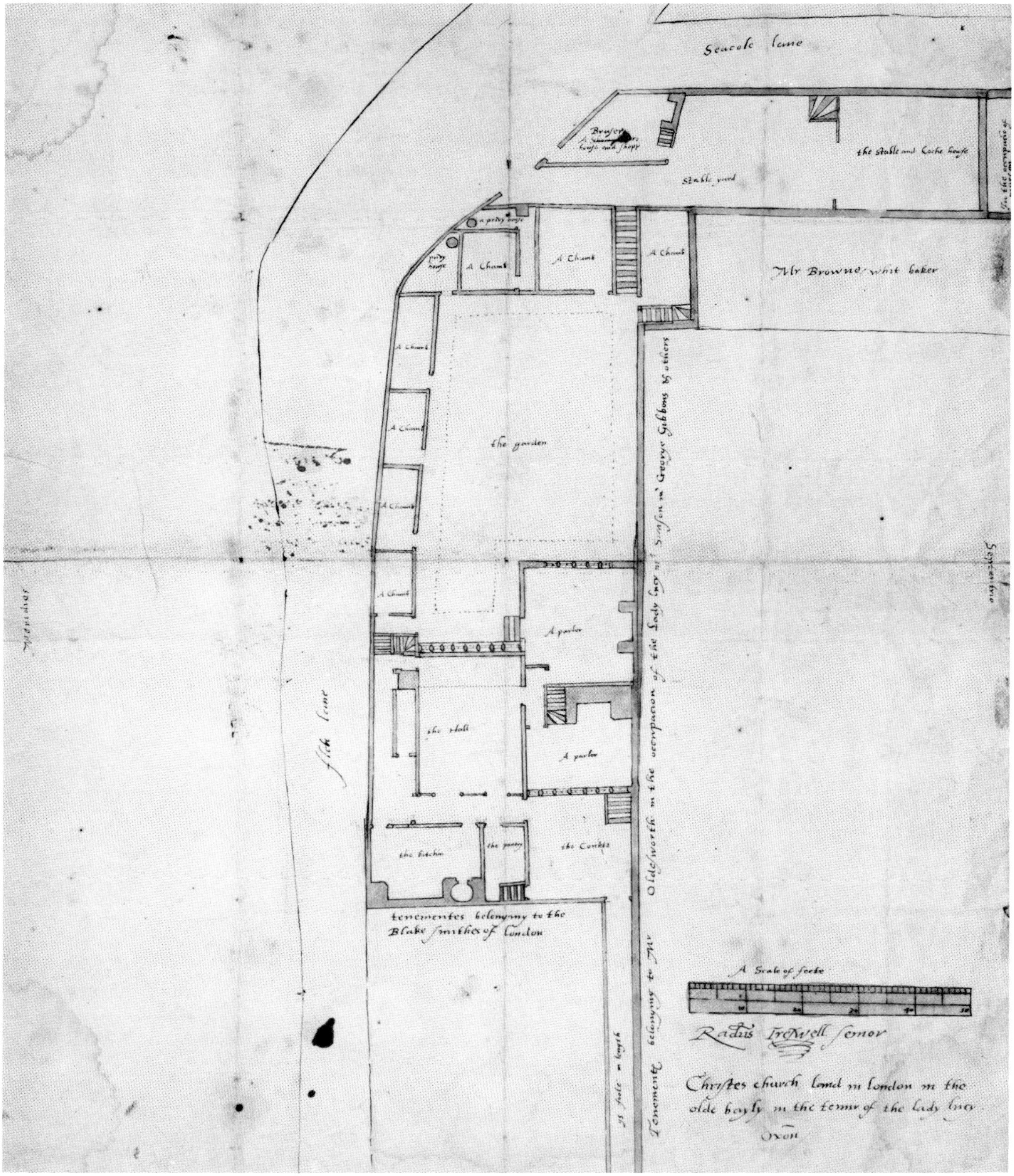

Figure 36. **32.** Lady Lucy's house, later Dean's Court, Old Bailey (1:300). North is to the right of the plan.

33. 3–4 Pancras Lane (formerly Needlers Lane)

Evidence Book, 4; HG, 1:Cheapside, St Pancras Soper
Lane, Fig 6

The detailed history of this site has been traced in
Keene and Harding's *Historic Gazetteer (HG, 1;
Cheapside*, site **145/14–15**). The property,
perhaps originally two separate tenements, was
united by the late thirteenth century. It was
probably inhabited by Simon Corp, pepperer, in
the early fourteenth century, and by William de
Causton, mercer, in the mid fourteenth century
(for those eminent merchants, see Thrupp 1948,
333, 329). In 1587 Arnold James, brewer, leased
part of the property to Thomas Thorowgood,
draper, and attached to the lease is a small
schedule of fittings which included wainscot
around the parlour, a wainscot portal and door; in
the chamber above the parlour chamber, one
portal and door of wainscot; two counting houses
next the chamber over the parlour, ceiled with
wainscot; the chamber over the parlour chamber,
with a portal and door of wainscot; and the
kitchen with a cistern of lead weighing 4½cwt and
a pump. The house was bought from James by
Christ's Hospital in 1602 out of £500 bequeathed
to them by Peter Blundell (GL MS 12935).

When surveyed for the hospital by Ralph
Treswell, the property was divided between two
main tenants. This is one of only three Treswell
plans which include details of windows
(cf. **32, 53**): two prominent four-light stone windows to the hall and parlour, and a third in the
slighter E wall of the hall, probably of timber.
There is no accompanying text, but the upper
floors of most of the buildings may be reconstruc-
ted from a lease of 1611 (GL MS 12935) to one of
the tenants, Edward Baber. The buildings appear
to be only two storeys high, with garrets. Especially noteworthy is the room with pillars, which

was not, as may appear, an open yard, but as the
schedule attached to the lease makes clear, an
enclosed space.

The brick wall which divided the garden was
inserted just before the lease was drawn up, to
divide Baber's tenancy from that of Jackson;
evidently Baber was taking over some of Jackson's
rooms. It therefore seems likely that the plan was
drawn in or shortly after 1611.

Schedule, 1611

Mr Baber: (2) A chamber over the kitchen, with a
chimney on the E side 42′ × 13½′ with a house of office
in it on the E side and a little void room with a passage
out of the same chamber on the NW corner into one
other chamber with a chimney, and a door into a little
study, which chamber being next the yard on the
W side 18½′ N–S × 17½′ E–W and out of that is a
door into another chamber at the NW corner over the
warehouse 24′ 9″ × 11½′; a little square room
9½′ × 8′ 8″ next the little yard; A chamber over the
long hall with a chimney and a door and portal of
wainscot 27′ × 17′; A little chamber over the buttery at
the N end of the same chamber wholly ceiled with
wainscot 13½′, with a stone wall, × 7′ 3″; next the little
yard is another chamber next the new yard wholly
ceiled in wainscot, about 16′ × 11½′, with a passage
up and down to the other rooms; Another chamber
with a chimney next the said yard 23′ 9″ × about 17′.
(3) A chamber next the new yard with a door and
portal of wainscot 17′ × 14′ within the walls; A garret
on the same floor 16½ × about 8½; Another garret
next the same 15′ 4″ × 15′ 9″; Another garret adjoining
the same, of the same measure; One other garret next
the new yard 14′ × about 18½′; Another garret
18½′ × about 13′ 9″; also a lead adjoining the last
mentioned garret, being on the E side, of the same
length × 3′ (GL MS 12935).

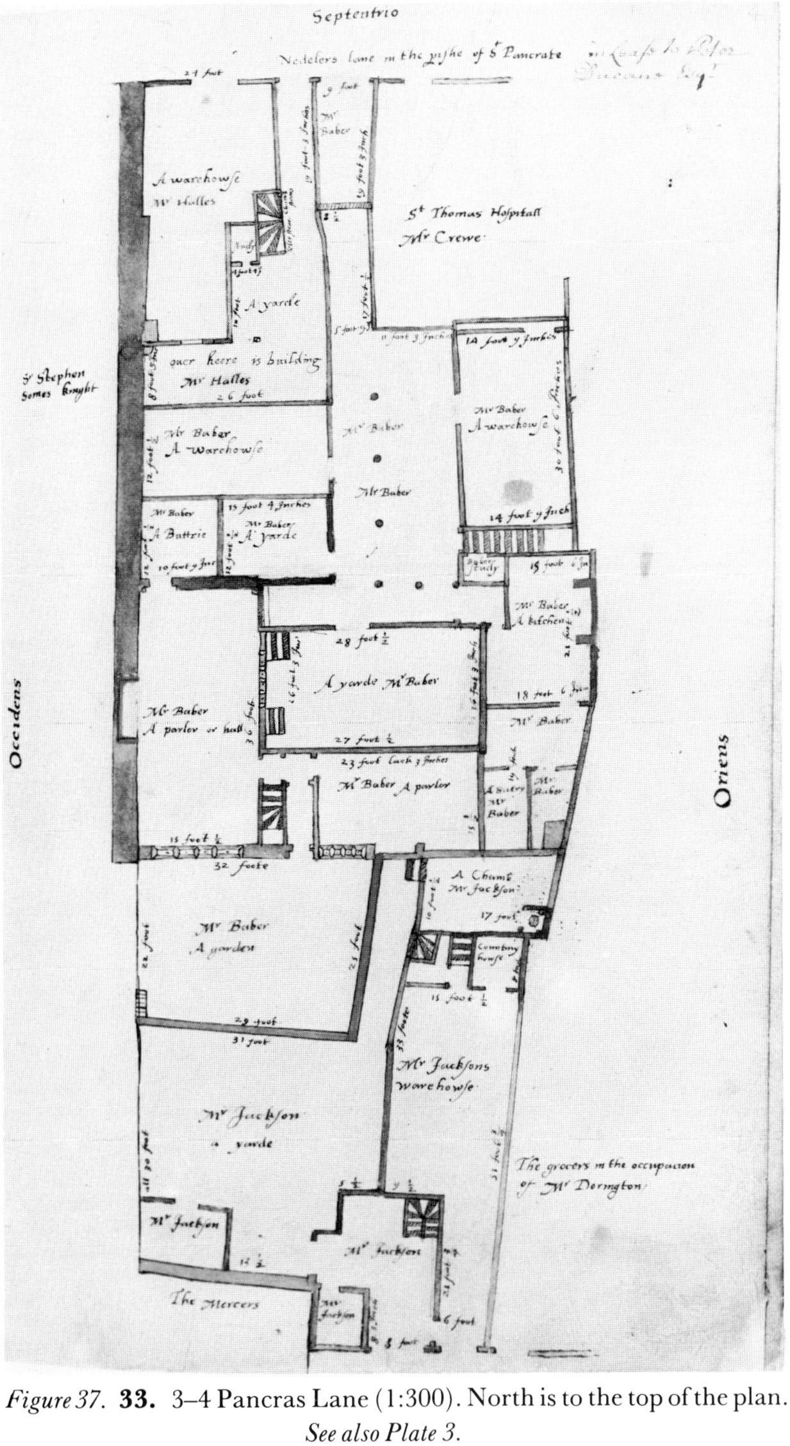

Figure 37. **33.** 3–4 Pancras Lane (1:300). North is to the top of the plan.
See also Plate 3.

34. Smith's almshouses, [St] Peter's Hill

Evidence Book, 16

David Smith, embroiderer to Elizabeth I, in his will (proved PCC 1587; *PCC 1584–1604*, 382) devised *inter alia* to the governors of Christ's Hospital, for a term of 1000 years after the death of his widow Katherine, six tenements built in 1584 upon the back part of a mansion (Woodmongers' Hall, now part of the College of Heralds), thereafter to be known as the 'poor widdowes Alley' or 'poore widowes Inne' for the use, rent free, of six widows, aged at least fifty-six years, who had been resident in the parish (of St Peter, Paul's Wharf) or the ward (Castle Baynard) for twenty years (GL MS 13813, 13814). The Hospital took possession in 1607 (CHMB I, 105 v). The site of the almshouses is now beneath Queen Victoria Street.

The six almshouses were all of a uniform plan. Each comprised a ground-floor chamber of brick with chimney, and a first floor and garret, probably timber-framed, which jettied one foot into the court. The upper chambers were not heated, but each had a 'howse of office'.

The imposing stone building next to the almshouse included an upper room called Woodmongers' Hall. The plan and text of Treswell's survey indicate that Thomas Swayne held a cellar and two rooms on the ground floor; the S wall of this edifice on the ground floor was a stout stone wall with two buttresses. There is no further information from the 1611 survey about the upper floors of this building, or about the part of it called Woodmongers' Hall; but details are available in a view of 1628.

View, 1628

[ground floor] A kitchen, stair and entry 25½′ × 29′; (2) A hall with a closet or study taken out of it E–W from the streetside 26′ × 27′ within the staircase; over Swain's house, a bedchamber behind the same hall 18′ 6″ × 21′ with a chimney; another chamber behind 18′ 4″ × 21′ with a chimney; (3) A fair large room called the Woodmongers' Hall over the aforesaid hall with the entry 28′ × 25½′ with a chimney and a closet, a bedchamber behind the said room 18′ 5″ × 21½′ with a chimney, another chamber behind the same 18′ × 21′ with a chimney; (4) A garret with a study behind the same at the E end, another garret on the same stair with a bedchamber at the E end of it; [5] another garret over the same garret (CH View Book 1, 65).

Text of reference, Evidence Book (1611)

Margaret Davis widow: [2] A chamber 12½′ × 9′ with a house of office in it, also a garret over the aforesaid chamber 12½′ × 9′.

Mary Taylor widow: [2] A chamber 12½′ × 9′ with a house of office in it, also a garret over the same 12½′ × 9′.

Johan Evered widow: [2] A chamber 12½′ × 9′ with a house of office in it, also a garret over the same 12½′ × 9′.

Johan Harrison widow: [2] A chamber 12½′ × 11′ with a house of office in it, also a garret 12½′ × 11′.

Elizabeth Castell widow: [2] A chamber 12½′ × 9′ with a house of office in it, also a garret 12½′ × 9′.

Welthian Watkin widow: [2] A chamber 12½′ × 11′ with a house of office in it, also a garret 12½′ × 11′.

Thomas Swayne hath two chambers and a seller as in the plott appeareth.

[   ] Price: [the tenancy to the W, fronting on to St Benet's Hill] [2] A chamber next the street 16½′ × 10½′, a chamber over the kitchen next the street with a chimney 27′ × 16′; [3] A chamber over the aforesaid chamber with a chimney 19½′ × 24½′, a garret with chimney of the same measure, decayed. A chamber over Thomas Swayne's house with a chimney 17½′ × 18½′, another chamber over Swayne's house 19′ × 17½′; [4] Two other chambers over the aforesaid chambers whereof the furthest hath a chimney being both of the aforesaid measure [i.e. as the chambers below].

28 foote 3 Inches

4 foote
3 Inches

9 foot ½

a hall

28 foote

Mr Smithes
howses

a larder

27 foote

A peare in
Docter
Papes howse

15 foote

Mr Smithes howse

4 foot ¼

8 foot ¼

all 19 foot ¼
Thomas Swayne

8 foot

Mr Smith a yarde

10 foote

a yarde
Mr Smith

a yarde

Swaynes
privy

18 foote

Thomas Swayne hath
thes 2 romes with a
seller 37 foot longe pte
wherof is 8 foot brode
and pte 4 foot ¾

well

15 foot

11 foot ½

Johan Evered

9 foot

9 foot 3 Inches

welthian
watkin

Mr Smithes
howses

11 foote

9 foot 3 Inches

Mery Taylor

11 foot ½

Elizabeth

the Almeshouses
on St Peters hill

11 foot ½

8 foot

9 foot ¼

Mararek Davis

11 foot

Johan Harrison

10 foot

11 foot 3 Inches

12 foote ½

St Peters hill

The Harroldes office called Darby place

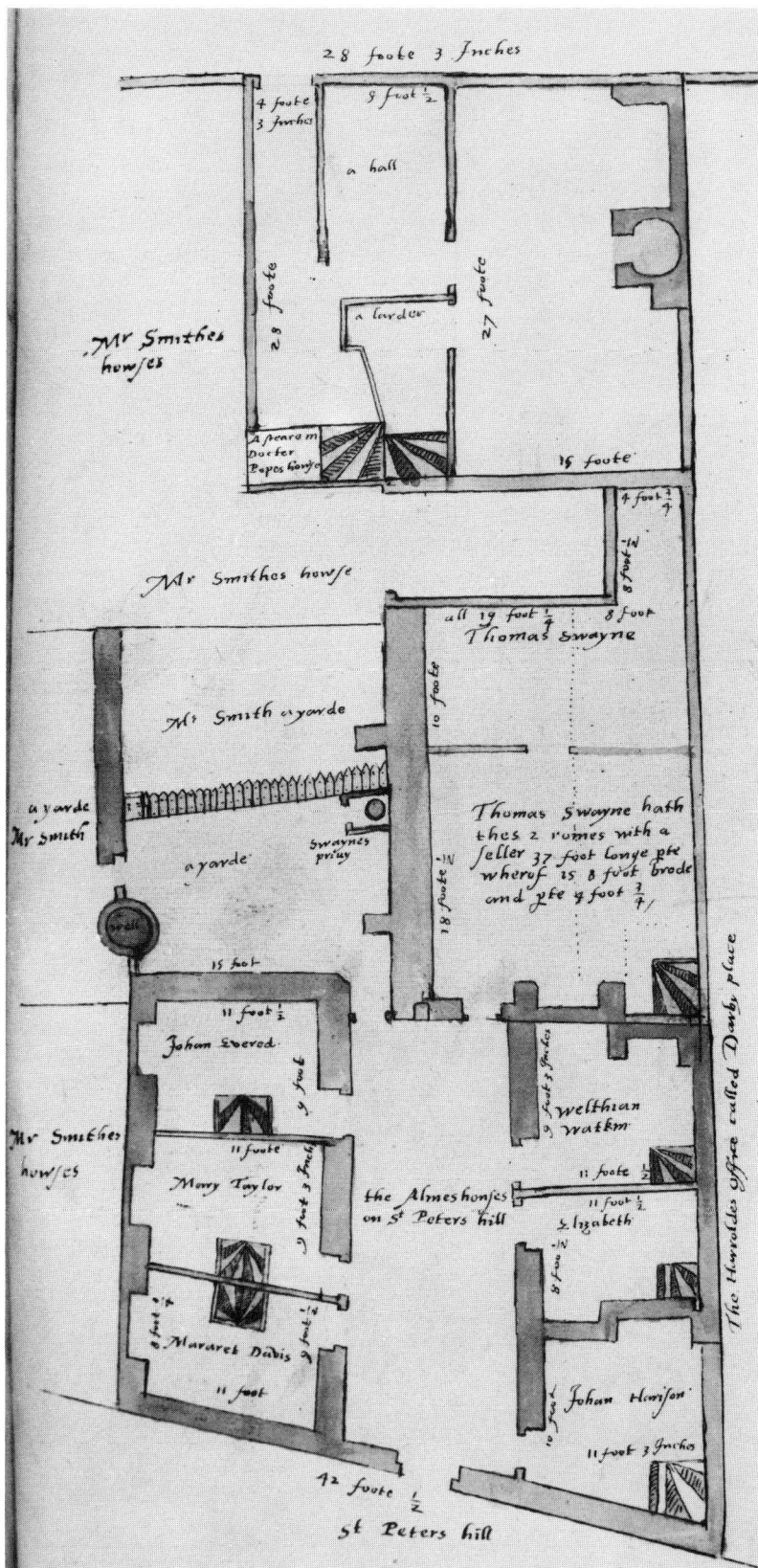

Figure 38. **34.** Smith's almshouses, [St] Peter's Hill (1:150). North is
to the right of the plan. *See also Plate 8.*

35. 28 Pudding Lane

Evidence Book, 12

This tenement, formerly chantry property, was granted in 1549 by Edward Welsshe and Simon Aynesworth to Nicholas Howe, butcher, and his wife Helen. By 1556 Howe was dead and his widow was married to John Gylmyn; they made an arrangement whereby they conveyed the property to Sir Roland Hill, who conveyed it back to them with reversion on Helen's death to the hospital (GL MS 13184). In 1573 Helen, now married to her third husband Cornelius de Vos, but acting on her own behalf, presumably in the supposition that he was dead, leased the property to Richard Holgate, a carpenter, on the condition that within two years he take down the stone wall on the street side and set up a substantial timber frame of two storeys (GL MS 13186); it was by then known as the Boar's Head. Cornelius de Vos did however reappear, since he and his wife Helen granted the reversion of the property to the City in 1577 (GL MS 13187).

The front of the building in the plan of 1611 (Fig. 39) was probably as Holgate built it in 1573–5; both tenancies were two storeys with garrets. The measurements of the chambers and the ground floor agree to suggest that they were all 19½′ deep and that there was no jetty at all to the street. How old the 'stone wall' of the frontage which Holgate removed may have been is not ascertainable from the deeds.

Text of reference, Evidence Book (1611)

Thomas Myles: [2] A chamber with a chimney 19½′ × 14½′; [3] One other chamber over the same before 20½′ × 14½′ with a chimney; [4] A garret over all 19½′ × 13½′; also a cellar under the shop.

Henry Dowsing: [2] A chamber next the street 14½′ × 11½′ with a chimney, stairs and entry between, one other chamber over the back room with a chimney 12½′ × 11½′; [3] A garret with a chimney over the room before mentioned, a garret next the street 19½′ × 7½′.

Daniell Kirby: [2] A chamber 11½′ × 11½′ with a chimney, also a gallery over John Dorrell's coalhouse and his own 14½′ × 4′ besides the stairs.

John Dorrell: [2] A chamber over the hall with stairs and chimney 23′ × 12′ 2″ with a little closet at the end thereof 7½′ × 3½′, also an entry and stairs leading to other chambers 13½′ × 5′, also a chamber or garret over the kitchen 15½′ × 12¼′; [3] A chamber next the the yard and over part of the hall afore mentioned 13½′ × 10½′, one other chamber over the other part of the chamber over the hall with a chimney 12½′ × 10½′; [4] A garret over all with a chimney and other funnels 25′ × 14½′.

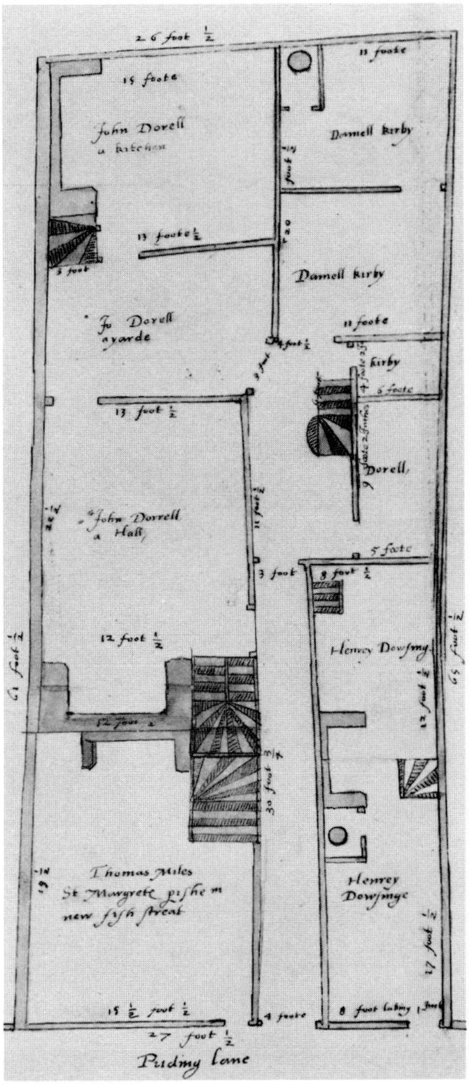

Figure 39. **35.** 28 Pudding Lane (1:150).
North is to the left of the plan.

36. Dudley Court, Silver Street

Evidence Book, 7

In 1547 Thomas Colley purchased much property which had belonged to Holy Trinity Priory Aldgate, in Silver Street. His estate passed to John Dudley of Hackney, sergeant of the pastry to Elizabeth I, and his son Thomas, grandson of Thomas Colley. The estate of Thomas Dudley was thereafter partitioned among his five sisters, Lucy, Bridget, Mirabelle, Susan and Barbara (GL MS 13242A–F). Three of the tenements of Bridget's portion passed to Arthur Jackson, clothworker, from whom they were purchased in 1599 by Christ's Hospital with part of a covenant made by Dame Dorothy Edmonds in 1596 (GL MS 13242F; *Charity Comm*, 101). The properties shown in the plan by Treswell were burnt down in the Great Fire of 1666 and the main plot rebuilt as a terrace of four houses with an alley down the W side (plan in lease of 1668, GL MS 13244). North is to the top of the plan (Fig. 40).

The two small tenements let to James Yates and Benet Ivett are of a form common in the Treswell plans: one room on each floor with newel stair in one corner, often attached to the chimney stack, facing the entrance. Both houses were 3½ storeys

high. As they backed onto neighbouring property which provided a fixed vertical plane, their upper-floor measurements may reliably be taken to indicate the amount of jettying of the upper storeys. Yates' tenancy would therefore jetty 1½' on the first floor, and another 6" on the second, which was flush with the garret; while Ivett's would jetty 2' on the first, and 3" on both second and garret.

Text of reference, Evidence Book (1611)

James Yates: [2] A chamber with stairs and chimney 14½' × 10'; A chamber with stairs and chimney 15' × 10'; [3] A garret over all 15' × 9½' with funnels of chimneys, stairs and a house of office.

Bennet Ivett: [2] A chamber with stairs and chimney 15' × 10'; [3] One other chamber over the same, with stairs and chimney 15¼' × 9'; [4] A garret over all, with funnels of chimneys and stairs and a house of office 15½' × 10'.

John Cowndley: [2] and [3] A chamber over the parlour with a chimney 20½' × 17½'; Another chamber over the other before mentioned 19½' × 10'. Two other chambers: one with a chimney 19' × 13½', a chamber over the kitchen and entry 18' × 11' with a funnel of a chimney; Also a house of office 9' × 4'.

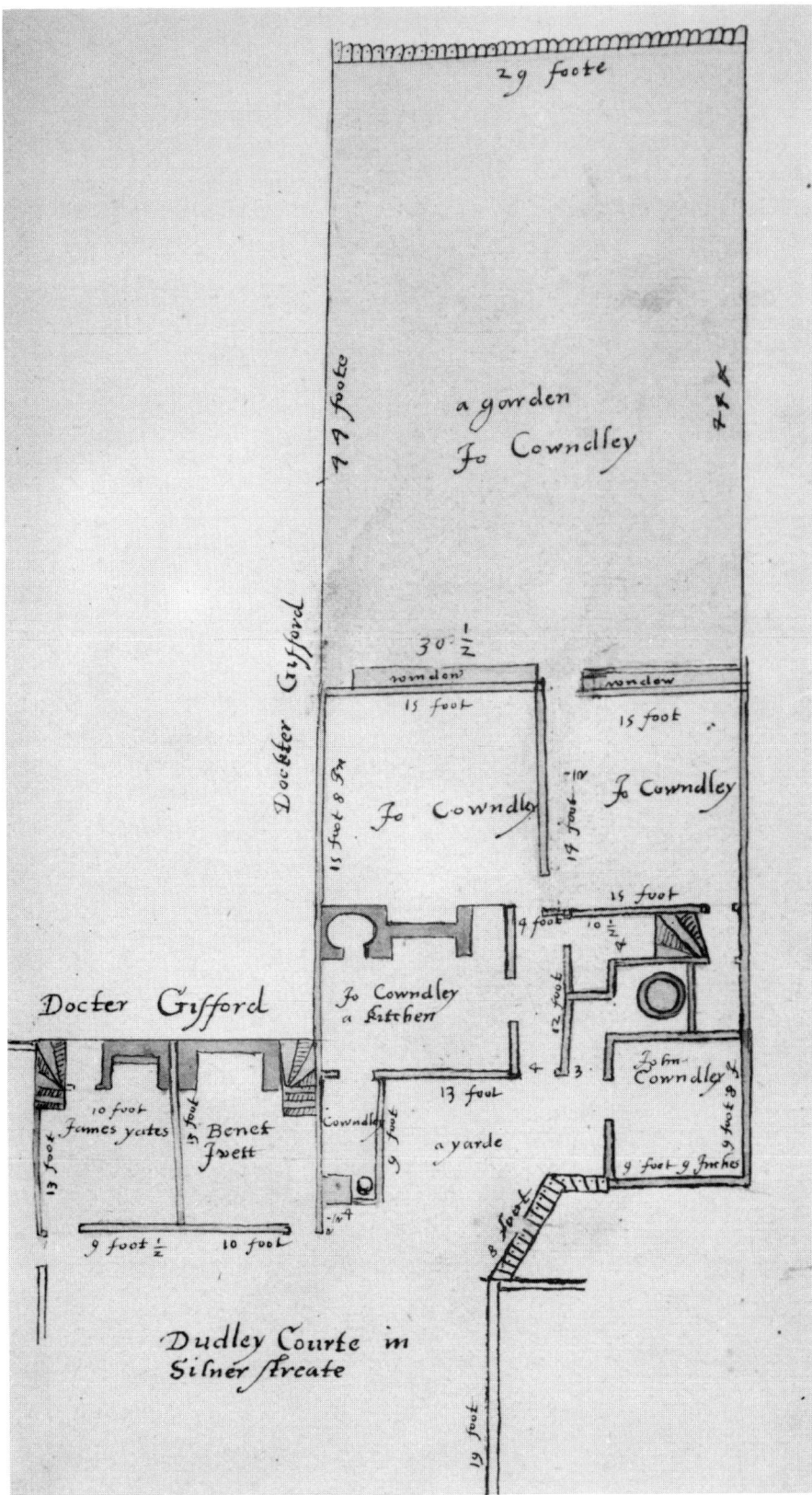

Figure 40. **36.** Dudley Court, Silver Street (1:150). North is to the top of the plan.

37. House in St Swithin's Lane

Evidence Book, 8

This house was one of a number of properties conveyed to Christ's Hospital by Sir Martin Bowes in 1565 (GL MS 12949).

No deeds can at present be traced prior to the conveyance. The house in St Swithin's Lane must have been near the N end, for it was sold in 1833 to the City of London under the provisions of the London Bridge Approaches Act (*Charity Comm*, 93), and presumably it lies beneath King William Street.

The compass directions on Treswell's plan (Fig. 41) appear to be wrong, for St Swithin's Lane runs N–S; it is not clear on which side of the lane the house stood. It was 3½ storeys high.

Text of reference, Evidence Book (1611)

Arthur Chastmore: [2] A hall over part of the shop 14′ × 12′ 3″, a chamber adjoining to the hall being next the street with a chimney 15½′ × 12′ 3″, a kitchen with a chimney 5′ × 8½′, also a little corner with house of office in it 5′ × 4′; [3] A chamber next the street 11′ 3″ × 13′ and the S and N ends 10½′ broad, another chamber of the same floor [*sic*] 16½′ × 10′; [4] A garret chamber in 1. with the staircase 17½′ and in b. 12½′.

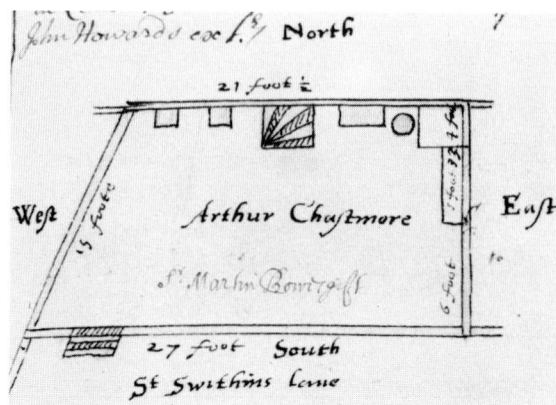

Figure 41. **37.** House in [St] Swithin's Lane (1:150). The direction of north is not known.

38. House in Fish Street Hill [New Fish Street], now part of 127 [Lower] Thames Street

Plan Book, 27

Part of Sir Martin Bowes' gift to Christ's Hospital in 1565 (GL MS 12949); augmented by a plot added from the parish of St Magnus in 1722, this property occupied the SE corner of Fish Street Hill and Lower Thames Street, now 127, Lower Thames Street.

The house in the plan of 1611 (Fig. 42) was apparently 5½ storeys high, with one or two small rooms on each floor. The compass points are wrong, as the street, to the left, should be to the W.

Text of reference, Evidence Book (1611)

Mrs Jane Bruskett: [2] A hall over the shop 17½′ × 13¼′ with a little buttery and stairs; [3] A chamber over the said hall with a chimney and a little closet hanging into the street 8½′ × 8½′; [4] A kitchen and a little room adjoining over the aforesaid chamber 17½′ × 33½′; [5] A chamber over the kitchen with a chimney of the same bigness; [6] A garret over all of the same measure.

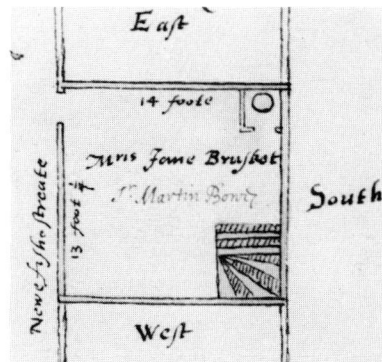

Figure 42. **38.** 127 [Lower] Thames Street (1:150). North is to the top of the plan.

39. All Hallows Lane, [Upper] Thames Street

Plan Book, 29

This lane, leading from Thames Street to the Thames at the W end of the church of All Hallows the Great, was known as Haywharf Lane in the fourteenth and possibly fifteenth centuries, but as Church Lane or Allhallows Lane during the sixteenth century (Harding 1980, 15). In 1480 William Gardyner bequeathed his property in the lane to the Shearmen's Company (CDW). When the property appeared in the Clothworkers' accounts for 1529, it had seven tenants (RW Accts).

When surveyed by Treswell in 1612 (Fig. 43), the property comprised nine buildings of single-room plan on the W side of the lane. A tenth building, also single-roomed in plan, is shown on an inset somewhat to the N since the adjacent Steelyard lay along the lane in between. The buildings, of utilitarian aspect, were 2–3½ storeys high. The five to the N were shared between two tenants; three units had no internal stairs to upper floors, though in two cases the tenant probably gained access by adjacent stairs. From one chamber a large vat protruded to the S, possibly into a small yard.

At the S end was a half unit 'open to the steares', i.e. the Clothworkers' Stairs which are shown adjacent to the common stairs at the end of the lane. The Clothworkers' Stairs were frequently repaired during the period 1528–1612 covered by the company accounts. In 1553 the need for repairs was blamed on the clothworkers' washing of their 'bukkes' (baskets), which was banned (CCO 1536–58, 235v). In 1562–3 72 loads of rag and 20 loads of flint were brought from Limehouse for repair work, which went on during night tides. A second load of 36½ loads of rag came by lighter, the total cost being £118.10.10*d* (RW Accts 1562–3). In 1565–6 the wooden steps were replaced (RW Accts 1565–6), and further major repairs to the stairs and end house carried out in 1597–8 (QW Accts 1597–8); this may be the 'newe house' noted by Treswell on the plan.

The S end of the lane and the stairs are shown by Hollar in his engraving of 1647 (Schofield 1984, Fig. 97). The company stairs are shown, but not the separate common stairs; this is an error common to all the panoramas except the unique woodcut of London of *c.* 1560 in the Pepysian collection (*ibid.*, Fig. 107). Immediately to the N Hollar shows a single-storey building of two gables, which must be the unit shown 'open to the steares' by Treswell, and then six buildings of two or perhaps three storeys with garrets. This suggests that the buildings shown by Treswell were roofed individually on their long axis, as would be expected, at right angles to the lane.

Text of reference, Plan Book (1612)

Mr Nelson: (2) A chamber with a chimney in it which chamber is divided into three parts all 26′ × 17½′ with the chimney and stairs.

William Browne, tenant to Mr Reynolds: (2) A hall with diverse partitions 30′ with the stairs × 26½′, three other chambers adjoining, one with a chimney in it, all 29′ × 26′; (3) Diverse garrets over all 39½′ × 26′, one little square garret lately builded over the N end of the garret aforesaid.

Edward Morton: (2) A chamber with a chimney, one other chamber or kitchen adjoining with two other little rooms; (3) Two garrets over all, one with a chimney.

Lawrence Taylor: (2) A chamber 26′ × 18½′ with the chimney and the stairs; (3) A chamber with a chimney and a kitchen adjoining with a chimney, both 26′ × 18½′.

Richard Wallis: (2) A chamber divided into two parts 26½′ with the chimney × 23½′; (3) Three garrets over the chamber aforesaid 26½′ × 23½′.

Widow Constantyn: (2) A chamber with a chimney being over the oven and warehouse 18½′ × 15½′, one other chamber with a chimney adjoining 17′ × 11′, also a little garret over the same.

Peter Wilkinson: (2) A chamber with a chimney divided into two parts 25½′ × 10¾′; (3) A chamber with a chimney and a little room adjoining 12′ × 12½′ with the chimney; (3) (*sic, rectius* (4)) A garret over all 26′ × 12½′.

Abraham Clarke: (2) A chamber with a chimney and a kitchen adjoining with a chimney both 28′ × 20′ 9″; (3) A garret over the same, 29′ × 20′ 9″.

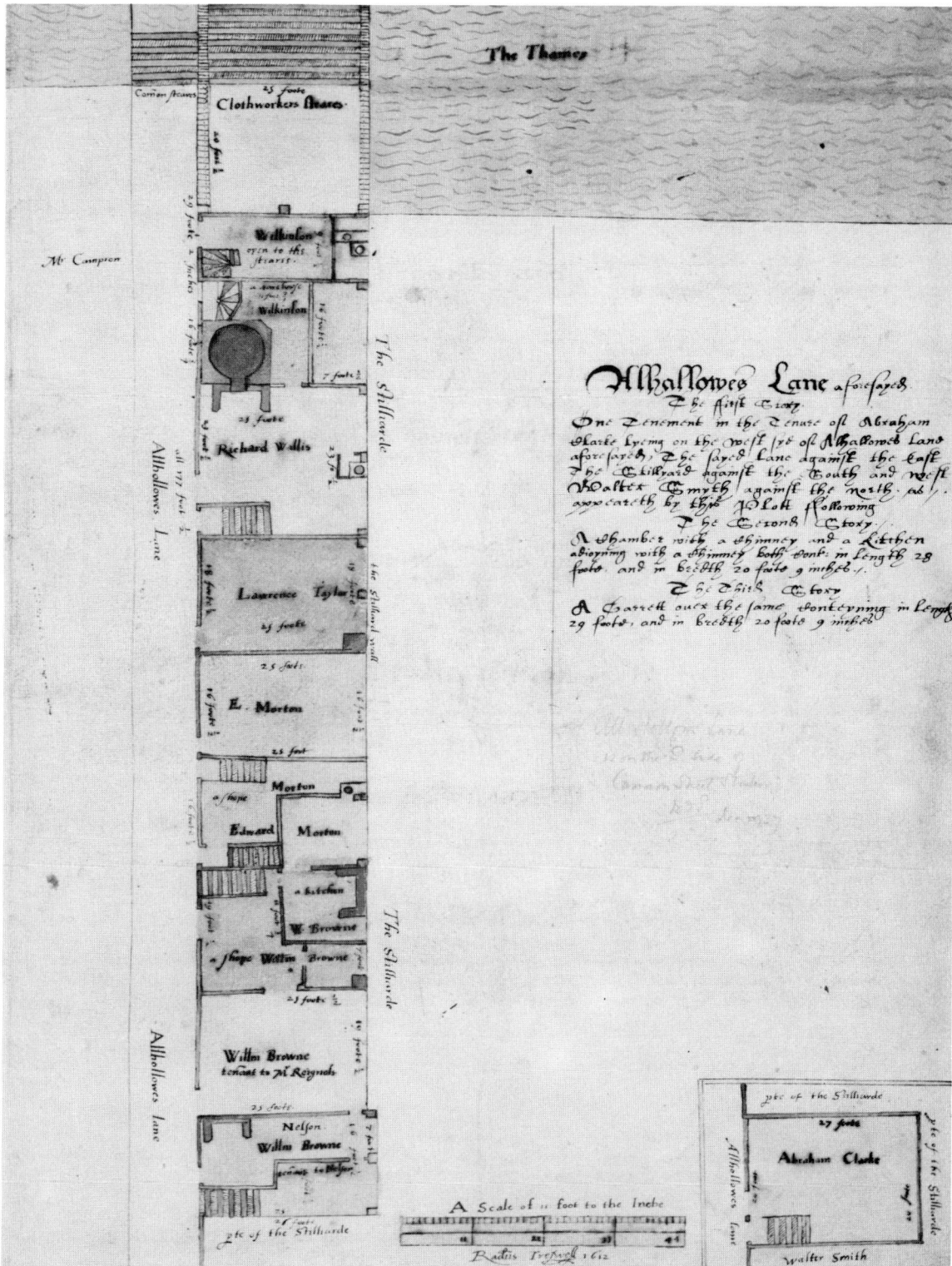

Figure 43. **39.** All Hallows Lane, [Upper] Thames Street (1:300). North is to the bottom of the plan.

40. Haywharf Lane, [Upper] Thames Street

Plan Book, 31

The medieval history of this prominent tenement, Sir John Pulteney's Coldharbour, has been elucidated by Vanessa Harding (1980). In the thirteenth century the property belonged to John de Gisors, one of the merchant oligarchs of the period (*ibid.*, 17). Pulteney, who was mayor four times, granted £80 rent from Coldharbour in 1347; he died in 1349. Thereafter the house went through a succession of aristocratic owners for a time; part was given to the adjacent church of All Hallows the Great to enlarge it and make a cemetery in 1398. From 1408 however it passed into industrial uses, including brewing; tenants (though not necessarily occupying the property) included a dyer, shearmen and a carpenter. In 1509 James Fynch granted the property to the Shearmen's Company, and the property thus became part of the Clothworkers' Company estate in 1528 (*ibid.*; CDW, 9). In 1509 the property included 36 tenants; in 1528 there were 30, some holding only a cellar or a garret (RW Accts). By 1553 however the rent was paid by three major tenants who sublet, and by 1560–1 only one major tenant, the Campion family, is named.

In 1537 the Company accounts mention 'bricking up of the whole of the Crane' (RW Accts). In the years 1553–7 the Company several times required the major tenant, Elizabeth Gates, to take down a rotten stable and hayloft (CCO 1536–1558, 252, 268, 275v).

Treswell surveyed 'the Brewhouse and two tenements sometime in twelve tenements' in 1612 (Fig. 44). The lane and its buildings were still in three tenancies, the major one of William Campion, Clothworker, and two subtenants, Atlee and Browne. Campion leased the adjoining property with its dyehouse in 1597 (Harding 1980, 15, 19), and Treswell notes 'Mr Campion's Brewhouse' on the next property to the W. Campion's buildings on the Clothworkers' property included a kitchen and boulting house, but they may be structurally incomplete on the plan, for the boundary to the W slices them off rather sharply. The text of reference describes this major building complex as of 3½ storeys, including a large parlour on the first floor; the ground-floor plan measurements suggest that a large timber-framed house comprised both E and W sides of the lane, and that all the major rooms lay on the first floor. To the N along the lane were seven small tenancies, of 2½ storeys.

Forming the E boundary of the whole long property lay the Common Sewer or Wolsey's Lane. This appears to have been, in 1612, a strip of ground rather than a channel; though it was crossed by walls and fences several times, and by privy buildings which blocked it twice. In 1569 Henry Campion was accused of having enclosed and stopped up a lane at Thames-side near Coldharbour with a brick wall, and the Chamberlain of the city was instructed to open it up and repair the stairs so that it could be a common lane as before (Repertory 16, 498; 17, 365) — evidently to no effect.

Below the text of reference, alongside the plan (but omitted from Fig. 44), is Treswell's record of a view of the property in July 1613 (i.e. exactly one year after the surveys had been conducted) by the Master and Wardens, Treswell, Thomas Haydon, carpenter, John Morgan, bricklayer, and others. The viewers noted that two plates engraved with the Clothworkers' name (*sic*, evidently not merely a badge) were set on the S waterside corners of the property; and they decided that four further plates should be set up to delineate the N bounds.

Text of reference, Plan Book (1612)

William Hunter, tenant to Mr Campion: (2) A chamber with a chimney on the N side 20½′ × 17′ with the stairs and study; (3) Another chamber divided into two parts 22½′ × 18½′, a half garret over the same.

William Hunter, one other tenement: (2) A chamber divided into two parts with two chimneys 20½′ × 17½′; (3) A chamber over the chamber aforesaid 20½′ × 17½′.

Raphe Whetenhall, tenant to Mr Campion: (2) A hall next Haywharf Lane and a chamber adjoining with a chimney, both 21′ 3″ × 20½′, one little chamber with a chimney adjoining 14½′ × 9½′; (3) Another chamber divided into three parts having one chimney all 23′ × 17½′, also one half garret over the same.

Raphe Whetenhall, one other tenement: (2) A chamber over the said lane 13½′ × 10½′; (3) Two chambers both 23′ × 17½′ with a chimney; also a half garret over the same.

William Bigges: (2) A chamber with a chimney 20′ E–W × 17′ with the stairs and chimney; (3) Another chamber divided into two parts 20′ × 17′; (4) A garret over the chamber aforesaid 20′ × 17′.

One other tenement wherein dwelleth diverse widows: (2) A chamber divided into diverse parcels wherein dwell diverse widows, 20′ × 17′; (3) Another chamber in two parts with two chimneys, 23′ × 17′, also a garret over the same with a chimney.

One other tenement: (2) A chamber divided into diverse parts 22½′ × 17′; (3) Two chambers with two chimneys 22½′ × 17′, also a half garret over the same of the like bigness.

One other tenement: (2) A chamber divided into two parts with a chimney 22½′ × 17½′; (3) Another chamber with a chimney 22½′ × 17½′.

Mr Campion: (2) On the W side, a study or chamber with a chimney [no measurements], a parlour with a chimney 21½′ × 14½′, a fair hall with a chimney 42½′ N–S × 14½′, another parlour over the way with a chimney 21′ × 15½′; on the E side, a fair parlour with a chimney from N 26′ × with the chimney 21½′, a buttery adjoining to the same 20½′ × 15′, a long loft or warehouse 54½′ × 23′; (3) On the W side, two chambers with two chimneys [together] 40′ × 23′, a fair chamber with a chimney 30′ × 17′, a gallery over part of the hall and over part of the parlour over the yard 30′ × 30′ at the E end and 11′ at the W end; on the E side, a loft or warehouse 54½′ × 21½′, a fair chamber over the Great Parlour aforesaid 27′ N–S × 22½′ E–W with the chimney; (4) On the E side, a long garret over the loft or warehouse aforesaid, two chambers with two chimneys [together] 30′ × 22′.

George Atlee, tenant to Mr Campion: (2) A hall and kitchen with two chimneys in them; (3) Two chambers with two chimneys in them; (4) A garret over the same.

John Browne, tenant to Mr Campion: (2) A hall and kitchen with a chimney 23½′ × 17′; (3) A chamber in three parcells with a chimney 23′ × 17′; (4) A garret over the same.

9

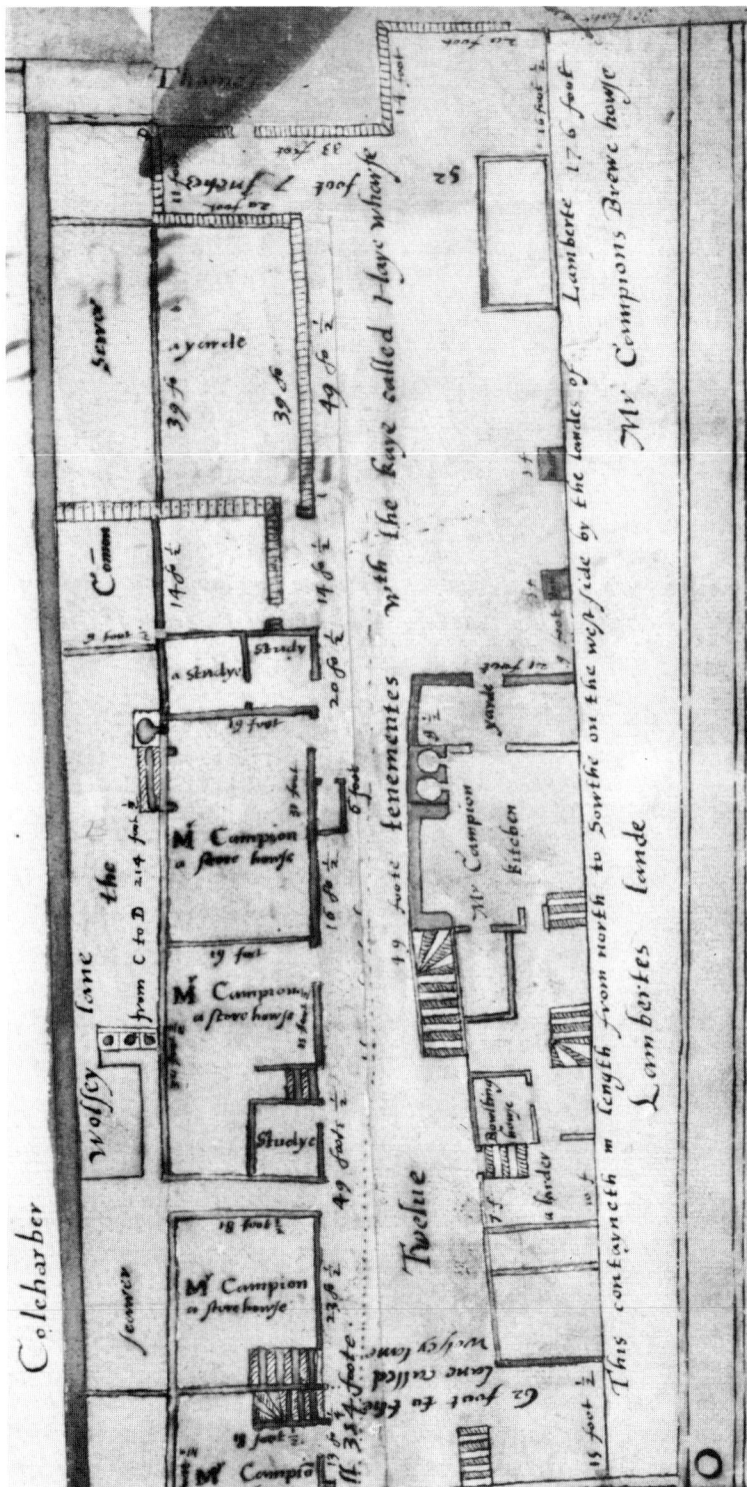

Figure 44. **40.** Haywharf, [Upper] Thames Street (1:300).
North is to the bottom of the plan.

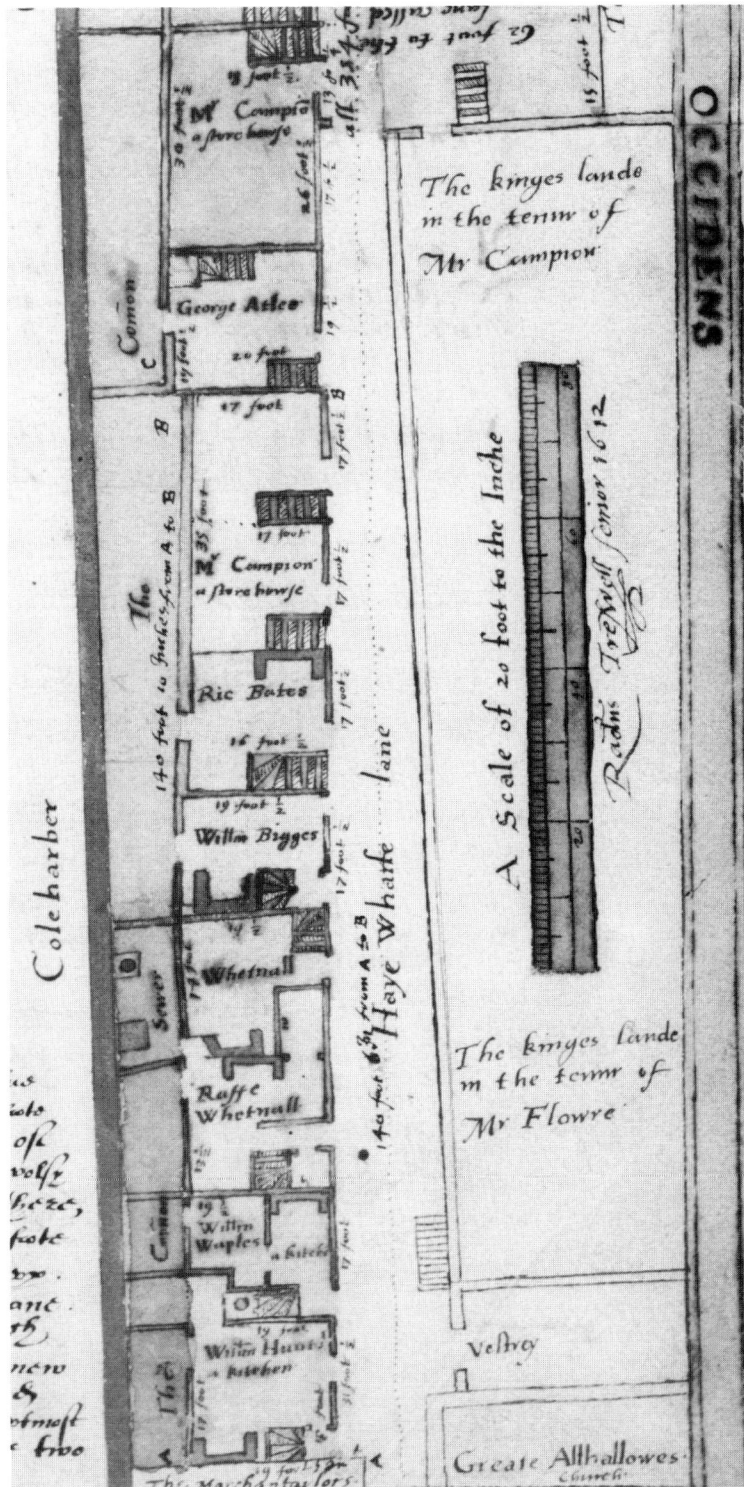

The kinges lande
in the tenw of
Mr Campion

OCCIDENS

A Scale of 20 foot to the Inche

Radus Treswell Senior 1612

The kinges lande
in the tenw of
Mr Flowre

Vestry

Greate Allhallowes
Church

Coleharber

Mr Campion
a storehouse

George Asten

Comon

The ... 140 foot to Inches from A to B

Mr Campion
a storehouse

Ric Bates

Willm Bigges

Sewer

Whetnall

Raffe
Whetnall

Willm
Waples

a kitch

Willm Hunte
a butcher

The Marchantaylors

Haye Wharfe lane

41. 174 [Upper] Thames Street

Evidence Book, 8

This small property on the N side of Thames Street was bequeathed to the Clothworkers' Company by William Frankland in 1574 (Hare 1860, 34). There are no pre-Fire deeds in the Company's possession.

By the time of Treswell's survey in 1612 (Fig. 45) there were two tenants; it is possible that the house had earlier been occupied by one. The building was of 2½ storeys, with a separate kitchen on the ground floor now used by one tenant only. No cellars are mentioned.

Text of reference, Plan Book (1612)

Widow Chapman, in the tenure of Christopher

Robotham: (2) A hall or chamber next the street, 15′ × 14½′ with the chimney and closet, a chamber over the coalhouse and kitchen 23′ × 14½′ with the chimney, 13½′ wide at the N; (3) A chamber or garret over the chamber aforesaid, 13½′ at the N end × 24½′, another garret next the street 15½′ × 14½′ with the chimney.

Widow Chapman, in the tenure of Ferdinando Boate: (2) A chamber next the street, 14′ × 13½′ with the chimney; one other room adjoining 12½′ with the stairs × 11½′ with the chimney; (3) Two garrets, one next the street with a chimney, both 29′ × 13½′.

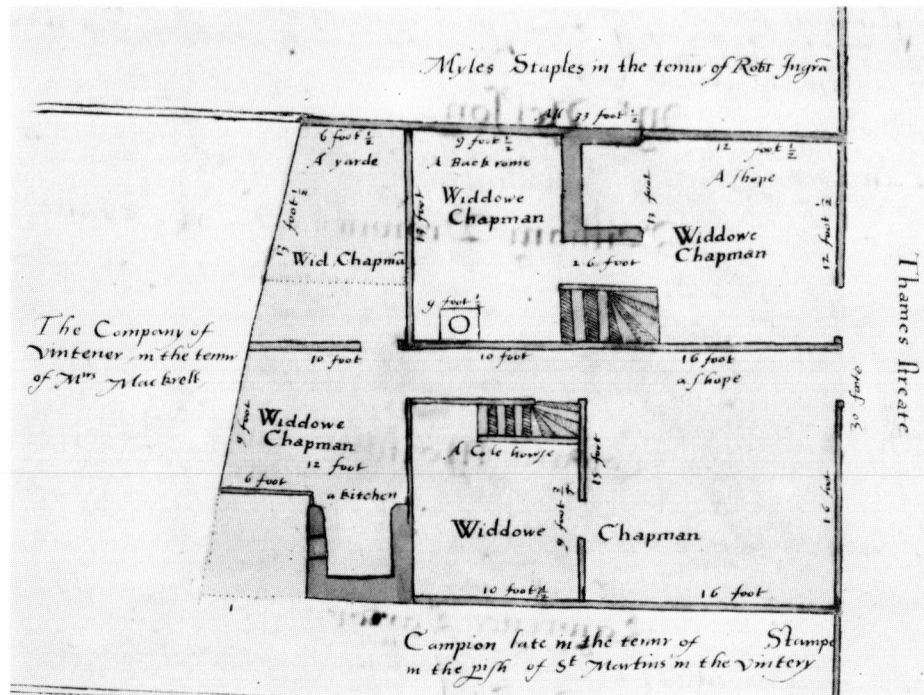

Figure 45. **41.** 174 [Upper] Thames Street (1:150). North is to the right of the plan.

42. 31–2 Throgmorton Street, 9–13 Copthall Court

Plan Book, 33–4; LTS Pubn 74 (vi) (1940)

Thomas Ormston, Clothworker, in 1556 bequeathed his property in Lothbury (the E part, later named Throgmorton Street) to the Clothworkers' Company on the death of his wife (*Charity Comm*, 218–9). The property does not appear in Company accounts until 1592–3, when it was let as a great house and four tenements (RW Accts).

Although obscured by recent expansion by the principal tenant (Fishburne), the arrangement shown in Treswell's survey of 1612 (Fig. 46) was a division of the site into two parts, E and W, shown clearest by the gardens. On the W lay a large house at the back of a small court entered from Throgmorton Street (Fishburne); the street range (Fishburne/Conyer and Cooke) was 3½ storeys high. The large house had a semi-octagonal baywindow facing the garden, and this continued up to the first floor (the 'round window'). A long gallery led towards the garden on the first floor, on the E side of the inner yard, from the chamber over the kitchen. The gallery seems to have ended at the N end, by the garden, in a baywindow. One feature of the street-range was unusual for a major street frontage: at the W end stairs led to the first-floor and higher chambers of Johnson, who had no ground-floor room (although he held the cellar beneath Fishburne's warehouse).

Along the E side of the great house, and entered by its own alley, was a row of three tenements with five tenants (Copthall Alley): two of the three ground-floor tenants (Curtis, Shirbrooke) had one room each, and the third (Martin) had in addition a first-floor room above his own, but without internal access to it. The first floor over the other tenants was occupied by two further tenants, Teder and Hall, each with a room and garret over, reached by a stair.

Text of reference, Plan Book (1612)

Richard Fishburne: (2) A chamber on the W side the yard or court from E to W with the chimney 12¾' × 25' N and S, one other chamber over the parlour from E to W 21' × 19½' N and S besides the round window and with the chimney, a chamber over the kitchen from E to W besides the entry between 13' × 19½' N and S with the chimney, also an entry out of the same in to the long gallery, which gallery from E to W 11' × 30' N and S beside the window, there is also an entry over part of the court; (3) A chamber on the W side the court from E to W with the chimney 13½' × 25' N and S, four garrets from E to W 37' × 19½' N and S, also garrets over the long gallery; (4) A garret over the chamber on the W side the court; A cellar under the building on the W side the court from E to W 10' × 55' N and S, one other cellar from E to W 9' × 14½' N and S.

Mr Fishburne, a tenement late Mr Colyer's: (2) A chamber next the street with a chimney from E to W 18' × 12½' N and S, a kitchen adjoining from E to E 11½' × 11½' N and S besides the chimney, also a little buttery adjoining the entry between, a chamber over the warehouse 18' × 18' besides the chimney; (3) A chamber next the street with a chimney, another room adjoining and another chamber adjoining the same, also a little room over the countinghouse, and another fair chamber with a chimney, all from N to S 48' × 19' from E to W; (4) Two garrets over all with a house of office in them with a door out into the leads; A cellar with a partition in the middle 46½' × 16'.

John Cooke: (2) A chamber next the street with a chimney and a kitchen adjoining with a chimney and oven both from E to W 20½' × 25' N and S; (3) A chamber next the street with a chimney with a chamber adjoining from E to W 20½' × 26' N and S; (4) A garret over all from E to W 18½' × 27' N and S; A cellar under all from E to W 11' × 19½' N and S.

Launcelott Johnson: (2) A hall next the street with a chimney and a kitchen adjoining with a chimney both from E to W 11' × 24½' N and S; (3) Two chambers one with a chimney from E to W 18½' × 25¾' N and S; (4) Two garrets over all 28' × 17½'; A cellar under Mr Fishburne's warehouse from E to W 17½' × 10½' N and S.

Copthall Alley, Throgmorton Street

Bartholomew Teder: (2) A chamber over Margarett Curtis from E to W with the chimney and oven 13½' × 21½' N and S; (3) a garret over the same of the like measure.

Widow Hall: (2) A chamber over Widow Shirbrook's chamber from E to W 12½′ × 18′ N and S with the chimney; (3) A garret over the same.

George Martin: (2) A chamber over his lower room with a chimney in it.

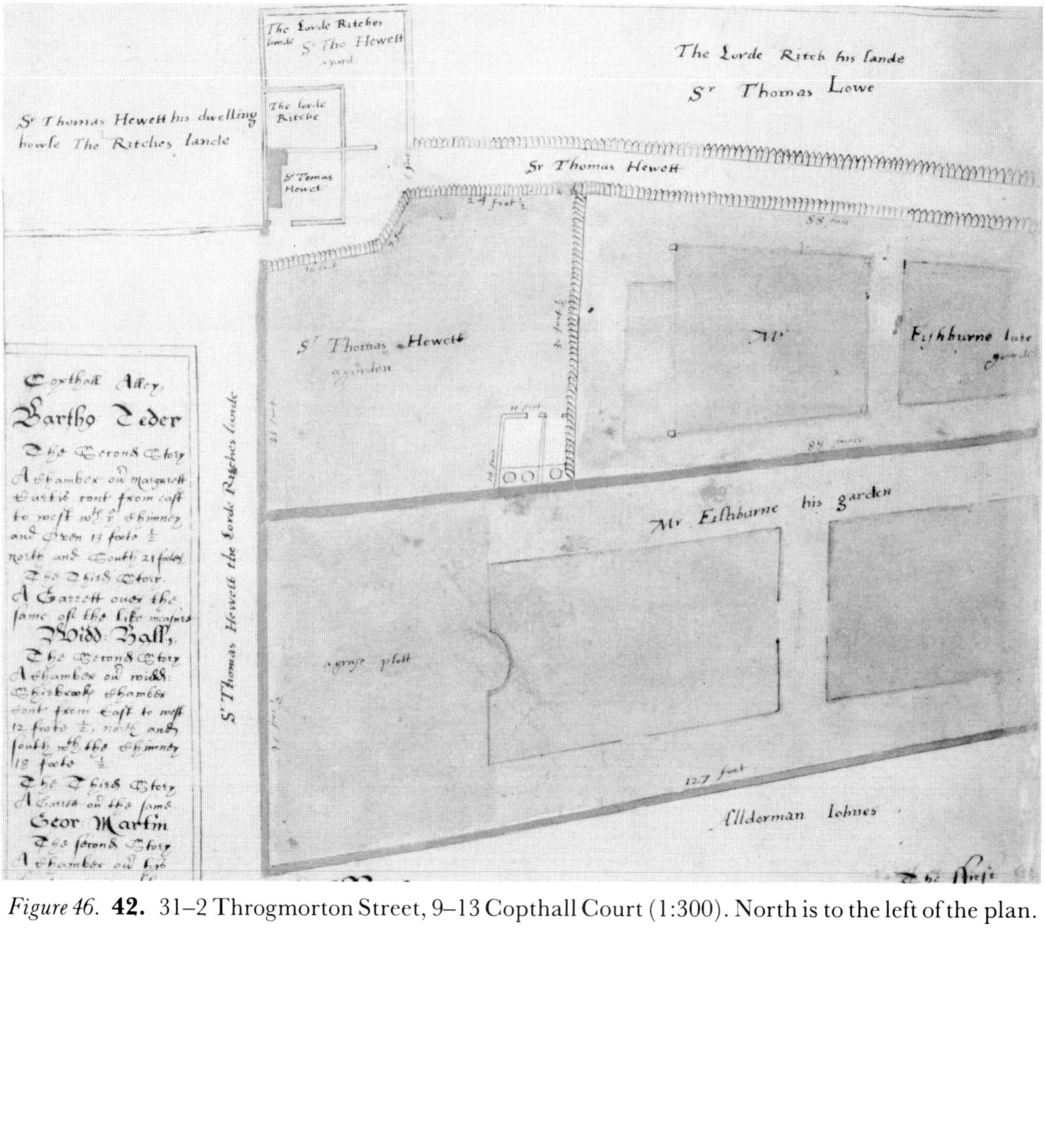

Figure 46. **42.** 31–2 Throgmorton Street, 9–13 Copthall Court (1:300). North is to the left of the plan.

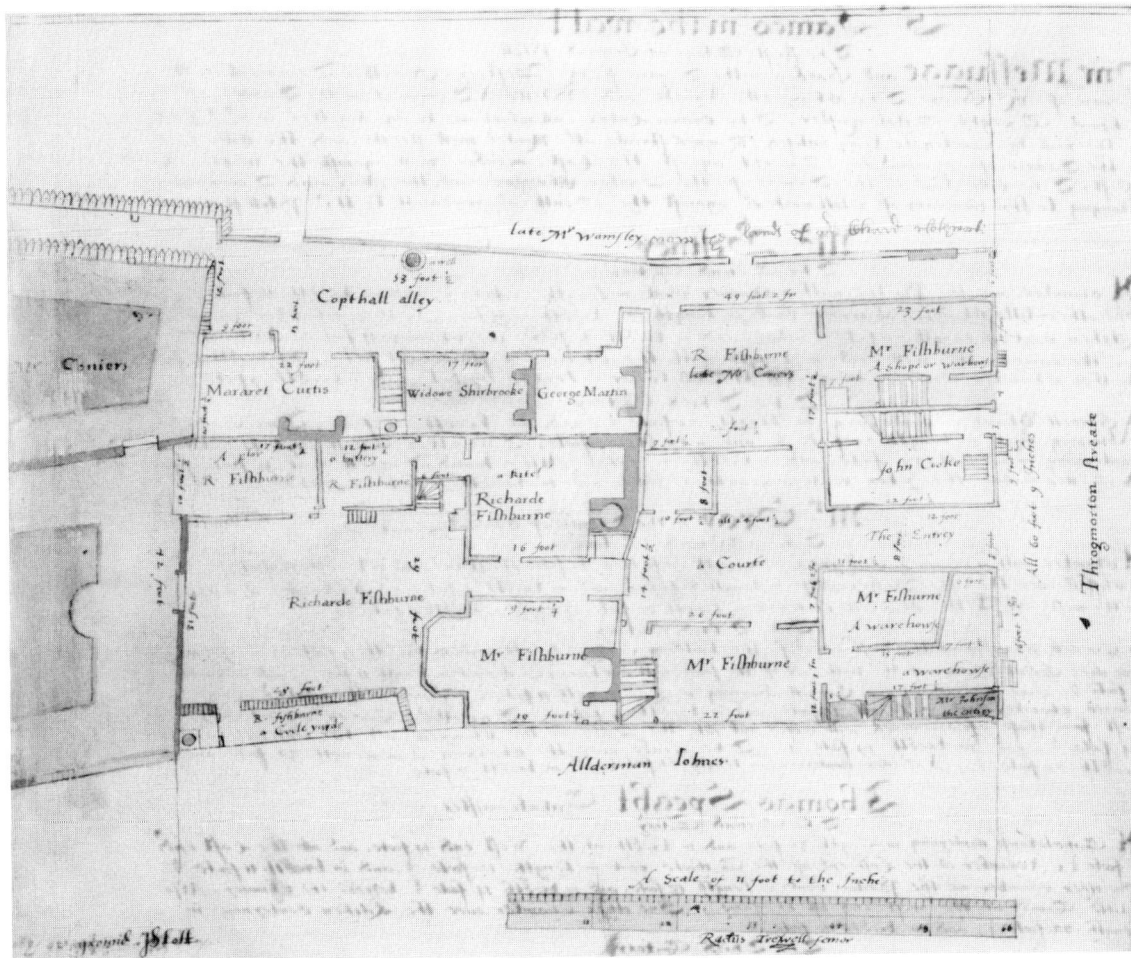

43. 21–2 Trinity Lane (formerly Knightrider Street)

Evidence Book, 9; Schofield 1983, Fig. 44

In 1553 Nicholas Bristowe and Lucy his wife granted one large messuage called the White Hart in Knightrider Street to Henry Roberts, brewer; Roberts leased it for twenty-one years to John Jackson, found (*Inq PM*, ii, 68–9). In 1563 Roberts demised the property to Jackson and Andrew Palmer, goldsmith, for their lives, with reversion to his own heirs (*ibid.*); at this time the White Hart was described as three messuages (i.e. it had been subdivided). Under Roberts' will of 1566 his widow Elizabeth took possession of the property (*op. cit.*, 70). In 1589 the owner of the White Hart, then a brewhouse, was Thomas Haselwoode, brewer; two tenants, Robert Cawsey and James Alcocke, were named (*op. cit.*, iii, 131).

William Mascall, mercer, by his will of 11 September 1608 gave £160 to Christ's Hospital, out of which the hospital appears to have bought the property shown in Treswell's survey, though no deeds showing the actual investment of the money survive. These houses were however in the possession of the hospital in 1605, before the gift, and it is possible that the governors 'decided to appropriate them as an investment of Mascall's gift, or rather as a security for the performance of his intention' (*Charity Comm*, 109).

The houses were 3½ storeys high. On the first floor of Abraham Fryth's tenancy, part of the floor was open to give light to the drinking rooms on the ground floor below; perhaps this was some form of gallery. The stone walls, two of which are (uniquely in the surveys) back-to-back, seem to comprise the relics of a medieval stone house. In the tenancy of Thomas Alcocke (presumably a relation of the James Alcocke recorded in 1589) are shown pipes for two privies on upper floors, passing behind the ground-floor privy to the pit below.

Text of reference, Evidence Book (1611)

Abraham Fryth: [2] A chamber or room with a chimney 19½′ long besides the stone wall on the W side which is 2′ thick and the paper wall on the

E side and part of this room is open on the floor to give light; One other room with a chimney and the funnel of the kitchen chimney 20′ × 13′ with a house of office 6′ × 3′ at the one end and × 4′ at the other with a shed next the same 8′ × 7′; [3] A chamber with a chimney 14′ × 12′ with a study 7′ × 3½′, some part lying on the stone wall next the gate, one other chamber with a chimney besides the passage 14½′ × 12½′, one other chamber with a chimney 11½′ × 11′; [4] A garret with a chimney 19½′ × 12′, a garret next the street 14½′ × 13½′ and [a garret?] 20½′ × 13½′; A cellar N–S 49½′ × 17½′ at the S end × 25½′ at the N end with a corner.

Thomas Alcoke: [2] A hall with stairs and chimney 14½′ × 14½; one other room next the hall 16′ × 8′, with the chimney, stairs and study; [3] One other chamber over the hall 16′ with stairs × 14½′ with a chimney; [4] One garret above all 16′ × 14′; Also a cellar 11½′ × 10′.

Thomas Alcocke in the occupation of George Eakines: [2] A hall over the shop 16′ with chimney and stairs × 14½′, one other chamber 12½′ × 8′, a kitchen with a chimney 15½′ × 8′; [3] One other chamber over the chamber over the chamber before (*sic*) 16½′ with stairs and chimney × 15½′; [4] A garret over the chamber before 16′ × 15′; Also a cellar under the shop with a trap door 14½′ × 11½′, with a little nook under the stairs.

Robert Rowse: [2] A hall over the shop 15½′ with stairs and chimney × 14½′, one other room with a funnel of a privy out of the room above 15½′ × 10½′, a kitchen on the S side with stairs into the garret 15½′ on the E side to the stone wall 13½′ on the N side 15½′; [3] A garret over his house divided into several partitions with a stone wall.

Thomas Chilton: [2] A chamber the W side in 1. with two pairs of stairs 17′ besides the chimney, and in b. on the S side, E and W in part 8′, one other chamber over West's shop 11′ × 10½′ with stairs up; [3] A chamber over the other with chimney and stairs 19′ × 11½′, at the N end of the chamber 8½′, then on the E side 6½′, the turning 2½′, the rest of the E side 11½′, this room hath a privy in it; [4] A garret 19½′ × 11½′, also a chamber over his hall 16½′ × 11½′, then a little room over Rowse's hall 8½′ × 5′.

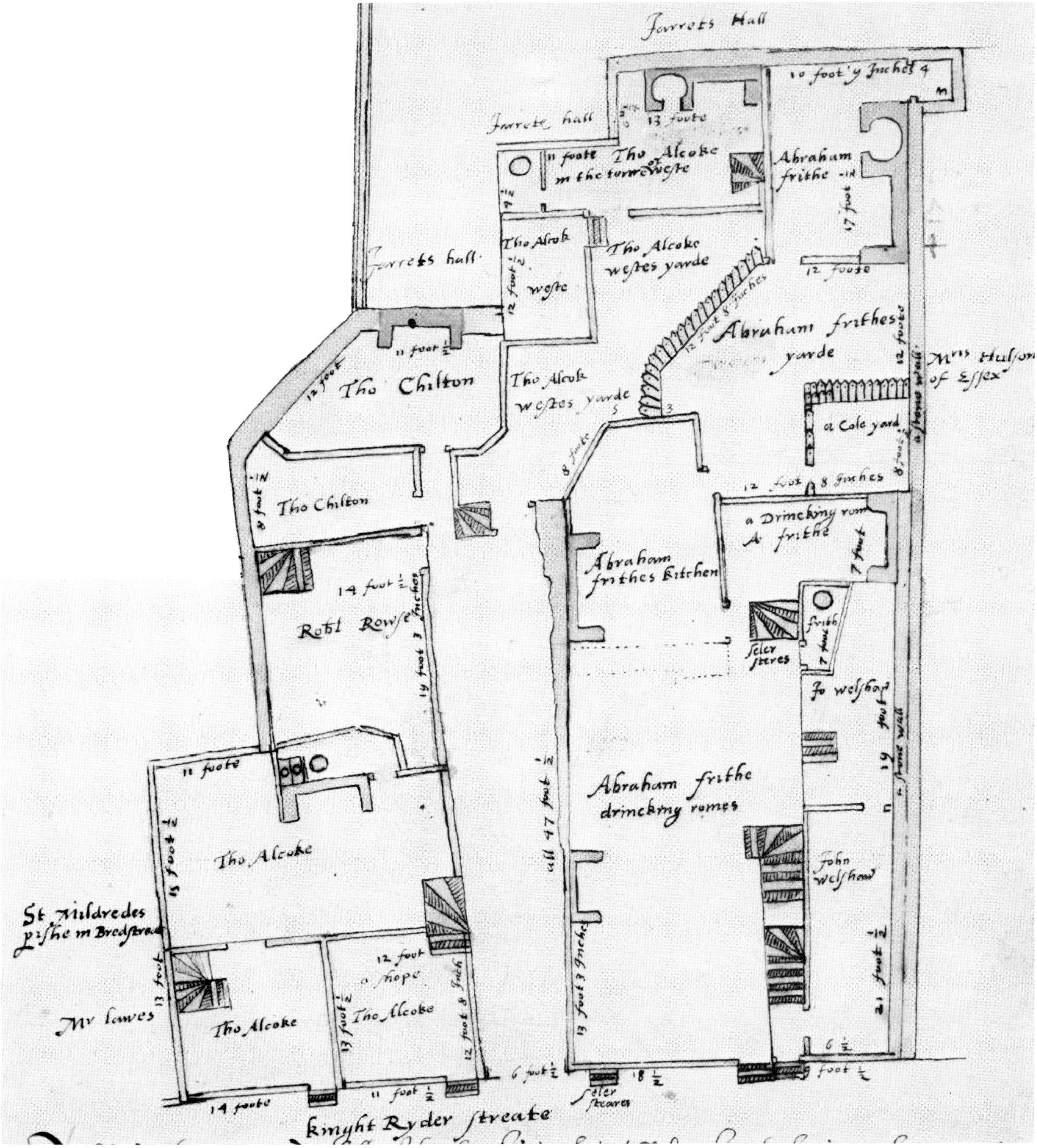

Jarrets Hall

Jarrete hall

Jarrets hall.

10 foot 'y Inches 4

5 ⁰/₀ 13 foote

11 foote Tho Alcoke in the torne weste

Abraham frithe

7 ¹/₄

Tho Alcok weste

Tho Alcoke westes yarde

17 foot

12 foot ¹/₂

12 foote

12 foot 8 Inches

Abraham frithes yarde

Mrs Hulson of Essex

12 foote

a stone wall

11 foot ¹/₂

12 foot

Tho Chilton

Tho Alcok westes yarde

a Cole yard

12 foot 8 Inches

8 foote

5

3

8 foote

a Drincking rom A· frithe

8 foot

9 foot

Tho Chilton

Abraham frithes kitchen

7 foot

14 foot ¹/₂

Robt Rowse

14 foot 3 Inches

frith

7 foot

seler steres

Jo welshod

11 foote

all 47 foot ¹/₂

13 foot 3 Inches

Abraham frithe drincking romes

14 foot ¹/₂

a stone wall

Tho Alcoke

13 foot ¹/₂

John welshod

St Mildredes prishe in Bredstreat

Mr lawes

13 foot

12 foot a shope

12 foot 8 Inch

21 foot ¹/₂

Tho Alcoke

13 foot ¹/₂

Tho Alcoke

6 ¹/₂ foot ¹/₂

14 foote

11 foot ¹/₂

6 foot ¹/₂

18 ¹/₂

seler steares

knyght Ryder streate

Figure 47. **43.** 21–2 Trinity Lane (formerly Knightrider Street) (1:150). North is to the top of the plan.

Thomas Alcock in the occupation of West: [2] A chamber over Frythe's kitchen with stairs and chimney 14½' × 11½', a chamber 20' × in b. at the W end 7' 9" with a chimney; [3] Two garrets with stairs and chimney 26' × 12', also at the NW corner of one of these garrets is a corner 5' one way and 7' another way being no part of this house but supposed to be of Jarrards Hall; A cellar under the shop with a privy in it 14½' × 7'.

John Welshaw: [2] A chamber 12½' × 9½' with a chimney and stairs, a chamber or a kitchen with a chimney 15' × 8' 3", a chamber 8½' × 8½', note that all the E side of this house standeth on a stone wall, next to a stone wall belonging to the said parish [Holy Trinity the Less]; ?[3] A chamber next the street with chimney and study 14½' × 12½', a chamber 12' × 8'; ?[4] A chamber 12' long, at the S end 7' 10", at the N end 5½'; ?[5] A garret next the street 14½' × 11½', a garret 8½' × 15½'.

44. Countess of Kent's almshouses, later 28–30 Tudor Street

Plan Book, 33

Margaret, Countess of Kent, built a row of five timber-framed almshouses on the site of a garden within the Whitefriars' precinct shortly before 1538, when she entrusted them to the Cloth-workers' Company as part of an endowment of property (see also the Tennis Place, Fen-church St, **21**). This was confirmed in her will of 1540 (CDW).

The almshouses comprised ten single rooms, five on the ground floor and five on the first floor, reached by a stair at one end and a long gallery (Fig. 48). The ground-floor chambers varied slightly in size around 13′ square; the chambers above were of similar dimensions. All had indi-vidual chimneys and houses of office. The tenants comprised seven old women and the Countess's porter in the 1540s (e.g. RW Accts 1543–4), but in 1612 there was a full complement of ten women whose names are given below the plan in the Plan Book.

Text of reference, Plan Book (1612)

[the tenants are listed below the text, but not assigned to individual rooms in the survey]

First house: (2) A chamber part over the entry and over the first chamber on the ground 18½′ E–W × 13½′ N–S with the chimney and the house of office.

Second house: (2) A chamber over the second cham-ber on the ground 15′ E–W × 13′ N–S with the chimney and house of office.

Third house: (2) A chamber over the third chamber on the ground 12½′ E–W × 12½′ N–S with the chimney and the house of office.

Fourth house: (2) A chamber over the fourth cham-ber on the ground 12½′ E–W × 22½′ N–S with the chimney and the house of office.

Fifth house: (2) A chamber over the furthest cham-ber on the ground eastwards 14½′ E–W × 12½′ N–S with the chimney and the house of office.

All which five chambers in the second storey have a long gallery leading into them all which gallery is jettied over into their yard [3½′] [scratched with the pen, but not inked].

Hereafter followeth the names of those poor people now dwelling in the Almeshouses in Whitefriars aforesaid:

In the first storey [i.e. ground floor]
Katherine Greene widow aged 71
Agnes Skinner widow aged 78
Elizabeth Midleton widow aged 83
Elizabeth Leighton widow aged 80
Agnes Pilsworth widow aged 97

In the second storey [i.e. first floor]
Suzan Hill widow aged 50 years
Robert Johnson porter aged 86 years
Margaret Williams widow aged 72
Margaret Tompkin widow aged 61
Agnes Akerland widow aged 65 years.

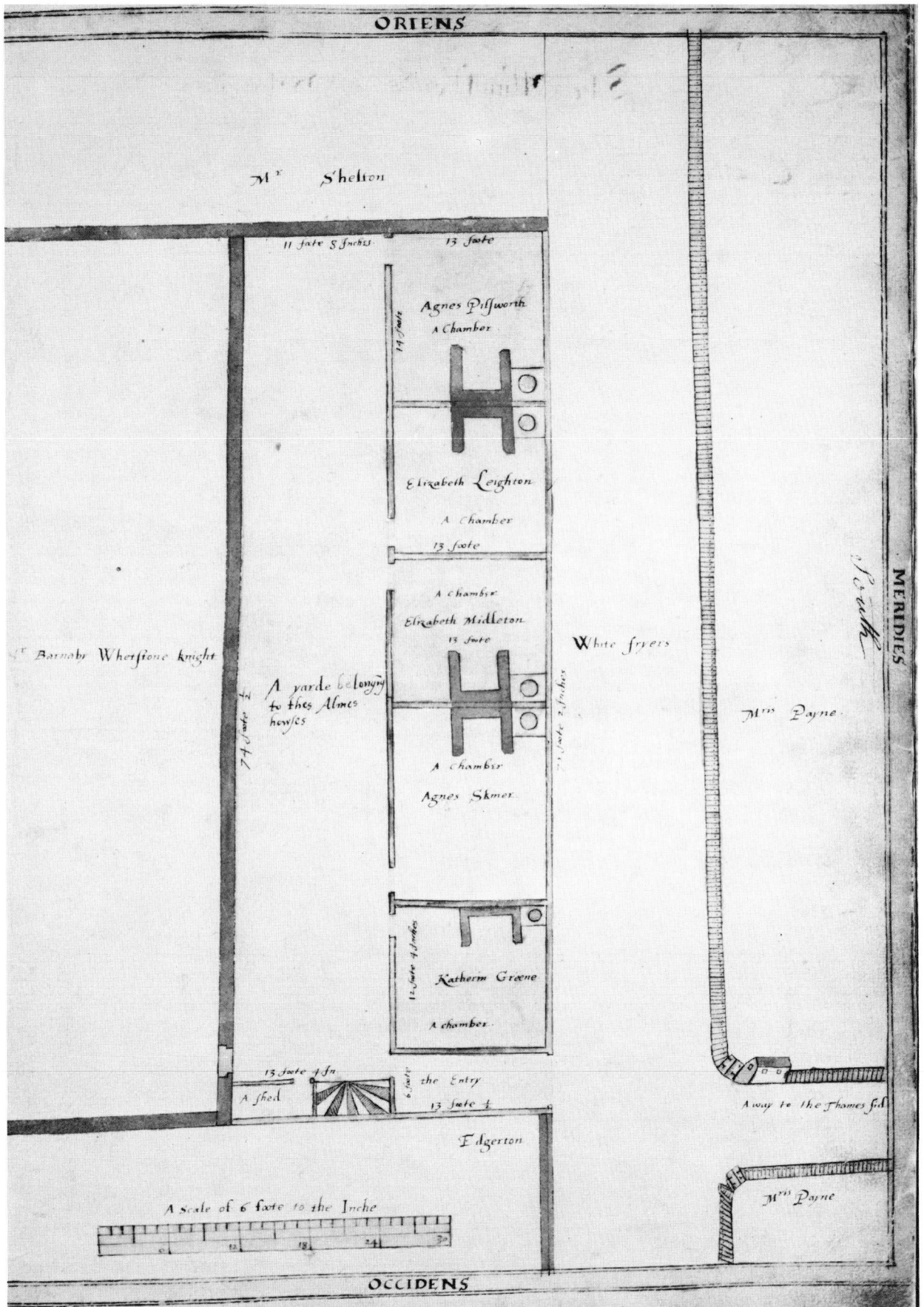

ORIENS

MERIDIES

OCCIDENS

Mr Shelton

11 fate 5 Inches   13 fote

14 fote

Agnes Pilfworth

A Chamber

Elizabeth Leighton

A Chamber

13 fote

A chambr

Elizabeth Midleton

13 fote

White fryers

Mr Barnaby Wherfftone knight

7 fote ½

A yarde belonging
to thes Almes
howfes

7 fote 2 Inches

Mrs Payne

A chambr

Agnes Skiner

South

12 fote 4 Inches

Katherin Greene

A chamber

13 fote 4 In

A fhed

6 fote   the Entry

13 fote ½

A way to the Thames fid

Edgerton

A Scale of 6 fote to the Inche

Mrs Payne

Figure 48. **44.** Countess of Kent's almshouses, later 28–30 Tudor Street (1:150). North is to the left of the plan.

45. Walbrook and Bucklersbury (4–5 Woolchurch Haw)

Plan Book, 25

The detailed history of this site from the early fourteenth century has been traced in *HG 3*, site **118/14**. The property was granted to the Clothworkers' Company by the will of John Rogers, clothworker, in 1558, when it comprised four old houses (CDW, 77–86). By 1571 it comprised three tenements; and in the text of reference of the Treswell plan of 1612, they are called 'those two tenements sometimes three and now one'. The structure reflected the three-part division, with three street doors; but Treswell notes only one tenant. A structural division is present between the shop on the S and the other two units to the N, presumably reflecting the time when the three parts were only two.

Text of reference, Plan Book (1612)

Johanne Ward: (2) A hall or chamber at the N end, 14½' E–W × 17' N–S with the chimney, a chamber adjoining 16½' N–S with the chimney, 15' E–W besides a buttery over the oven, a parlour and kitchen with two chimneys 17½' E–W × 16½' N–S; (3) A chamber at the N end 15' E–W × 16½' N–S with the chimney, one chamber adjoining 15' E–W × 17½' N–S with the chimney and the closet, a chamber over the parlour and kitchen 18½' E–W × 17½' N–S; (4) Three garrets over all with a chimney at the S end, 51½' × 14½'; A cellar under the N end 11½' E–W, 15½' N–S, another cellar adjoining 11' E–W × 15½' N–S, another cellar at the S end 12' E–W × 16' 3" N–S.

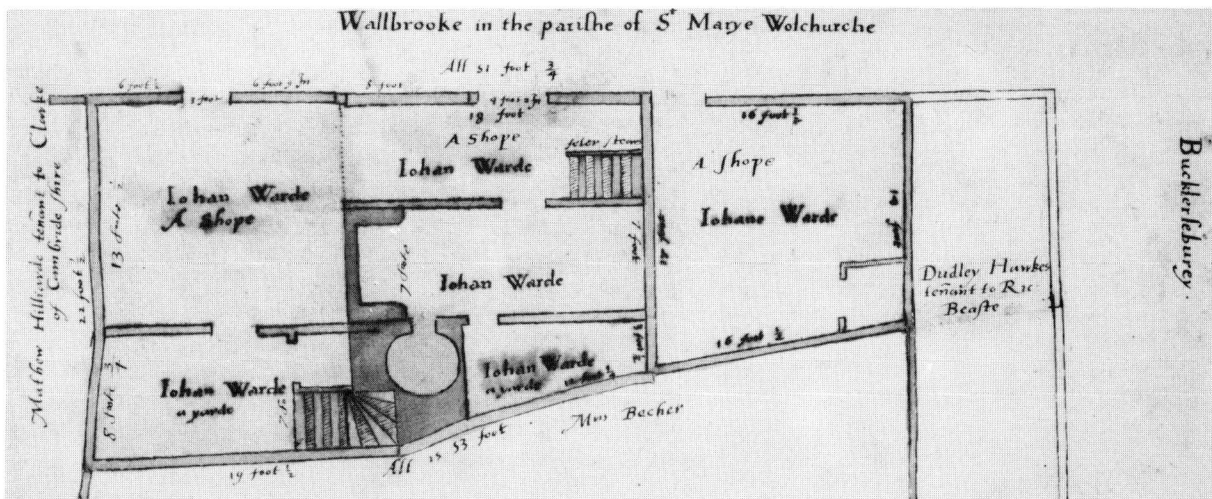

Figure 49. **45.** Walbrook/Bucklersbury (4–5 Woolchurch Haw) (1:150). North is to the left of the plan.

46. 90–4 West Smithfield, 28–30 Cow Lane

Plan Book, 41

In 1536 Thomas Cutbert, barber, brother and heir of Robert Cutbert, granted the Maidenhead in Cow Lane to Edward Barbour, Katherine his wife and others. In 1558 John Essex and Kathleen his wife, formerly wife of Edward Barbour, leased the Maidenhead and three tenements in West Smithfield to John Stevyns; in the same year however the property was leased to William Heron, woolmonger. By his will of 1580 Heron bequeathed the lands to the Clothworkers' Company. In 1603 the Company leased them to John Walker on condition that he rebuild four small tenements on the S side, between Smithfield and the entry to the Maidenhead, which his will of 1609 records he did at an expense of £200 (all deeds in CD Box 52).

When surveyed by Treswell in 1612, the Heron estate comprised five large two-room plan houses facing Smithfield, all with prominent chimneys and ovens, the four tenements rebuilt by Walker on the Cow Lane frontage and the Maidenhead, then called Pheasant Court. Presumably the Maidenhead had been a hostelry; by 1612 it was certainly divided into a number of individual tenancies, some of them single chambers. Ten tenants had ground-floor rooms; seven of these had upper chambers also. Subtenants were of two kinds: Edward Lee, who apparently lived ('dwelleth') in a cellar with a chimney beneath the tenancies of Hill and Pott, and two widows, Howell and Lee, who each had a first-floor chamber over Procter's tenancy.

The building forming the tenancies of Ashpoole and Procter is interesting as being of lobby-entrance plan, a form otherwise found only in the more open, outlying parts of the city (see **13**).

Text of reference, Plan Book (1612)

Edward Drewery: (2) A hall and a chamber, together 17½′ × 15½′ with a little buttery adjoining, a chamber over the kitchen 20½′ with the passage and the chimney × 12½′, also a little room at the W end of the same chamber 8′ square; (3) A chamber over the hall, of the same size, a garret backwards; (4) A garret over the previous chamber, 20½′ × 14½′; A cellar under the kitchen, 11½′ × 11′.

Christopher Askwith: (2) A chamber with a window jettied out towards the Pennes, 17½′ × 15½′ with the chimney; A chamber backward and adjoining 21½′ with the passage and jettied window × 12½′ with the chimney; (3) A chamber 19′ with a jettied window × 15½′ with the chimney, another chamber 22′ × 12½′ with the chimney; (4) Two garrets; A cellar under the shop, 14½′ square, an adjoining cellar 11′ × 8½′, and a cellar under the kitchen, 11½′ × 10′.

Christopher Askwith, in the tenure of George Shelton: (2) A chamber next the Pennes 22½′ with the chimney × 10½′, another chamber adjoining over the kitchen 16½′ with the chimney × 13′; (3) A garret over the last mentioned; A cellar backward, 11½′ × 10′.

Christopher Askwith, in the tenure of Thomas Wescott: (2) A chamber over the shop with a chimney, 22½′ × 10½′, another chamber over the kitchen, 16½′ with the chimney × 13′; (3) A garret over the last mentioned chamber; A cellar backwards, 12′ × 10′.

Peter Clarke: (2) A chamber next the street, 18½′ × 17′ besides the chimney, a chamber over the kitchen, and a chamber over the back room 15′ with the chimney × 13′; (3) A chamber with a chimney, divided, and a garret under the back room; (4) A garret next West Smithfield with a chimney; A cellar under the shop 16½′ × 14½′, and a 'long slype' W out of the cellar, 20′ long.

Robert Seger: (2) A hall 17½′ × 15½′ with a chimney; (3) A chamber with a chimney 17½′ × 16′; (4) Two garrets, together 17½′ square; A cellar as a kitchen with a chimney 13½′ × 12′ 9″, and a house of office under the stairs.

Tobias Harvist: (2) A chamber 21′ × 12′ besides chimney and the stairs; (3) A chamber with a chimney of the same size; (4) A garret; A cellar 17½′ × 16′.

Thomas Brettnor: (2) A hall 18′ × 15½′ with a chimney, a little chamber over the kitchen, 10′ 8″ × 7½′; (3) A chamber with a chimney 19′ × 15½′, a little chamber at the N end; (4) A garret, with a little room at the N end with a chimney, 26′ × 15½′ and a house of office in it.

Blewbore Alley

Mr Webster

Samson Pott
George Backhows
Charles Hill
Willm Ashpoole A chamber
Willm Procter A Chamber
Richard Lightburne
Richard Andrewe
Henrey Perkins A Shope
Thomas Anderson A Shope
Nic Ashley A chamber

Phesante courte
Phesant courte
Phesant courte

Edward Drewry A stable or shed
E. Drewry
E. Drewry A kitchen
Edwarde Drewry A shope
E. Drewry A yard
E. Drewry A yard
E. Drewry

Christopher Askwith A kitchin
Christopher Askwith A Shope
A shed Shelston
G. Shelstone
George Shelstone
George Shelstone A shops

Tho Welcott A yard
a shed
Peter Clarke
Tho Welcott kitchen
Thomas Welcote A shope
Peter Clarke A kitchen
Peter Clarke A shope

Willm Haslome
a shops
Tho Brettnor
Tho Brettner
a kitchen
John Showell
Tho Brettna A shope
Tho Breckna
Tobias Harvile A shope
A shope
Robert Seger
A shope

The Parish land belonging to St Mary Overy now in the tenure of Henry Perkins All is 406 foote

All is 30 foote
All is 85 foote
All is 86 foote

Cowe lane
Cow lane
Cowe lane
Smithfielde penes

A Scale of 5 foot to the Inche

Radus Treswell senior 1612

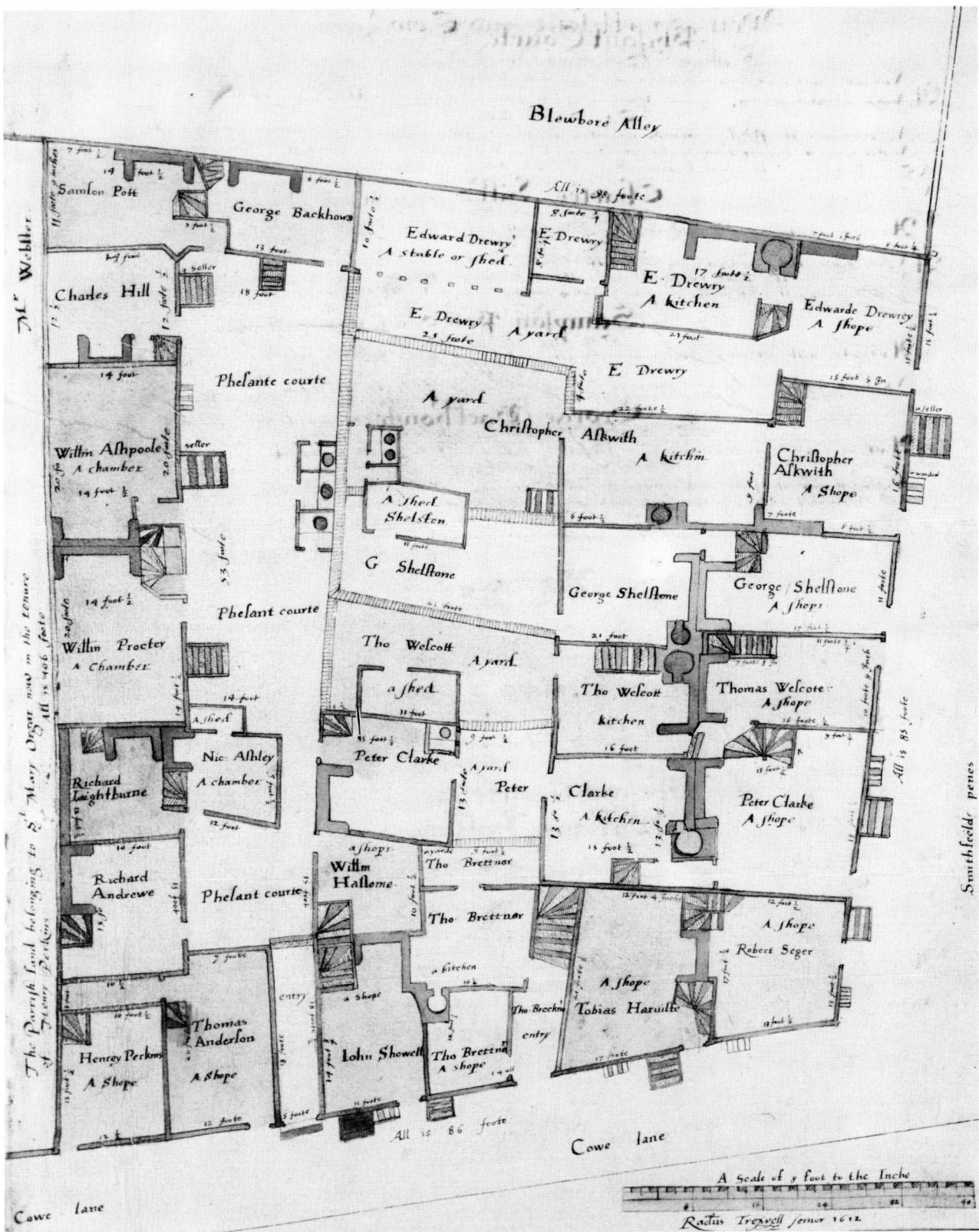

Figure 50. **46.** 90–4 West Smithfield, 28–30 Cow Lane (1:200). North is to the top of the plan. *See also Plate 5.*

John Showell: (2) A chamber 19' with the chimney × 15'; (3) A chamber with a chimney 20' × 16'; (4) A garret with a chimney 21' × 16½'; A cellar 16½' × 15' with a house of office in it.

Thomas Anderson: (2) A chamber 16½' × 12½' with a chimney; (3) A garret 16½' × 12½'.

Henry Perkins: (2) A chamber 16½' × 13' with a chimney; (3) A garret 16½' × 12'.

Pheasant Court

William Haslom: (2) A chamber 12' × 10½' with a chimney; (3) A garret with a chimney.

Richard Andrews: (2) A chamber 16' × 15' with a chimney; (3) A garret 16' × 15' with a chimney.

Richard Lightburne: (2) A chamber 13' square with a chimney; (3) A garret of the same size.

Nicholas Ashley: (2) A chamber with a chimney; (3) A garret with a chimney. Over Proctor's, Widdow Howell: (2) A chamber; Over Ashpoole's, Widdow Lee: (2) A chamber; (3) A garret 17' with a chimney × 15½', a garret adjoining 19½' with the chimney × 16'; Two cellars under the same building, one in the tenure of John Crippes.

Hill: (2) A chamber 15' × 12½' with a chimney; (3) A garret 16' × 12½' with a chimney; A cellar under this and Samson Pott, 22½' with a chimney × 13', wherein dwelleth Edward Lee.

Pott: (2) A chamber with a chimney 17½' × 10½; (3) A garret 18½' × 11½' with a chimney.

Backhouse: (2) A chamber with a chimney 15½' × 12¼'; (3) A garret 18¼' × 12¼'; A cellar 8' square.

47. 77 Wood Street

Plan Book, 43

Two houses on this property are first mentioned in 1364, when John, son of John Casewell, fishmonger, granted them to Robert de Esse (CD Box 56); in 1520 the property was bought by the Shearmen's Company from two shearmen, William Estwyk and John Olyver, and a merchant tailor. The houses became part of the Clothworkers' estate when the Shearmen and the Fullers united to form the Clothworkers' Company in 1528. During the sixteenth century the property was divided between two tenants; by 1612 (Fig. 51) there were four tenancies, respectively $2\frac{1}{2}$, $4\frac{1}{2}$, $4\frac{1}{2}$ and $3\frac{1}{2}$ storeys high on cellars.

The 'Callendring House' at the rear of the Talbot is the only clear example of industrial premises attached to the houses belonging to the Clothworkers' Company. The Calender was a large wooden box filled with stones cemented together, weighing 10 tons or more, which pressed finished cloths by rolling over two rollers on a table (Singer *et al.* 1957, 177–8). It was moved backwards and forwards by means of ropes winding on a shaft turned by a horse-gin or treadmill; in this case apparently by horse-power.

Text of reference, Plan Book (1612)

John Beaumond: (2) A chamber next the street $14\frac{1}{2}'$ E–W × $12\frac{1}{2}'$ N–S with the chimney, besides the passage and house of office, one other chamber $12\frac{1}{2}'$ N–S × 11' E–W; (3) A garret next the street $16\frac{1}{2}'$ E–W × $12\frac{1}{2}'$ N–S, another garret 18' E–W × 12' N–S.

Frauncis Wright, 2 tenements now divided into three: [a] (2) A chamber or hall over the shop and entry 18' 4″ with the chimney × $12\frac{1}{2}'$; (3) A chamber over the hall aforesaid $19\frac{1}{2}'$ with the chimney × 12' at the E, 13' at the W ends; (4) Another chamber $19\frac{1}{2}'$ with the stairs and chimney × 13'; (5) A garret over the chamber aforesaid; A cellar under the shop.

[b] (2) A hall over the kitchen with a chimney 14' × $13\frac{1}{2}'$; (3) A chamber over the hall with a chimney 14' × $13\frac{1}{2}'$; (4) Another chamber with a chimney of the same bigness; (5) A garret over the chamber aforesaid; A cellar under the kitchen.

[c] The Talbot (2) A kitchen with a chimney over the horseplace $16\frac{1}{4}'$ × $13\frac{1}{2}'$, a hall adjoining over part of the Callendring House with a chimney 17' × 14', a chamber adjoining with a chimney and buttery $17\frac{1}{2}'$ × 13', a buttery over the stairs and the Goldsmiths' wall 6' × 6'; (3) A chamber over the kitchen with a chimney $14\frac{1}{2}'$ × $13\frac{1}{2}'$, another chamber adjoining $17\frac{1}{2}'$ × $12\frac{1}{2}'$ with a study in it, another chamber adjoining $17\frac{1}{2}'$ × $12\frac{1}{2}'$ with a chimney; (4) A garret $18\frac{1}{2}'$ × $12\frac{1}{2}'$; A cellar under the Callendring House arched with brick 16' × $15\frac{1}{4}'$.

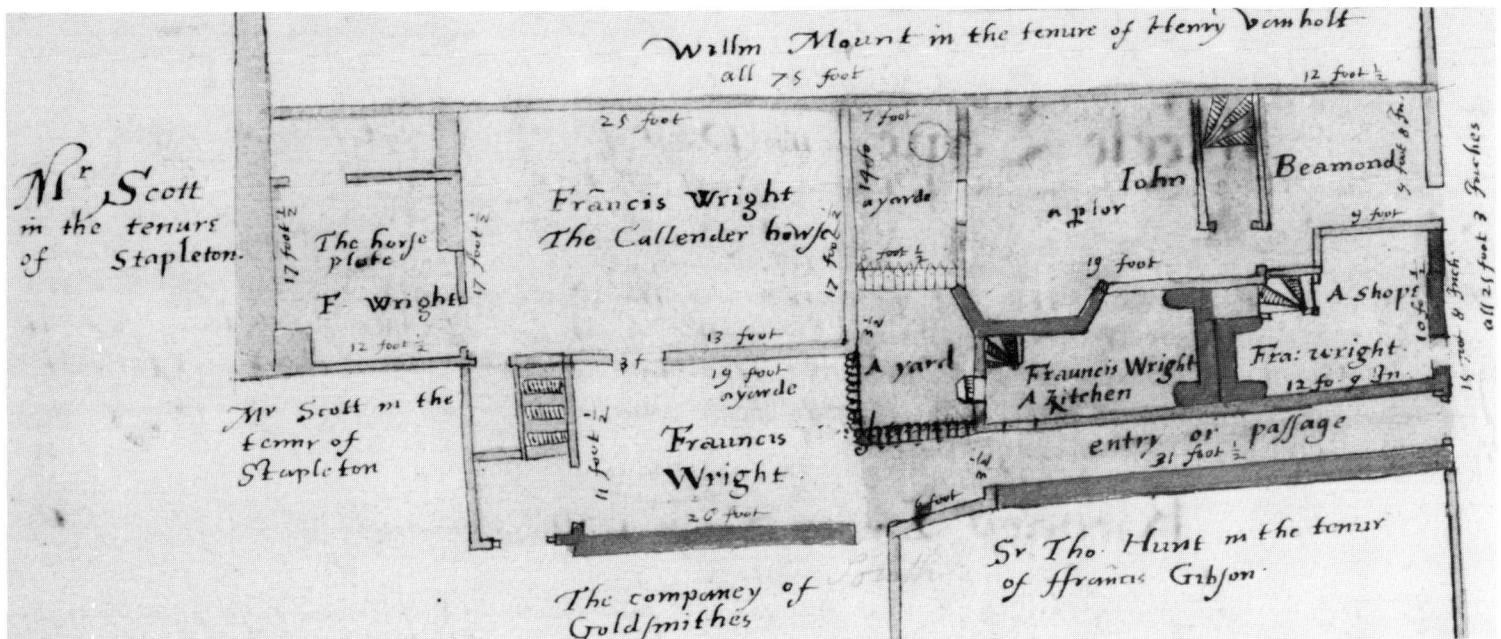

Figure 51. **47.** 77 Wood Street (1:150). North is to the top of the plan.

48. 4–18 Lower East Smithfield, 1–9 Dark Entry

Plan Book, 19

This triangular piece of land surrounded by ditches lay to the E of the Tower of London in East Smithfield. Originally a garden belonging to St Mary Graces priory, it was sold to the Clothworkers' Company in 1595 by Elizabeth Holligrave. The property was by then split into seven tenancies, the same number as in Treswell's survey of 1612 (CDW, 24–7: for a more detailed history, see *HG 2*, site 'Lower E Smithfield, Clothworkers' Co').

The site in 1612 divided into the wider N half (to the bottom of the plan) occupied by Arthur Parker and at least two sub-tenants (in the row of smaller sheds on the N boundary); and six tenancies arranged in E–W strips across the narrowing property, the S tenant Wood enjoying a garden at the end. All were of two storeys, some with garrets.

The site now forms part of St Katherine's Dock.

Text of reference, Plan Book (1612)

Robert Wood: (2) A chamber next East Smithfield 10½' square besides the study, one other chamber adjoining 17' with the chimney × 11'.

John Weekes: (2) A chamber with a chimney divided in two partitions, also a little-room over the kitchen 13' × 9'; (3) A half garret over the said chamber.

Geo. Burnam: (2) A chamber with a chimney 20' × 15', 2 chambers behind the same 22½' with the chimneys × 13½'; (3) 2 garret chambers over the said chamber, with a chimney, 20' × 15½', one other garret chamber behind the same 13½' × 12½'.

Anthony Reinolds: (2) A chamber with a chimney and 2 other chambers adjoining backward, both 17½' × 12½'; (3) 2 garrets over all.

Henry Whitson: (2) A chamber with a chimney, also one other chamber adjoining with a chimney, one other room over the back warehouse.

Michell Brooke: (2) A chamber 19½ × besides the chimney 10', one other chamber and buttery adjoining; (3) A garret over all.

Arthur Parker: (2) A chamber next the court 17½ × besides the chimney 11', one other chamber adjoining 17½' × 10½, two other chambers, one with a chimney 30' with the stairs × 13½'; (3) A garret of the two chambers aforesaid being of the same bigness, two other garrets 22½' × 17½';

[over the chambers in Parker's Alley]: (2) 6 chambers over the tenements aforesaid with chimneys in them all saving one; (3) 6 garrets over the said chambers.

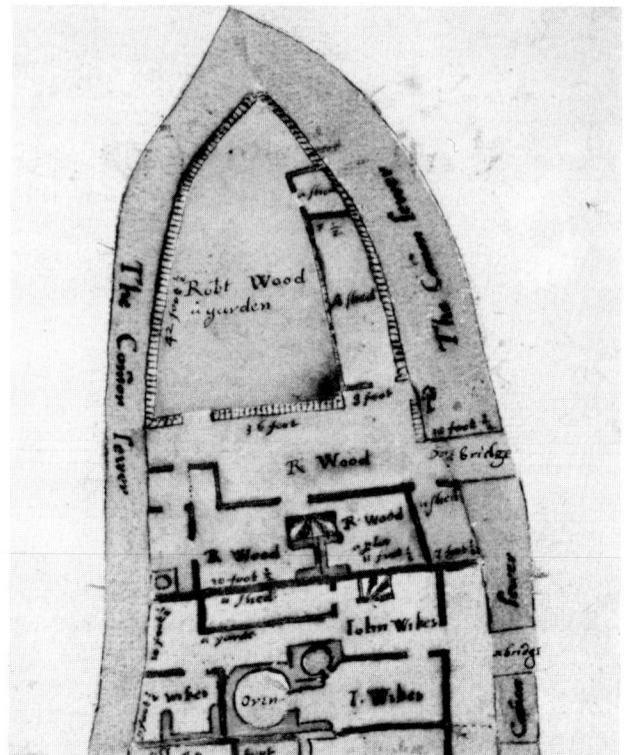

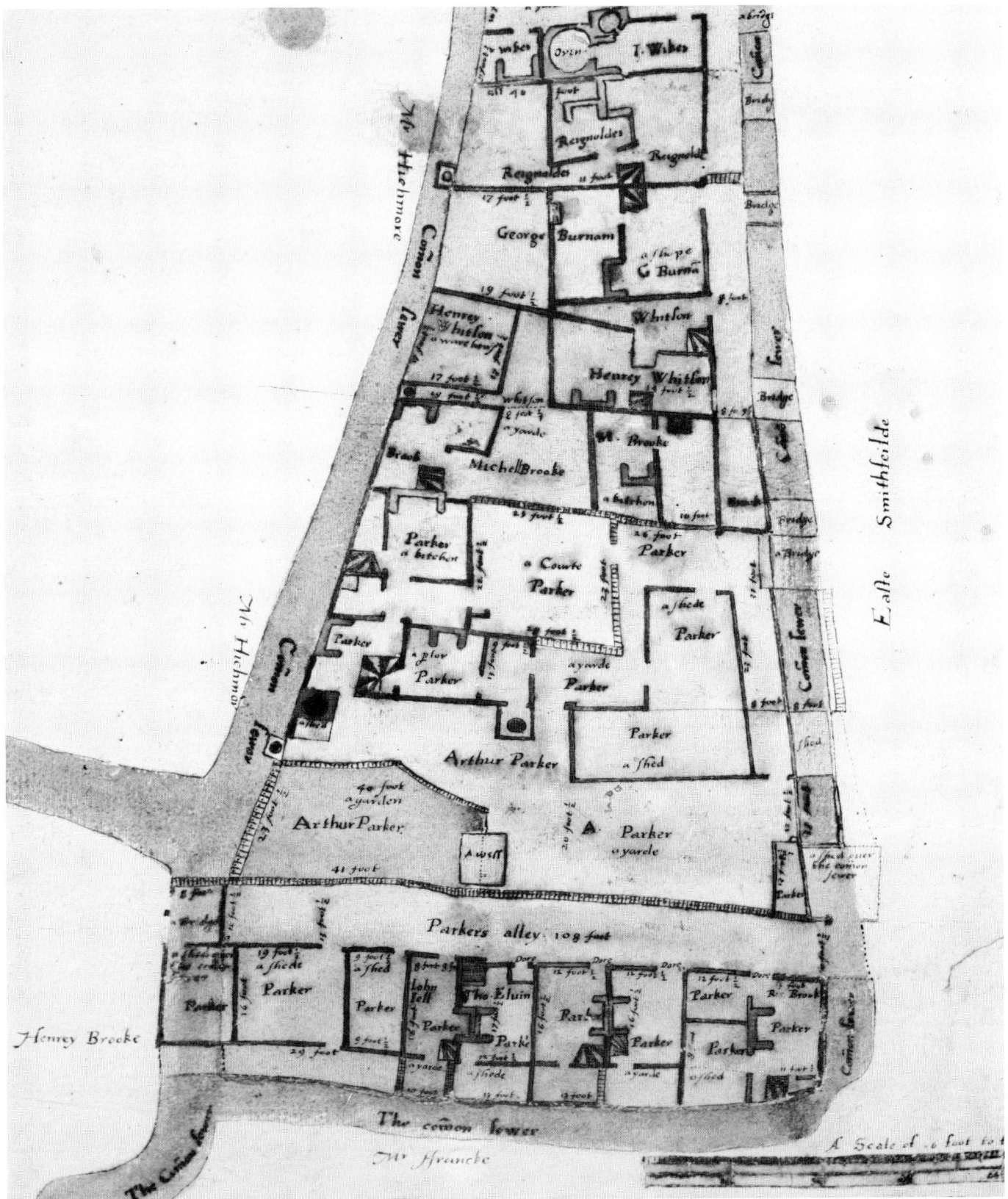

Figure 52. **48.** 4–18 [Lower] East Smithfield, 1–9 Dark Entry (1:300). North is to the bottom of the plan.

49. 44–8 later 34–8 Blackman Street, now 291–9 Borough High Street, Southwark

Evidence Book, 5; Thompson, Grew and Schofield 1984, Fig. 11

In 1537 the prior of St Mary Overey, Southwark, leased to William Cawsey, saddler, for 60 years two tenements in the parish of St Mary Magdalene, Southwark, on the W side of an unspecified highway; these are probably wholly or partly the properties described below (**50**) as in the Meal Market, Southwark. Also leased were six tenements and a garden in Blackmanstreet in the parish of Newington. By 1544 all these properties were in the hands of John Pope and Anthony Foster, who confirmed them to George Hoord; in 1559 a Richard Bortsek of Newington also quit-claimed his interest in the six tenements in Blackmanstreet to Hoord. By his will of 22 December 1562 (*PCC 1558–1583*, 158) Hoord left all his lands in Southwark to Christ's Hospital (GL MS 13387).

On the plan of 1611 in the Evidence Book (Fig. 53), however, seven tenements are shown; it is not clear which, if any, is an addition, or whether one of the properties had been subdivided by the time of the plan. Nor are the upper storeys of the houses described, since no text survives with Treswell's plan. The form of one of them is known from a lease of 1585 by the hospital to Gilbert Apperton, in which the tenant was required to rebuild the house 'of good, stronge, substanciall and well seasoned tymber of Oke, which shall contain two stories high and a half, the first of them to be tenne fote highe, the second storie eight foote and the halfe storie fower foote or more besides the rofe' (GL MS 13389); this is probably the house later no. 46, the tenancy of Richard Johnes in the plan. Thomas West, who leased the two houses to the S, was given a lease in 1611, previously only occupying the property as undertenant; this dates the plan to that year or later. His two tenancies were still standing, unaltered on the ground floor, in 1697, when they were again planned in a lease; the northern was rebuilt between 1713 and 1734, but the southern remained unchanged in plan of the latter year (GL MS 13390).

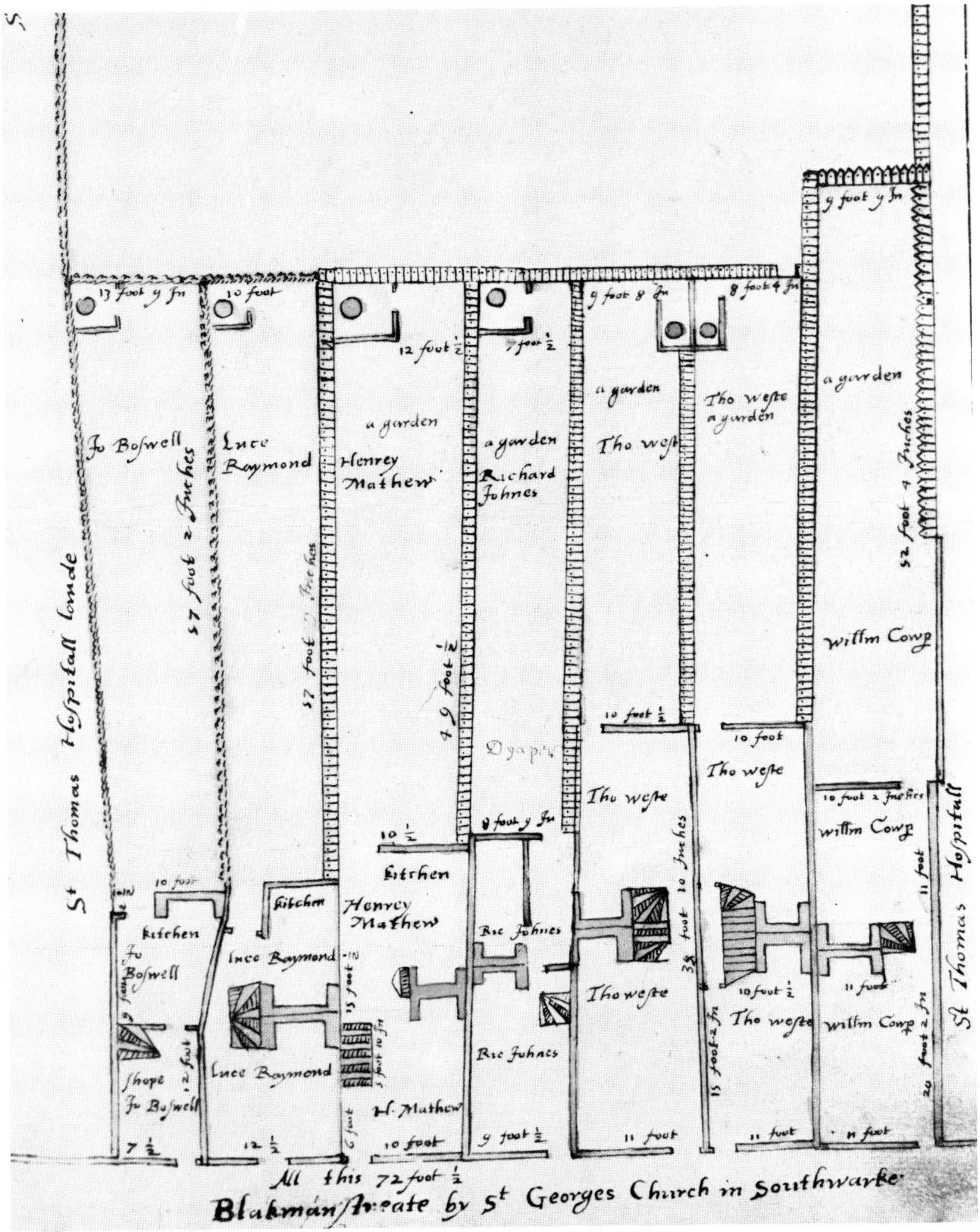

St Thomas Hospitall londe

13 foot 9 in   10 foot   12 foot ½   7 foot ½   9 foot 8 in   8 foot 4 in   9 foot 9 in

Jo Boswell   Luce Raymond   Henrey Mathew   a garden Richard Johnes   a garden Tho weste   Tho weste a garden   a garden

57 foot 2 Inches   57 foot Inches   57 foot Inches   49 foot ½   52 foot 4 Inches

Dyaper

Willm Cowp

10 foot ½   10 foot

Tho weste

10 foot 2 Inches

Willm Cowp

35 foot 10 Inches

kitchen   9 foot 9 in

kitchen   Henrey Mathew

kitchen

10 foot   Jo Boswell   Luce Raymond   Ric Johnes

kitchen

Jo Boswell   Luce Raymond   Tho weste

Ric Johnes   Tho weste   Tho weste   Willm Cowp

15 foot   15 foot 2 in

shope Jo Boswell   H. Mathew   10 foot ½   11 foot   Tho weste   Willm Cowp

7 ½   12 ½   6 foot   10 foot   9 foot ½   11 foot   11 foot   11 foot

20 foot 2 in

St Thomas Hospitall

All this 72 foot ½

Blakman streate by St Georges Church in Southwarke

Figure 53. **49.** 44–8, later 34–8 Blackman Street, now 291–9 Borough High Street, Southwark (1:150). North is to the left of the plan.

50. The Mealmarket, Southwark

Evidence Book, 6

These four tenements are probably rebuildings or fragmentations of the two tenements originally owned by St Mary Overey priory, Southwark, as detailed under 44–8 Blackman Street (**49**) above; in the Treswell plan there are still two main tenants, George Dalton and Johanne Stoke, the proprietress of the Red Bull. They were sold to the Commissioners for the Improvement of London Bridge in 1830 (*Charity Comm*, 92).

The houses were 3½ storeys high.

Text of reference, Evidence Book (1611)

George Dalton in the occupation of Henry Hurst: [2] A chamber over the shop 10½′ × 11′ 9″ with the stairs; A chamber next the yard with a hearth without a funnel 12′ × 10½′; [3] A garret over the first chamber 13½′ with the stairs.

George Dalton in the occupation of John Aldrich: [2] A chamber over Henry Hirst's first chamber [i.e. the shop] 18′ 9″ with stairs × 13½′ with the chimney; A garret over the same 19′ with the stairs × 14½′ with a chimney; A chamber over his shop 18′ × 12½′ with the chimney; Another chamber over the yard and buttery 12′ × 6′ 9″; Another chamber over the kitchen 12′ × 7, all these beside the staircase up and drowne [*sic*]; [3] and [4] A little chamber over the room over the buttery beforesaid 6½′ × 12½′; A chamber next the street with a chimney 19½′ × 12½′; A garret over the chamber aforesaid next the street 16½′ × 12½′; A chamber over the kitchen next the

yard 12½′ × 10′ with stairs and chimney; A garret over the said chamber 12½′ × 10′ 3″ with the funnel of the chimney; A woodhorse [*sic*] or shed in the yard 20′ × 4′ at the E end and × 6′ at the west end; A little room over part of the room aforesaid 10½′ × 4′ 3″; Also a cellar under the shop 21½′ × 15½′.

The Tavern called the Red Bull in Southwark — Johan Stocke widow in the occupation of Thomas Brackle: [2] A chamber with a chimney next the street 18′ × 9′ 3″; Another little room with a chimney 9′ × 6′; A large room over the cheesemonger's shop with a round jetty 18′ × [ ] with a chimney; Another room over part of the cheesemonger's back room, and part over another room below 19′ with the chimney × 12½′; Another room over the back room or cellar with a chimney 18½′ × 12½′; Another room over the kitchen 18′ × 15½ with the chimney; Also another room over the buttery 11′ × 9′ 3″, all these besides the stairs and passages; A large garret over the kitchen, buttery and entry 27′ × 16½′ with the chimney, stairs and a little closet, where is to be noted that there wanteth a piece over the entry to give light to the under rooms; [3] A garret over the chamber over the cellar 19′ × 13′, besides the stairs and passage to a stool of ease; A chamber next the street 20′ × 12′ 3″ with the chimney; Another chamber next the street 19½′ × 11′ 8″ with a funnel of a chimney; A chamber over the chamber over part of the cheesemonger's back room, and another room 19½′ × 13½′ with chimney; A cellar under the cheesemonger's shop and 2 other rooms 39′ × 18½′ at the S end next the street and × 10½′ at the N end.

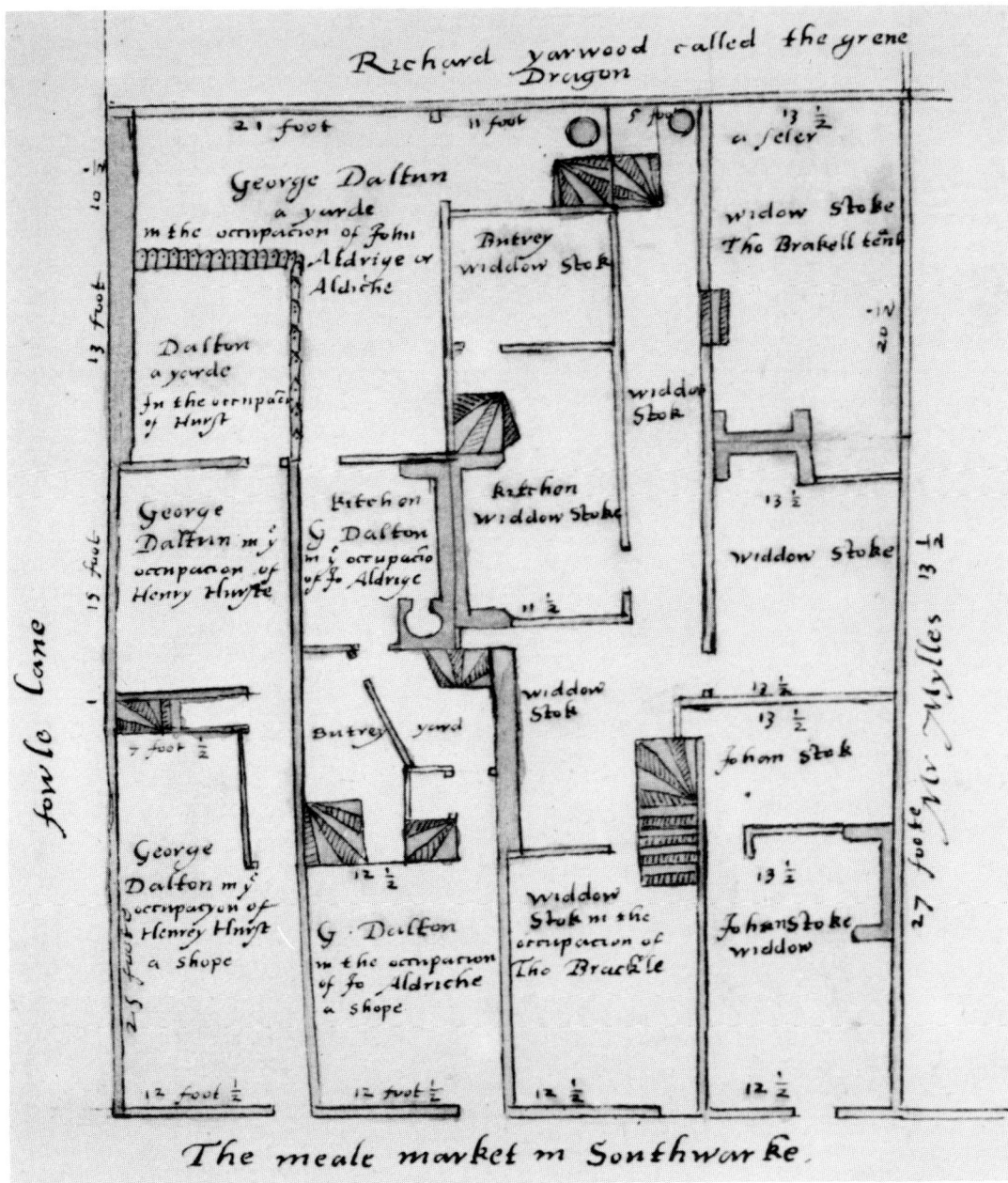

The plan is annotated with the following text:

Richard yarwood called the grene Dragon

21 foot   11 foot   5 foot   13½ a seler

George Daltnn
a yerde
in the occupacion of John
Aldrige or
Aldiche

widow Stoke
Tho Brakell tent

Daltōn
a yerde
in the occupacō
of Hurst

Butrey
widdow Stok

widdow Stok

fowle lane

13 foot
15 foot

George
Daltnn my
occupacion of
Henry Hurste

Kitchen
G Dalton
in ç occupacō
of Jo Aldryc

kitchon
Widdow Stoke

widdow Stoke

13½

7 foot ½

George
Dalton my
occupacyon of
Henry Hurst
a shope

Butrey   yard

widdow
Stok

12½
13½

12 ½

Johon Stok

27 foote Mr Mylles   13¼

25 foot

12½

G. Dalton
in the occupacion
of Jo Aldriche
a shope

Widdow
Stok in the
occupacion of
Tho Brackle

13½

Johan Stoke
widdow

12 foot ½   12 foot ½   12 ½   12 ½

The meale market in Southwarke.

Figure 54. **50.** The Mealmarket, Southwark (1:150). North is to the right of the plan.

51. Sun Tavern, King Street, Westminster

Evidence Book, 18

In 1556 Richard Castell or Casteler, cordwainer of Westminster, and Catherine his wife, granted to Christ's Hospital their estate in Westminster. This comprised three blocks of property:

(i) the Sun tavern, King Street (**51**) (GL MS 13008)

(ii) a block of four properties on the N side of Tothill Street (**52**) (GL MS 13009)

(iii) a large block of property N and W of the Woolstaple, on the N side of Old Palace Yard (**53**) (GL MS 13053).

The Sun tavern lay on the W side of King Street, opposite the turning into New Palace Yard. This property was a tavern in 1388, when it is described as being *iuxta* the gate of King's palace to the E; its position on the other side of King Street is however confirmed by subsequent leases (GL MS 13002; 13052). Richard Castell himself appears to be living at the Sun in 1549 (GL MS 13007). The property was probably of three storeys on cellars in 1611 (Fig. 55).

Text of reference, Evidence Book (1611)

Sun Inn, in the occupation of Thomas Larkine: [2] and [3] A chamber over the chamber beforesaid 16½′ × 16½′ with a chimney, a garret over the chamber aforesaid 18½′ × 13½′ with a chimney, a chamber over the parlour next the yard with a chimney 16½′ × 12½′, a chamber over the kitchen with house of office in it 12½′ × 8′, a chamber over the back room 19½′ × 14′ with a chimney, a cellar next the street 15′ × 13½′, a cellar under the back room 15½′ × 14′.

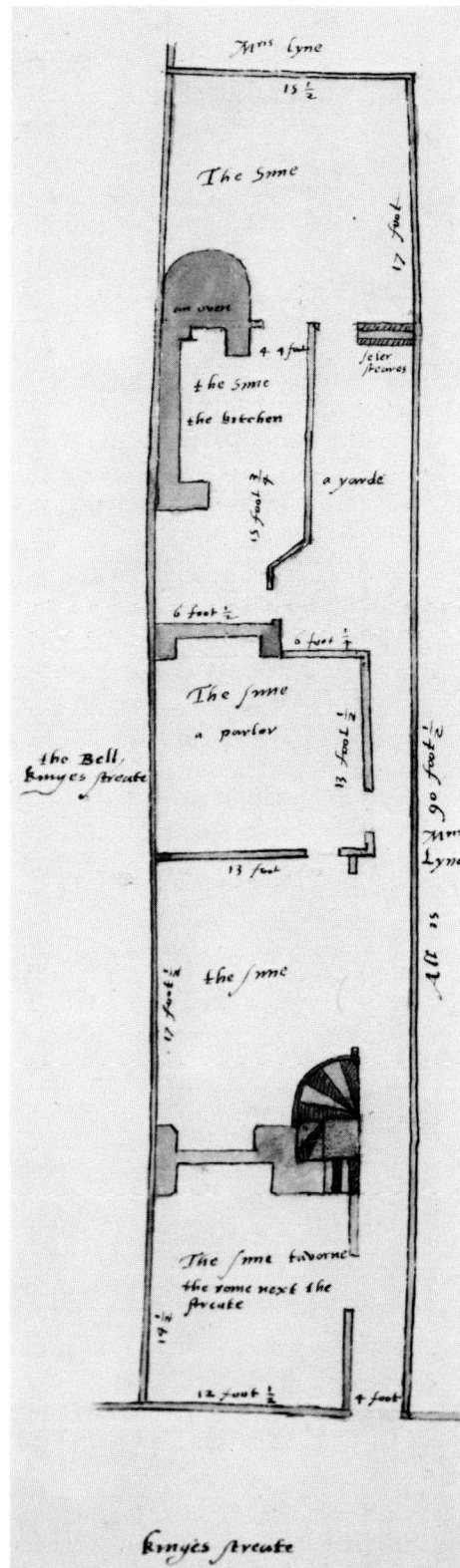

Figure 55. **51.** Sun, King Street, Westminster (1:150). North is to the right of the plan.

52. Tothill Street, Westminster

Evidence Book, 20; Glanville 1972, plate 6

This group of lands, on the N side of Tothill Street, was in the possession of the fraternity of the Assumption in St Margaret's church, Westminster, in the medieval period (GL MS 12993; 13010); by 1550 it was in the hands of Casteler (GL MS 12996), and formed part of his grant to Christ's Hospital in 1556 (see **51**).

Unlike the other London plans, this survey, which forms part of the Christ's Hospital collection of 1611 in the Evidence Book, presents the buildings in the usual 'rural' or matchbox style, with the facades along Tothill Street detailed (Fig. 56). The survey in the Evidence Book is clearly a slightly selective re-drawing of a loose survey which is attached to a lease of 1586 (GL MS 13057) (Plate 2); the tenants' and abutting owners' names are the same, as is the majority of the drawing, but in the loose version the facades of neighbouring houses (i.e. not those in Hospital ownership) are also shown; these are omitted from the Evidence Book version.

On both plans St James' park to the N is called the king's park; but in the lease of 1586, the queen's park. The plan is not mentioned in the lease.

Thus the loose survey appears to have been drawn up in 1586. It is possible that certain glosses, including the naming of the king's park, were added after 1603, possibly at the expiry of the 23 year lease of 1586, i.e. in 1609.

The Kinges p^{ke} called St James p^{ke}

173 yardes betwen the pales besides ye diche

A ponde

the Close now demised being an Orchard and a garden

Willm Main

The lande somtime the lady Vanyshaw and after Tho Persons now a garden platt late in the tenur of Sr Henry Maynard knight & in the occupation of Xtofer Byrom

72 yardes 2½ foot beside the Parke wall

a garden

the corner of the stone wall

82 yardes from the corner to the p^{ke} wall

Our ladyes ground somtime in the tenure of the lord Awdley and late the Earle of warwike and now the lady Graye

47 yardes & 2 foot betwen thes two pales

this is a barne and a stone wall

45 foot ¼   30 foot   14 yardes

a garden

Willm Mommys garden

the Deane and Chapter of westm^r in y^e tenur of Wm Main

87 foot

16 foot

Lewes Own garden

A Brewehowse wth other Buyldings

60 foot

Stanley

13 foot 7 Inches   17 foot   17 foot   16 foot

Tuthill streate

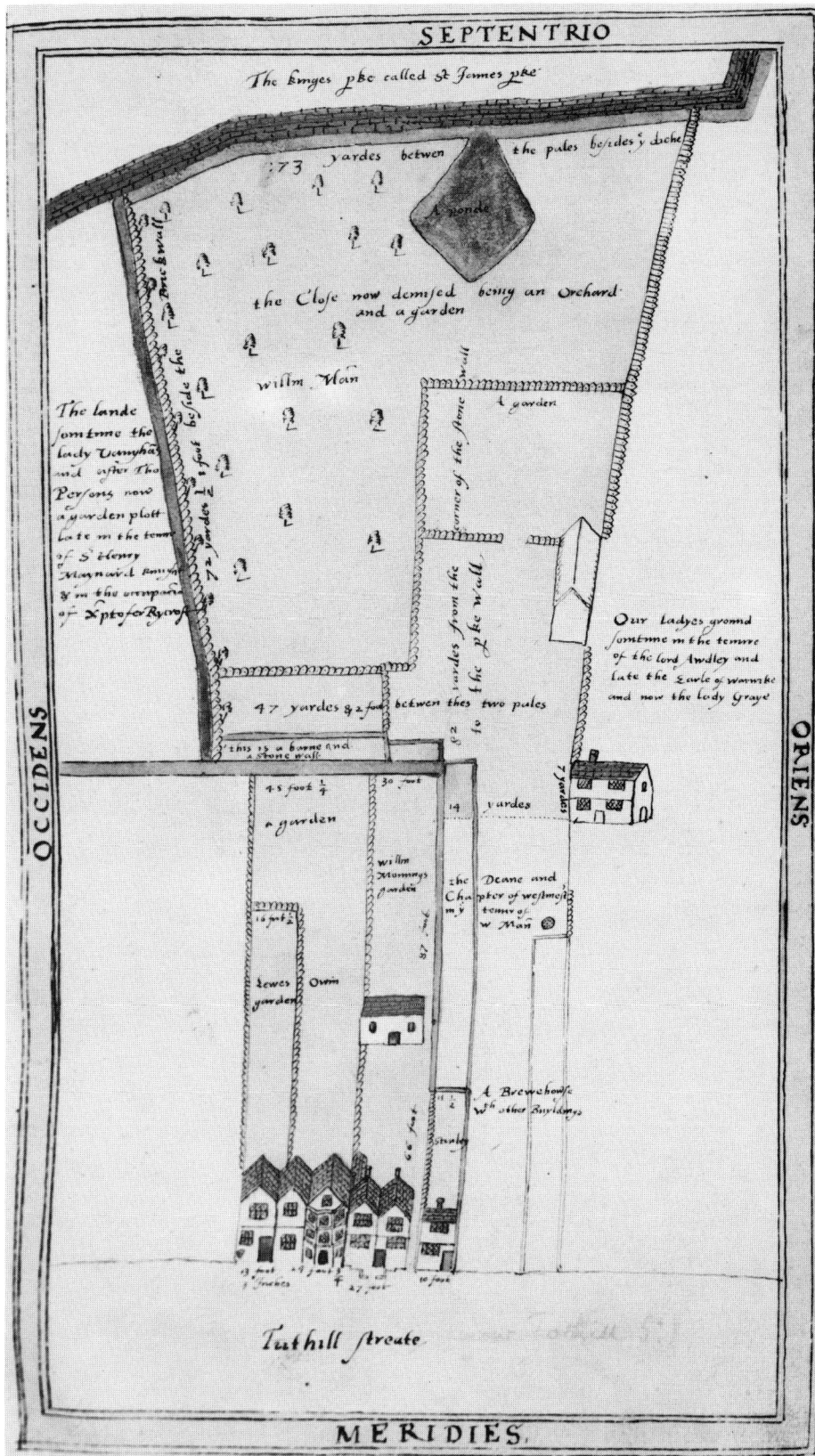

Figure 56. **52.** Tothill Street, Westminster. North is to the top of the plan.
See also Plate 2.

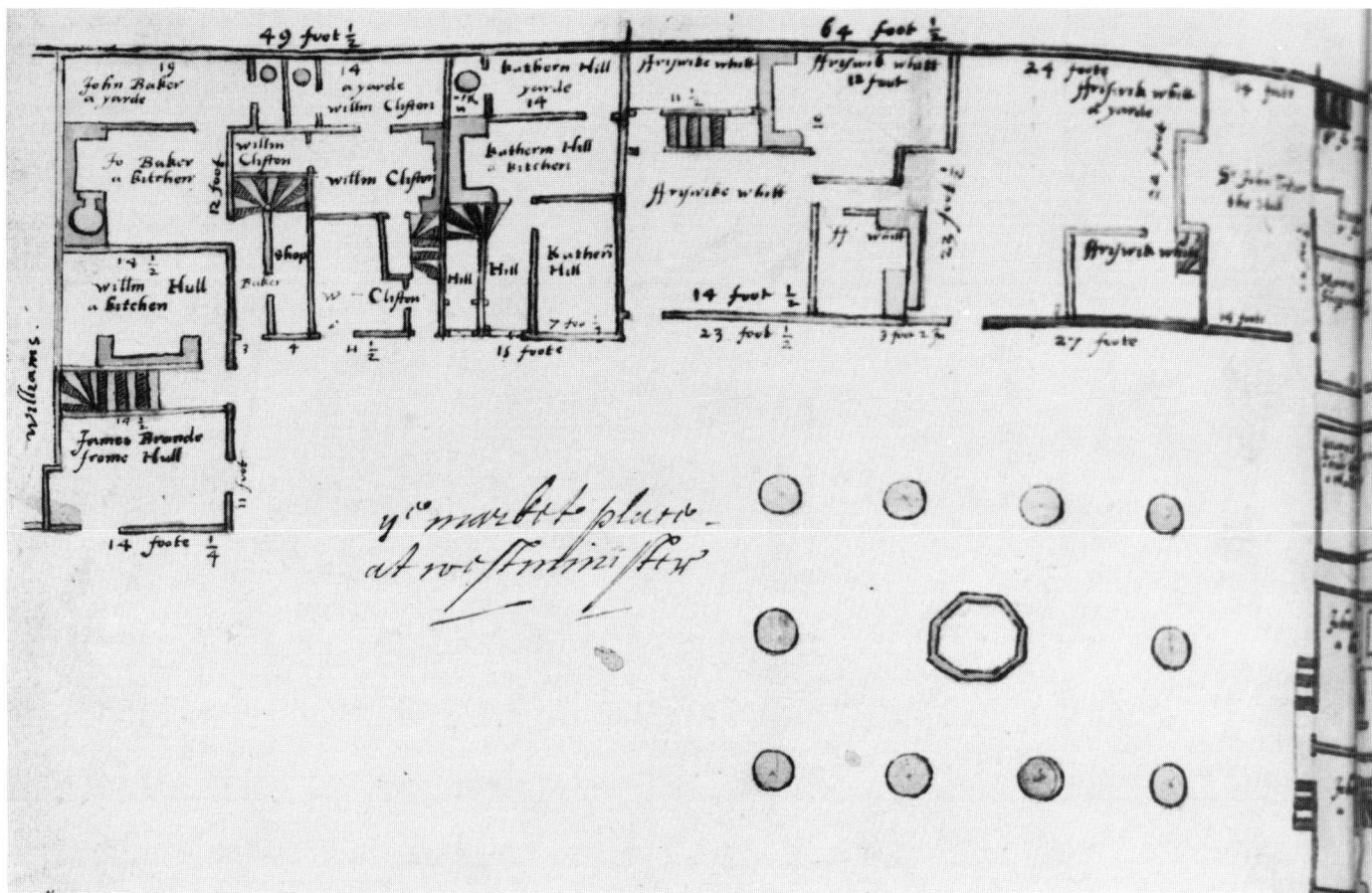

53. Woolstaple, Westminster

Evidence Book, 19

Buildings and gardens are recorded on the N side of Woolstaple Yard, behind the N frontage of Old Palace Yard, from the mid-fifteenth century (GL MS 12975; 12980). A large block of property forming the N side of the yard and part of the E side was acquired by Richard Casteler by 1549 (GL MS 13007), and formed part of his grant to Christ's Hospital in 1556 (GL MS 13053). By the time of Treswell's plan there were seventeen tenancies.

Treswell's plan can be dated to after 1603, when one of the tenants, John Binion, acquired his lease (GL MS 13033), and before 23 March 1609/10, when Sir John Trevor, another tenant, surrendered his lease (GL MS 13030). The plan can be divided into three parts: a strip of properties, mostly 3½ storeys high, along the N side of the yard; a row of seven houses of similar

Figure 57. **53.** Woolstaple, Westminster (1:200). North is to the top of the plan.

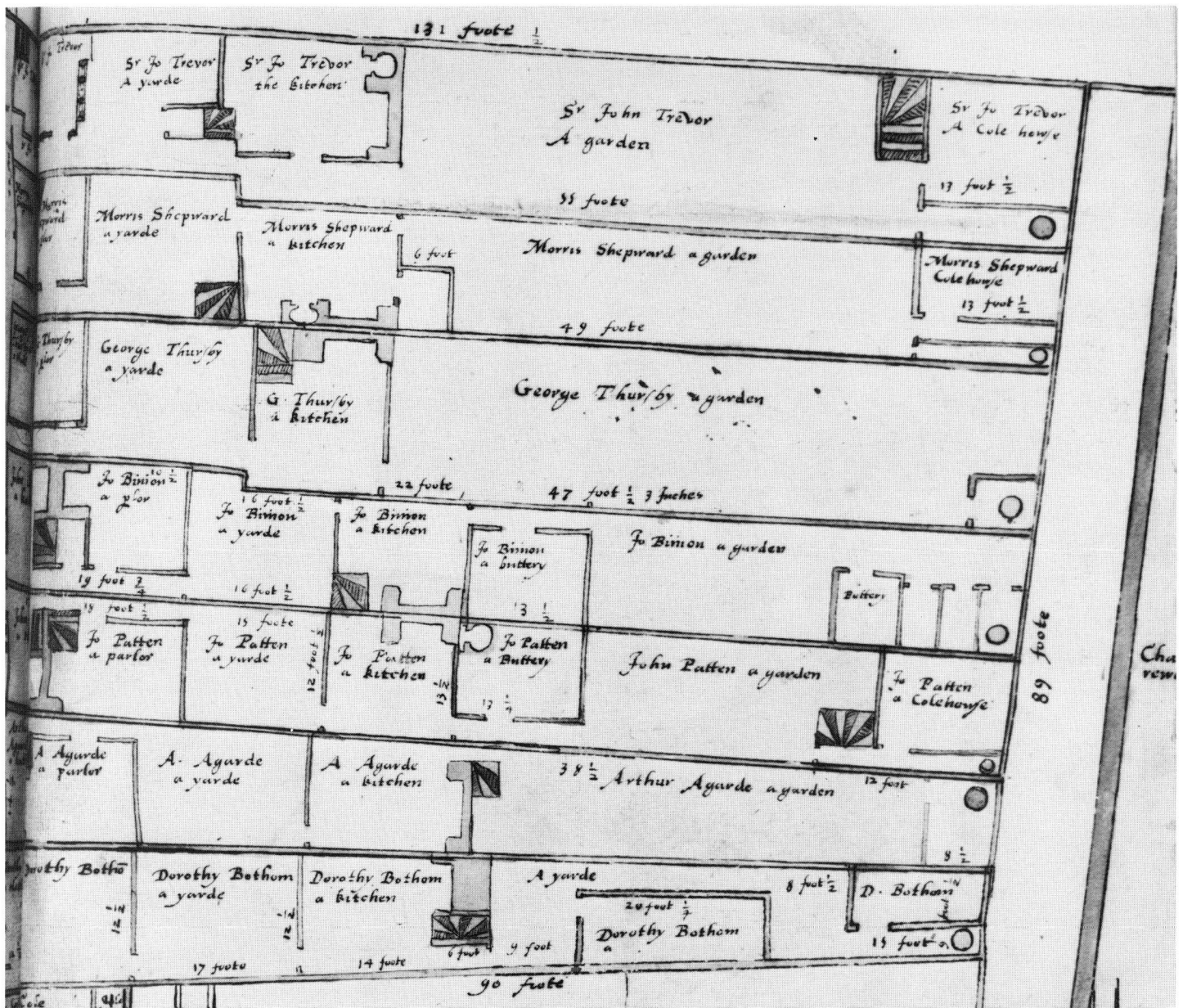

proportions along the E side of the yard, with outhouses (including separate kitchens) and gardens stretching to Canon Row in the E; and the Woolstaple building itself, shown as ten posts of circular section arranged in a rectangle around an octagonal feature which might be either a central pillar or a basin or fountain.

A separate and loose unsigned plan of one tenancy, that of George Thursby, is also extant (GL MS 22635/21). It is probably by Treswell.

An inventory of furnishings and linen sold to Trevor when he took over his tenancy in 1588 (GL MS 13029) is at present the sole indication of how a house surveyed by Treswell was furnished; though the inventory mentions only nine of the fifteen chambers and outhouses described in the text of reference.

Inventory of furnishings sold to John Trevor, 1588

In the great Parlour

Inprimis one table with a frame and five joined stools. A long settle and a side table. One little table fast to the wall and a walnut cupboard, three foot stools. A bedstead with green curtains and vallence, two featherbeds a bolster and two pillows. A pair of bellows. A screen. A little creeper. Three stools covered with black leather, and one great one covered with black leather, and one chair covered with black leather. A plate candlestick. A pair of tables. Two carpets of Darneck. Seven books and one chair covered with black leather.

In the great chamber over the parlour

Item a bedstead with tester of silk and blue silk curtains. A down bed two pillows and a bolster. Three joined stools. A chair with needlework, a mattress of canvas. A mattress of new buckram. A new coverlet of tapestry. Two white blankets. A black mantle. Five curtains of green cloth, and vallence of the same. A chair of Turkey work and a stool of the same. A mat for a bed. A pair of brasen andirons. A fire shovel. A pair of bright creepers. A pair of tongs tipped with brass. A chamber pot. A little cupboard. A long narrow press. Two little curtains of saye. A steel glass. An old chair of black leather.

The little chamber next the great chamber

Item two short ship chests. A candle box. A close stool. A pewter basin. Two little cosers. A bedstead with a featherbed, a bolster and painted cloths.

The chamber next the room

Item a bedstead. A straw bed, a featherbed, a bolster, two pillows, a rug. A canopy of red velvet with curtains of red silk. A curtain of yellow canvas. A folding table. A low stool. A creeper. A chamber pot. A red cloth chair. A table with a cross frame. The chamber hanged with painted cloths and two cosers of black leather.

The little parlour

Item a round table. A chair of red cloth. A table with a cross frame. A quossing of red cloth filled with wool. A little chest. A settle, two cosers. A pair of bellows. A

standish of pewter. The parlour hanged with painted cloths.

The chamber next the garret

Item a bedstead with a featherbed and a bolster. Two straw beds. A table with two trestles, two wool beds. A pillow. Two wool bolsters, two pairs of rough blankets rewed (?) at the end. A table with cross frame and two new ?huery coverlets.

The upper chamber with the chimney

Item a joined bedstead, a truckle bedstead. A rush mat, two featherbeds, two bolsters, two pillows. A hall cupboard, four old chairs. A joined stool, four old chairs of black leather, and a table with a cross frame.

The garret

Item a press. A long table with trestles. A hest for candles. A great wainscot chest. A wicker chair. A stilletory to set in brick, four bottles. A flask and a searse [sieve]. Five little curtains of canvas. Two new curtains of green saye, an old vallence for a bed of blue yellow saye. A vallence of linche wolsey. Four little carpets of green. Six new cushions of tapestry. Two long cushions of needlework, one pillow of down, two pillows of feathers covered with leather.

The kitchen

Item a garnish of pewter, eighteen porringers. Two dozen of plate. Twenty five trenchers. Four new pie plate. Six sallet dishes. Eight pewter potts. One flagon. Six candlesticks. Four candle cups. A tankard of a pint. One salt. One collander, one ladle. A jack of iron with weights. Three spets [?spits]. Two pairs of cob-irons. A paring shovel. A chopping knife. A frying pan. Two gridirons. A spade. Three iron bars for chimneys. Three pans. Two kettles. Three pots. One Skomer [skimmer]. Two little posnets. Two chasers. Two revets(?). A baking pan. A basin and a ewer. Two brasen mortars with pestles for spice. One chamber pot and two tankards of half-pint.

Linen

Item six pair of sheets of housewife's cloth. Six pair of pillowberes. Three pair of canvas sheets. Four dozen of napkins. Three table cloths, two towels, two square cloths of diaper. Two dozen of napkins and two towels.

Wooden stuff

Item six wooden trays. A half peck [measure]. Three wooden measures, a pair of little scales of wood. Diverse things of wood and iron. Five little kettles of brass with new ?bayeles, two pair of brazen scales, weights of brass and lead to them. Diverse iron and wooden things of small value.

Text of reference, Evidence Book (1611)

William Hull: [2] A chamber over the shop 16½′ × 15′ with a chimney; [3] A chamber over the said chamber 17½′ × 16½′ with a chimney; [? 2 or 3] A chamber 10½′ × 10¼′ next the street; [3] A chamber 19′ × 6′; [4] A garret over the whole house.

John Baker: [2] A chamber over Hull's kitchen 17½′ × 12′ with a chimney, a chamber over his own kitchen 9′ × 8¾′ with a chimney; [3] A chamber next the street 16′ × 12½′ with a chimney, a chamber 13′ × 9′; [4] A chamber 13′ × 12′ with a chimney, a garret 13½′ × 9′.

William Clifton: [2] A chamber next the street 12½′ × 8′ with a chimney, a chamber 16½′ × 8′ with a chimney; [3] A chamber next the street 14½′ × 9′ with a chimney, a chamber 16½′ × 7½′; [4] A garret 12′ × 15½′, a garret next the street of the same length and breadth.

Katherin Hill: [2] A chamber with a chimney next the street 12½′ square, a chamber with a chimney 11½′ × 8′; [3] A chamber over all the rest 22½′ × 11′ with a chimney; [4] A garret 16½′ × 11′, a garret 17½′ × 12′.

Friswike White: [2] A chamber next the street 16½′ × 13½′ with a chimney; [3] A chamber next the street 16½′ × 9′; [2] A chamber next the yard 11½′ × 8′, a room over the buttery 11½′ × 4′.

Sir John Trevors: [2] A chamber next the street 12½′ × 22½′, a chamber next the same 14½′ × 12½′, a chamber 14½′ × 12½′, a chamber 11½′ × 8′, a chamber next the garden 17½′ × 13½′ the stairs and entry between with a chimney; [3] A chamber over the chamber before of the same measure with a chimney, a chamber next the yard 15′ × 12½′ with a chimney, a chamber next the yard 10½′ × 8′, a chamber 13½′ × 8′ the stairs and entry between; [4] A chamber or garret next the street 24½′ × 11¼′ with a chimney.

Morris Shepward: [2] A chamber next the street 13½′ × 11½′ with a chimney, a gallery over part of the yard 17′ × 6′; [3] A chamber 13½′ × 16′ next the street with a chimney, a chamber 12′ × 16′, a gallery over the gallery afore mentioned 13½′ × 7′ with a closet at one end 7′ square.

George Thursby: [2] A chamber over the kitchen 14′ × 15′, a chamber 15½′ × 11½′ with a chimney, a chamber next the yard of the same measure; [3] A chamber next the street with a chimney 15½′ × 13½′ [storey allocations difficult for following except for last

two] A chamber over the same with a chimney of the same measure, a chamber next the yard 13′ × 12½′ with a chimney, a chamber or garret 13½′ × 12½′ with a chimney, a garret next the street 20½′ × 13½′ with a chimney, a chamber next the yard 13½′ × 12′ with a chimney; [2] A chamber over the kitchen 13½′ × 9½′ with a chimney, a chamber over the buttery 13½′ × 12½′.

John Patten: [2] A chamber next the street 18½′ × 12½′ with a chimney, a chamber [   ]; [3] A garret next the street 13′ × 10½′, one other garret adjoining to the same with a chimney of the same measure, a garret 12½′ × [   ], a chamber [   ]; [2] A chamber over the kitchen 13½′ × 10′ with a chimney, a chamber over the buttery with a chimney 13½′ square.

Arthur Agarde: [2] A chamber next the street 16½′ × 15½′ with a chimney, one other chamber with a chimney 14½′ × 12½′; [3] A chamber next the street 14½′ × 14′ with a chimney, a chamber with a chimney 14½′ × 13½′; [4] A garret next the street 22′ × 14½′, a garret 15½′ × 13′; [2] A chamber over the kitchen with a chimney 13½′ × 11½′.

Dorothy Botome: [2] A chamber with a chimney next the street 14½′ × 14′, a chamber next the yard with a chimney 14½′ × 12½; [3] A chamber with a chimney next the street 15′ square, a chamber next the yard with a chimney 14½′ × 13′; [3 or 4] A chamber next the yard 15½′ × 10¾′, a chamber 11½′ × 10′, a chamber next the yard 16′ × 13′; [2] A chamber over the kitchen 15′ × 10¾′.

Florance Cadwell in the occupation of Cole: [2] A chamber next the street 12½′ × 10′ with a chimney; [2 or 3] A chamber next the street 7′ square; [2] A chamber next the yard 11′ × 10′, one other chamber 12½′ × 7½′.

Florance Cadwell in the occupation of William Mullins: [2] A chamber next the street with a chimney 15½′ × 11½′; [3] A chamber over the same of the same measure with a chimney; [3 or 4] One other chamber over the chamber before with a chimney 14½′ × 12½; [2 or 3] A chamber with a chimney 15½′ over Cole's house, a chamber 11′ × 8′; [3 or 4] A garret 13′ × 8′, one other garret 15½′ × 8′.

Florance Cadwell in the occupation of Raufe Henn: [2] A chamber next the street with chimney 13½′ square; [3] A chamber over the same of the same measure; [3 or 4] A chamber with a chimney 13′ × 9½′ with a chimney, a garret 14′ × 13′; [2] A gallery over a shed in Cole's yard 19½′ × 4′.

BIBLIOGRAPHY

Basing, P., 1982	*Register of the fraternity of the Holy Trinity and SS Fabian and Sebastian in St Botolph without Aldersgate* London Record Soc 18
Black, W. H., 1871	*History and Antiquities of the Worshipful Company of Leathersellers*
Girtin, T., 1958	*The Golden Ram*
Glanville, P., 1972	*London in Maps*
Harben, H. A., 1918	*A Dictionary of London*
Harding, V., 1980	'The two Coldharbours of London' *London Topographical Record* 24, 11–30
Hare, T. H., [1860]	Mr Hare's Report [to the Charity Commissioners] on the Clothworkers' Company charities, 1880 [1860]
Harvey, J., 1954	*English Medieval Architects*
Loftus-Brock, E. P., 1872	'Notes on the Norman crypt', *Journ Brit Archaeol Assoc* 28, 176–9
Schofield, J., 1983	'Ralph Treswell's surveys of London houses *c* 1612' in *English Map-Making 1500–1650* (ed. S. Tyacke), 85–92
Schofield, J., 1984	*The Building of London from the Conquest to the Great Fire*
Sluger, C., Holmyard, E. T., Hall, A. R. & Williams, T. T., 1957	*A History of Technology: III, c 1500–c 1750*
Strype, J., 1720	*A Survey of the Cities of London and Westminster . . corrected . . . and brought down from . . . 1633 . . . to the present* (3 vols)
Thrupp, S., 1948	*The Merchant Class of Medieval London*
Weinstein, R., 1980	'Clothworkers in St Stephen Coleman Parish, 1612' *London Topographical Record* 24, 61–80

INDEX

Numbers in italic refer to figure numbers.

Pudding Lane, 19, 27, 110, *39*
Pulteney, Sir John, 118
pumps, 20, 106, *5; see also* wells
Purbeck, Isle of (Dorset), 6

Q

Quatremayne, Richard, 100
quays, *44*
Queen Victoria Street, 108

R

Radstone (Northants.), 7
ragstone, *see* stone
Ramsden (Essex), 6
Ramsey (Remys), Mary, 19, 21, 23, 64, *19*
ranges, 85, *29*
Rawse, William, 59
Raymond, Luce, *53*
Red Bull, Meal Market, Southwark, tavern, 21, 140, *54*
Reinolds, Anthony, 136, *52*
Revell, (?Nicholas), carpenter, 74
Rewley Abbey (Oxford), estate, 58
Reynolds, Mr, 116, *43*
Rice, Thomas, 79–80, *26*
Richard, chaplain, 39
Richard I, king, 97
Richardson,
    Henry, 20
    Hugh, 70, *23*
Rickling (Essex), 2–3, 7
Ringwood alias Burnham Channel (Essex), 6
Ritche Robert, Baron Rich, *18, 46*
Robert, Friar, hermit, 97
Roberts,
    Henry, brewer, 126; Elizabeth his widow, 126
    Tewthe, vintner, 2
Robertson, *see* Robinson
Robinson,
    Alice, 7
    Mrs, *31*
Robinson (Robertson), Anne, 18–9, 72, *24*
Robotham (Robotom),
    Christopher, 122
    Richard, 78, *25*
Rogemonde,
    John, 74
    John his son, 74
Rogers,
    John, clothworker, 131
    Mr, *25*
Rolf, Edward, *31*
Rome (Italy), 9
roofer, *see* trades
roofs, flat, 25–6; *see also* leads
Rose, John, 97, *34*
Rowse, Robert, 23, 126, *47*
Royal Exchange, 65–6
Runwell (Essex), 6
Rymell (Rimell), Humphrey, 92, *31*

S

saddler, *see* trades
St Albans (Herts.), 1, 8n
St Andrew Baynard Castle, estate, 44
St Augustine Watling St, estate, *35*
St Bartholomew's Hospital, estate, 6, 8n, *29*
St Benet's Hill, f10238
St Botolph Aldersgate, 2, 34, 42; parish, 2; *see also* Holy
    Trinity, Fraternity of
St Botolph (without) Aldgate, 39; cemetery, 39; estate, *30*;
    parish, 39; vestry house, 40
St Botolph (without) Bishopsgate, [street near], *10*
St Christopher le Stocks, parish, 66
St Dunstan in the East, parish, 94
St George, Blackman Street, Southwark, *53*
St Giles Cripplegate, estate, *34*
St Giles in the Fields, Westminster, parish, 1, 6
St James Garlickhithe, parish, 84
St James' Hermitage (Lambe's Chapel), Monkwell Street, 21,
    24, 26, 29, 97, *34*
St James' Park, Westminster, 144, *56*
St Katherine Cree, parish, 74
St Katherine's Dock, 136
St Magnus, estate, 115
St Margaret, Westminster, Fraternity of Assumption in, 144
St Martin in the Fields, parish, 1, 6
St Martin Orgar, parish, estate, *50*
St Mary Graces Abbey, 136
St Mary Magdalene, Southwark, parish, 138
St Mary Overey Priory, Southwark, 138, 140
St Mary Spital, (without) Bishopsgate, hospital, 46, 74
St Michael le Querne, 1, 5, 9, 11, 56, *15*
St Nicholas Lane, 15, 100, 102, *3, 35; see also* Foxe's Court
St Pancras (Middx), property near, 8n
St Paul's Cathedral, estate, 17
St Paul's Churchyard, gate, 56
St Peter Paul's Wharf, parish, 108
St Peter's Hill, 15, 28, 108, *38*
St Sepulchre, parish, 7, 104
St Swithin's Lane, 114, *41*
St Thomas Apostle [Street], *12*
St Thomas Hospital, 9, 11; estate, *37, 53*
salter, *see* trades
Salters' Company, almshouses, *34*
Samways, Joseph, 62, *18*
Saunder(s), John, shearman, 100; Agnes his daughter, wife of
    Oliver Claymond, 100; Mary his daughter, wife of Richard
    Nicholl, 100
Saunders, John [another], *24*
Saxton, Christopher, surveyor, 9, 11
Scafe, Richard, *26*
schools, 97, 99
Scott,
    Thomas, 79, *26*
    Mr, *51*
screens, 148
screens passages, 18, 102, *26, 32*
scrivener, *see* trades
Seacoal Lane, 104, *36; see also* Fleet Lane
Seares, John, 21
Seger, Robert, 20, 26, 133, *50*
Serege (?), Matteo Dominico de, physician, 100

U